TREADING THE BAWDS

Manchester University Press

WOMEN, THEATRE
AND PERFORMANCE

SERIES EDITORS
MAGGIE B. GALE AND VIV GARDNER

Already published

Auto/biography and identity: women, theatre and performance
EDS MAGGIE B. GALE AND VIV GARDNER

Women, theatre and performance: new histories, new historiographies
EDS MAGGIE B. GALE AND VIV GARDNER

TREADING THE BAWDS

Actresses and playwrights on the Late-Stuart stage

GILLI BUSH-BAILEY

Manchester University Press
Manchester and New York

distributed exclusively in the USA by Palgrave

Copyright © Gilli Bush-Bailey 2006

The right of Gilli Bush-Bailey to be identified as the author of this work has been asserted by her in accordance with the Copyright, Designs and Patents Act 1988.

Published by Manchester University Press
Oxford Road, Manchester M13 9NR, UK
and Room 400, 175 Fifth Avenue, New York, NY 10010, USA
www.manchesteruniversitypress.co.uk

Distributed in the United States exclusively by
Palgrave Macmillan, 175 Fifth Avenue,
New York, NY 10010, USA

Distributed in Canada exclusively by
UBC Press, University of British Columbia, 2029 West Mall,
Vancouver, BC, Canada V6T 1Z2

British Library Cataloguing-in-Publication Data is available

Library of Congress Cataloging-in-Publication Data is available

ISBN 978 0 7190 7251 2 paperback

First published by Manchester University Press in hardback 2006

This paperback edition first published 2009

Printed by Lightning Source

Contents

	Series editors' foreword	page vi
	Acknowledgements	vii
	Introduction	1

Part I: Background

1	In the company of women	27
2	United we stand	51
3	Control and influence on the Late Stuart stage	76

Part II: The Players' Company at Lincoln's Inn Fields

4	New moves, new voices	107
5	Competition and criticism	135
6	Re-forming the stage	157
7	Old stories, new histories	179
8	Certainly not a conclusion	203
	Bibliography	208
	Index	223

Series editors' foreword

This series, *Women, Theatre and Performance*, has its origins in the work of a number of feminist theatre academics from the 1980s and 1990s – a period when interest burgeoned in the part that women have played in theatre over the centuries. That interest was in its turn the daughter of the 'Second Wave' women's movement, the women's theatre movement and the women's history movement from the previous two decades. It was with some delight that women theatre workers, spectators and scholars alike discovered that women *did* have a significant history in performance, and these women – and some men – have continued to investigate, interrogate and work with their histories. Feminist performance analysis and women's theatre history has now become an established part of performance practice and theatre studies at both a university and a more popular level.

In the 1990s, the journal *Women and Theatre Occasional Papers* became the host for the documentation and dissemination of contemporary research and innovation in theatre practice and scholarship in Britain. The emphasis on history and historiography was a considered decision. It was felt that at that time no consistent outlet existed for all the work that carried on the feminist retrieval project of the 1980s which was emerging from theatre and drama departments in Britain and elsewhere. This emphasis on history did not – and does not – preclude engagement with contemporary practice. On the contrary, it was felt that our history was very much part of our present and that the two could, and should, be studied side by side. This series seeks to continue that original project and to make the research and debate available on a more than 'occasional' basis. The series will consist of themed volumes that consider theatre as part of a wider nexus of social and cultural practices. Women's contribution to all areas and types of theatre and performance will be included, from opera and acrobatics to management and dramaturgy. Continuities and consistencies will not be sought, though they may be found within the transhistorical and transcultural organisation of the material.

The series is designed for students at all levels, teachers and practitioners, as well as the interested enthusiast who wishes simply to 'fill in the blanks' where women have been hitherto 'hidden' in theatre histories.

Maggie B. Gale and Viv Gardner

Acknowledgements

Acknowledgements tend to be a short history of collaboration and influence: the following is true to that tradition. My thanks go first to my editors, Maggie Gale and Viv Gardner, for their thoughtful comments and encouragement, not least by including this book in their series Women, Theatre and Performance, which has contributed to my writing and thinking over the past five years. Then, to Richard Everett for his support and understanding during the many changes that the journey from professional actress to academic have brought to us both; to Kingston University for accepting my unorthodox preparation for undergraduate work and especially to Dr Sarah Sceats, for encouraging me to pursue postgraduate research. The Department of Drama and Theatre at Royal Holloway has been my place of study and work over the last decade: fellow research students and former tutors have become colleagues and friends and I am grateful for the generous support they continue to offer. Finally, I would particularly like to thank Professor Jacky Bratton for her invaluable criticism and comments on my work, at all stages of its development and, above all, for her own writing which continues to break new ground in the field of women's theatre history. She is simply the best theatre historian, mentor and collaborator – without whom …

This book is dedicated to three special theatre women:
Evelyn Howard, Joan Berly and Rebecca Everett.

Introduction

Consciousness of history is all-pervasive at the start of the twenty-first century. Wherever we look, it is present[1].

Twice a day, from Monday to Saturday, the Theatre Royal Drury Lane offers backstage tours to groups of schoolchildren, students and tourists. Clutching tickets admitting entrance 'Through The Stage Door', we are instructed to gather – in the foyer.[2] This impressive front of house space is positioned behind the four large double pillars that dominate Catherine Street on which this, the fourth Theatre Royal Drury Lane, now stands.[3] A statue of Shakespeare, commissioned to adorn the portico of the theatre in 1820, now occupies a corner on the left hand side of the foyer, while on the other side the seated figure of Noel Coward, cigarette in hand, guards the set of doors leading through to the Lower Rotunda. Above the doors are two ornately carved wooden plaques with gold embossed lettering: the larger of the two, nearest to Shakespeare, lists the roll call of 'Patent Holders, Lessees and Managers' from Thomas Killigrew in 1663 to Andrew Lloyd Webber, who took control of the building in 2000. The other pays honour to the less well-known names of 'actors, musicians, writers and workers for the stage who have given their lives for their country' in the Great War (1914–1918). The whole works to impress upon us the cultural significance of the building and those who have contributed to its place in theatre history. On the opposite side of Catherine Street stands a pub, Nell of Old Drury. It too boasts wooden plaques with gold lettering, impressing on the reader its own stake in royal and theatrical history: 'Our pub owes its name to Nell Gwynn, who was King Charles II's favourite mistress. She had been an orange seller in Covent Garden and was an actress.' An image of Nell (after Verelst, c. 1680)[4] hangs over the pavement, suspended above the heads of passers-by.

The tour guide greets us and we move through the foyer doors, into the Lower Rotunda to be introduced to the lives and works of the great men of the theatre. The grave-looking statues of Kean, Garrick, Shakespeare and Baume tower above us as the guide lists their achievements. The story is then taken up by a second guide who appears in costume as the archetypal gossiping cleaner, 'Margaret Mopp'. With a wave of her duster, we move from the guide/tourist to performer/audience relationship as she regales us with tales of the altercation between royal father and son, a rather less than regal wrestling match between George III and the Prince Regent, 'right where we're standing', which resulted in the creation of two sides to the theatre, identified by their separate royal boxes: the King's side and the Prince's side. We are reminded that this is 'not a museum but the oldest working theatre in Europe' – so photographs of the stage and the set of its latest offering are forbidden 'for copyright reasons': the business of theatre is after all a commercial concern. We can, however, take photographs of the King's box and the live performance of the theatre's history moves to audience participation as two unsuspecting young male tourists are selected to re-enact the moment in 1916 when King George V knighted actor Frank Benson – with a prop sword. Crossing to the Prince's box, the first guide admits us to the backstage area and the labyrinth of passageways beneath the stage. We are promised sight of the oldest parts of the theatre which date back to the Restoration in 1660 and its founder, Sir Thomas Killigrew, who built the theatre in 1663 to provide entertainment for its royal patron. King Charles II, recently returned from exile in France, famously decreed that theatres should be re-opened, actresses should replace the boy actors who had previously played all female characters and, as the Drury Lane backstage tour has it, London's audiences were to enjoy 'fun' after the eighteen years of public theatre closure enforced by Cromwell and his Puritan government.

Before long we are standing in the lower depths of the building, surrounded by the detritus of the current production: abandoned music stands, lighting cables, and empty costume rails clutter the narrow corridors. We are gazing at a shallow archway, now bricked up but once a tunnel through which, we are assured, Charles II would journey beneath the streets to visit the infamous orange seller and sometime actress Nell Gwynn: 'this tunnel led straight to the brothel Nell and her mother ran in the Strand'. Nell is then brought to life, carrying a basket with a requisite number of oranges, to lead us beneath the stage and finally – out 'Through The Stage Door' that opens on to Russell Street. The disembodied image of Nell of Old Drury looks down upon her embodied impersonator who bids us farewell on the steps to the theatre with a rhyming couplet that ends: 'may the stardust of Drury Lane shine for ever in your hearts'. We are, as the street signs remind us, in 'Theatreland', a logo that hints at the Disneyfication of the history of

London's West End and points to the popularisation of that historical past as part of a very present theatrical economy. The quotation at the head of this introduction speaks of the 'all-pervasive' consciousness of history that has resulted in a shift from the image of unwieldy dusty books on library shelves to a vibrant presence with 'an unexpectedly broad popular appeal',[5] as the twice daily tours of Drury Lane theatre demonstrate. Evans argues that the explanation for this rising interest in the popular presentation and reception of history 'is about identity, about who we are and where we came from. At a time when other sources of identity such as class and region have declined, history is stepping in to fill the gap.'[6] Adaptations of historical novels, television series and docu-dramas re-enacting the 'great', and not so great, moments in our history fill the small and large screen alike and, as Evans notes, the theme of the individual battling aginst the tyranny of social and cultural repression have made films such as *Gladiator* and *Titanic* ... among the highest-grossing movies of all time'.[7] The theatre too has proved a fruitful and commercially successful topic in the bid to cash in on the big screen entertainment value of the historical past: *Shakespeare in Love* (1998) with Joseph Fiennes as the young bard and Gwyneth Paltrow as the object of his adoration, playing out *Romeo and Juliet* in 'real' life and on the stage of the carefully reconstructed Rose Theatre. A central thread to the dramatic narrative of this film revolves round Paltrow's character, Viola De Lesseps, a gentlewoman who cross-dresses in the disguise of a boy player in order to appear on the public stage. The potential danger of a woman appearing publicly in the male bastion of Elizabethan theatre is all part of the dramatic tension that contributes to her inevitable success before a packed theatre audience that, surprisingly, includes the Queen herself, making an incognito visit to the public playhouse – as Evans wryly notes, 'Hollywood movies have scant regard for historical accuracy if it interferes with the prospects of a good profit'.[8]

The fate of the boy actor and the introduction of women to the public stage is the subject of *Stage Beauty* (2004), a film about the life and work of Edward Kynaston, the 'last' actor to perform female characters on the Restoration stage before the arrival of the 'first' actress. Richard Eyre, former artistic director of the Royal National Theatre, has followed his front-of-camera presentation of the history and development of Western theatre practice in the docu-series *Changing Stages* (2001), by turning his directorial hand to this key moment in theatre history which is, as Eyre writes, 'set in a theatre that I'm not familiar with, a theatre without women – at least on the stage'.[9] In the film's account of the homosocial world of Edward Kynaston's theatre, the arrival of the actress is seen as not so much an economic threat as a personal threat: 'Ned's fate is something more than artistic redundancy ... it also deprives him of his identity ... Who he is professionally and what he is sexually are inextricably bound together. The question that the film explores is this: who is he now?'[10] The film's emphasis on Ned's sexual identity is, perhaps, reflective of a more twenty-first century anxiety but the threat to his economic identity is rooted in a deeper resistance to women's successful presence in the public sphere. The commercial potential for the exploitation of 'real' women on the public stage is made clear, especially in a scene when 'Mrs Hughes' is sitting for her portrait and is persuaded to bare a breast to prove she is a woman and thus boost box-office returns. When women are visibly making money by performing 'themselves', questions are raised about personal and economic agency: who is exploiting whom? In *Stage Beauty*, Nell Gwynn is presented as a 'wannabe' actress who uses her sexual charms to persuade her royal lover to introduce the law that forbids men to play female parts. Eyre admits to the anachronism that places Nell's desire to act at the centre of the new decree but, interestingly, limits the admission to the fact that Charles II 'didn't meet her until eight years later',[11] rather than the fact that Nell Gwynn was actress first, royal paramour later: an interesting inversion of events that, none the less, continues the well-worn elision of actress and whore – a trope that feminist theatre historians continue to problematise.

Kirsten Pullen's *Actresses and Whores: On Stage and in Society* (2005) tackles the problem head-on by calling for new understandings of the distinction between the financial transactions implicit in the act of prostitution and the appellation of 'whore' which, she argues, was a far milder label for the wilful woman in seventeenth-century discourse: 'During the Restoration, the word "whore" was an insult, certainly, but one along the lines of the contemporary "bitch", designating an unruly woman rather than one who engages in commercial sex ... Transferring the language but not the meaning of seventeenth-century vernacular is one way historians elide the position of the Restoration actress.'[12] The difficulty with this approach is that the 'meaning' of the unruly, transgressive woman is inextricably bound up with her sexual and sexualised identity.[13] The enduring power of this essentially patriarchal construct has been the subject of feminist criticism for some thirty years or more. Its prevalence in historical discourse is demonstrated by the wealth of materials that Pullen can draw upon in her series of case-studies from the seventeenth to the twentieth century. This is not to undermine Pullen's central project of demonstrating the agency of performing women in creating alternative social and cultural narratives, nor indeed to question the weight of the opposition that works to occlude them – this book contributes directly to that same revisionist understanding. But the unavoidable issue here is that the hegemonic accumulation of sexualised meaning and meanings in the history of the actress has in fact prevailed. Those meanings have worked and still work to reinforce one another in multilayered histories that resist erasure and will simply ignore alternative strategies, such as the one Pullen suggests in her bid for a revised and reconfigured semiotic.

The representation of women in theatre as sexually transgressive is still vividly present in our histories, embodied by twenty-first-century actresses who perform the reconstructed lives of their predecessors and reinforced by our participation as tourists and filmgoers consuming its hegemonic assumptions. In the history of Drury Lane theatre, the actress is, at best, pushed to the edge of the 'real' narrative of male theatrical innovation and achievement. She is a sideshow entertainment which, like Nell Gwynn's image on the pub sign, is suspended 'outside', above the pavement, opposite the grand nineteenth-century columns of the theatre and only brought 'inside' as part of the reconstructed back-stage life of the theatre – a moment re-enacted beneath the stage. Her story, like the theatre's underground tunnels, with all their Freudian associations, is a subterranean journey of sexually charged imagination, weaving its way beneath the streets above. In *Stage Beauty*, Nell is the cheeky cockney – a Restoration Barbara Windsor – with a big heart and a cleavage to match, exchanging sexual favours for money, opportunity and fame. Sex sells – and the business of theatre, which includes these metatheatrical performances of history is, above all, a commercial venture.

The questions that this book addresses spring from this understanding of the theatre as primarily a profit-making enterprise but one that continues to trace a complex and often precarious path through the history of Britain's social and cultural economy. In the history of the theatre, the sexualised construction of its working women has remained at the heart of the narrative.[14] This book asks what the purposes of such histories might be and why, in spite of revisionist approaches, do we, as historians, theatre women and their audience perpetuate this 'story' in the twenty-first century? To return to Richard Evans: 'wherever we look, it is present'.[15]

Living with histories

The presence of the theatrical past, its influence and how we respond to that influence, have been central to the debates in contemporary makings of theatre history. In 1989 Thomas Postlewait and Bruce McConachie brought together a series of essays that offered new access to the theoretical and methodological approaches arising from the advance of academic interest in the widening field of cultural studies. *Interpreting the Theatrical Past* still stands as a benchmark in theatre history, not least for feminist historians who rose to the challenge of revising traditional narratives. Tracy C. Davis championed the revisionist strategies of feminist scholarship and set the pace for new approaches in her essay, 'Questions for a Feminist Methodology in Theatre History'.[16] Over the past fifteen years many have responded to this book's challenge and the dominance of canonical Western theatre histories has been nudged, although not entirely overturned, in the pursuit of alternative narratives of the historicised past – a task that, as yet, is far from complete.[17] Theoretical and methodological frameworks are tested and redefined and alternative strategies continue to be explored in collections of essays such as Worthen and Holland's *Theorizing Practice: Redefining Theatre History* (2003) in which Susan Bennett's essay 'Decomposing History (Why Are There So Few Women In Theater History)' demonstrates that the marginalisation and occlusion of female narratives is still taking place in the recording of twentieth-century theatre history.[18] Tracy C. Davis continues to ask provocative questions of feminist theatre historians in her essay 'The Context Problem', one of a number of new historiographical essays by leading North American theatre historians in a recent special issue of *Theatre Survey*.[19] Davis identifies the problems surrounding the creation of contexts to explore absences in theatre histories, the lacunae, the gaps that for feminist historians have been there for too long: 'What had been unseen to history may now be spoken and written about.'[20] But there is another contextual problem for women's theatre history, not one of absence but of presence: the presence of a theatre history that admits women only on its own terms.[21] In order to unpack the weight of this enduring story a little further, I will return for a moment to the Theatre Royal Drury Lane to consider further the assumptions that run through the theatre's representation of its own history: assumptions that are vividly present because they are deeply rooted in the historicised past.

Susan Bennett opened out the framework within which historical theatre and performance might be explored in her striking study, *Theatre Audiences* (1997), which considers the processes of spectatorship in the context of different theatres and their changing audience. Bennett draws attention to the social and cultural significance of the theatre building, arguing that 'the milieu which surrounds a theatre is always ideologically encoded and the presence of a theatre can be measured as typical or incongruous within it'.[22] Bennett is referring directly here to the geographical location of theatre buildings and how this affects their potential audience. In the case of the Theatre Royal Drury Lane, that cultural geography is further complicated and layered with ideologically encoded histories: 'The theatre building is a landmark as cultural institution. It is a physical representative of the art which dominant ideologies have both created and promoted.'[23] As the 'oldest working theatre in London' Drury Lane claims a direct link with the re-opening of the theatres at the Restoration in 1660 and, as I have described above, boasts of its innovative and sustained contribution to the production of dramatic art in Britain. But the present cultural position of the theatre presents something of an anomaly in this construction. There is an uncomfortable 'doubleness' at work here, revealing a series of splits and contradictions that places the theatre at odds with the dominant cultural identity it claims in the present, via its representation of the historical past.

The colonnade on the long, Russell Street side of the building marks a straight line to Covent Garden and Drury Lane's one-time competitor, the Royal Opera House.[24] The refurbished piazza now has shops and stalls merging with street performance, open-air restaurants and, sometimes, large screens on which the current Opera House offering is projected, free of charge, to a wider audience than can afford the prices: popularising art from the newly extended, and heavily subsidised, home of ballet and opera. In contrast, Drury Lane has, at least from the middle of the twentieth century, exclusively housed the lavish commercial musical with all its popular cultural associations. Between these two Theatres Royal stands the Theatre Museum, with its archives and exhibitions offering another inflection on the all-pervasive interest in history.[25] In a bid to offer an inclusive experience of all kinds of performance in Britain's theatre history, interactive exhibitions here are augmented with costume and make-up workshops. At the time of writing, a reverent exhibition devoted to the works of one of Britain's leading 'classical' theatre families, the Redgraves, is matched by a noisy, high-energy exhibition on the 'Making of the West End'. The Theatre Royal Drury Lane features prominently in the sphere of popular theatre – a good night out – rather than as a participant in the earnest justification for public subsidy at Covent Garden or the cries for a London base for the Royal Shakespeare Company. Yet in the telling of its own history, Drury Lane displays statues of Shakespeare, not Lerner & Loewe, Kean in *Hamlet* rather than Jonathan Pryce in *Miss Saigon*. These rather obvious comparisons draw attention to a fundamental split that is at the heart of our construction of theatre history: a binary established in notions of high/low art, the drama versus entertainment, the opera over the musical.

In this binaried construction of theatre, Drury Lane is firmly in the sphere of popular culture, competing more fiercely with the once illegitimate[26] theatres on the Strand than with its closer neighbour, the Royal Opera House, Covent Garden. The history of Drury Lane can be read as one that has moved over from high to low, from art to entertainment, but its self-presentation firmly rejects this approach by hanging on to and promoting its hegemonic history. The power of the historicised construct is clear; but how does it relate to the representation, or non-representation, of women in theatre?

Jacky Bratton's *New Readings in Theatre History* adds weight to current debates around theatre history and its place in a new millennium. As her title suggests, Bratton offers new ways of analysing theatre history through a range of materials discounted in the past but she also examines the historiographical methods and ideologies that have formed and inform theatre history itself. In challenging the way theatre history has been chronicled, she exposes the assumptions that have worked to marginalise women's theatre history.

> It was a necessary condition of the successful hegemonic control of the theatre that there was a binary division set up between 'the popular' and the theatre of art; that women's work within the public space should be disguised, discounted or appropriated to male control; and therefore entertainment, embodied as female, become the Other of the 'National Drama' of male genius.[27]

The elision of women and entertainment, women as object of the male gaze, the 'other' in a theatre created by and for male consumption underpins the history of early theatre women. There is a place for women in theatre history but it is a place prescribed and described predominantly within a phallocentric discourse interested in promoting theatre as part of a wider political project. Bratton identifies the 1830s as a key political moment in the development and creation of the ideologies that dominate theatre history today. She argues that in order for the 'grand narrative' to be formed, the terms on which theatre was determined and defined relied on the establishment of 'a system of difference – text and context, high and low, the written drama and the materiality of the stage'.[28] The marginalisation or occlusion of women as the 'other' in relation to male genius emerges from a critical sensibility that privileges text – specifically male-authored text – over performance. 'It was understood that Shakespeare, and writers for the theatre who followed his literary banner, were ill-served by harlequin – the actors and the managers ... all the material and emotional heritage of the stage – was viewed merely as the context which helped (or more often hindered) the realisation of the written dramatic text.'[29] The central suggestion here, that we should reject a literary theatre history in favour of one that privileges performers and performance, is one that has been accepted in academic discourse, not least by scholars working out of university departments of drama and performance studies. But the importance of Bratton's book lies in its argument that nineteenth century historiographical processes and agendas have underpinned and privileged a theatre history in which performance is appropriated to serve a literary project. Of most significance to my enquiry here is that Bratton demonstrates that this historiographical method was applied in retrospect – that earlier periods of theatre were subjected to a scrutiny which judged according to a nineteenth-century system of difference. In a bid to substantiate the definition of theatre in the 1830s, the theatrical past was re-viewed and re-used to underpin an essentially nineteenth-century cultural project: 'in pursuit of which a history of the stage since the medieval-Elizabethan point of origin was written – a history which was not substantially challenged until very recent years'.[30] In other words, the histories we have today say as much as, if not more about, nineteenth-century interpreters as they do about the theatrical materials from the past they were interpreting.

Old stories, new approaches

It is from this perspective that I begin the task of revisiting and re-viewing the histories of the first professional women working in the public London theatres. Thus far, I have focused on the historical representation of performing women but there were many other women working in and around the theatre in the second half of the seventeenth century: managers, trainers and, crucially, female playwrights. This book deliberately sets out to break down the binary between writing and performance by considering the impact of the dramatic discourse written *by* women *for* women to perform and, further, by looking anew at the performing woman's influence in the creation and realisation of the female characters written for her. Theatre histories represent writing and performing women as being tarred with the same 'whorish' brush but I will look beyond that branding to investigate other identities and suggest a different set of connections between theatre women. The methodology I shall employ is a historiographical approach that is necessarily self-conscious about the critical lens it uses. As Mark Fortier notes, 'Materialist criticism will seem simplistic and mechanical if it underplays the complexities of the relations between culture and society.'[31] In other words, if we are to challenge the histories we have, we need to be alert to the complexities of their influence, not only at the point they were created but also as part of the hegemonic ideology we have received. The story this book tells is, at some points, in direct conflict with the history we have inherited, not least by placing women in theatre at the centre, as the subject of this history, rather than on the edge, the 'other' beyond the narrative, beneath the public stage. This does not mean that men are excluded from the story, far from it, but they are not the subject of the narrative here. Their importance is in relation to the stories of the women I am reconsidering: the story of Elizabeth Barry and Anne Bracegirdle, *not* Thomas Betterton and Colley Cibber, Pix and Centlivre, *not* Congreve and Vanbrugh. This approach not only reverses the procedure of received history, as evidenced in the Drury Lane theatre tour, but also upends academic procedure, where critical studies of 'great' playwrights and actors still outnumber those of their female contemporaries. Even some recently published, 'alternative' grand narrative theatre histories place women in parenthesis to the main text, sometimes even allotting shaded boxes to the descriptive texts on the lives and work of early theatre women.[32] So what are the materials of a 'new' history and what tools are need for this particular archaeological dig?

The problem for projects of feminist historiography is largely one of evidence – material remains of the sort that can be verified as 'authentic' remain at the cornerstone of historiographical practice and the lack of them, the absence of 'hard facts' in the scientific, forensic model of doing history, leads to accusations of inauthenticity – of story-telling, even. But, as I have discussed above, the popular appeal of history at the beginning of the twenty-first century has much to do with *how* the story is told and *who* is telling it. Richard Evans notes that the 'personal point of view' of today's television historian or presenter 'is a sharp contrast to the style in which historical programmes were presented a decade or so ago, with their emphasis on authoritative and seemingly irrefutable neutrality'.[33] The point is, of course, that histories are always told from a personal, subjective perspective: neutrality, however appealing as an ideal, is not a practical option. Early feminist works spoke of 'herstory', a self-conscious but effective device to draw attention to the alternative subject position of their narratives. The term has now become unfashionable and largely dropped from feminist historical discourse but, interestingly, most television historian/presenters, in Britain at least, tend to be white males and it could be argued that '*his*tory' prevails. The material remains: the dates, performance calendars, play-texts, reviews, letters, lampoons – all the 'facts' the historian researches and gathers – may well be from the same source but the 'story', the narrative we present reflects the subjective perspective of each presenter, whether in front of a television camera or in an academic book.

Thomas Postlewait usefully explores the sometimes uneasy relationship between narrative and scientific historical methods noting that, 'increasingly, contemporary historians have acknowledged that scientific and narrative methods are necessarily interrelated'.[34] It is not then that 'history' can ever stand alone in any meaningful way but that as materials are gathered and sifted, turned over and viewed again in relation to other 'finds' from the same, or related, spot a narrative emerges – a new story is formed. As Postlewait explains, 'the task of describing and explaining what happened also includes the need to interpret how and why human events occurred. Narrative provides coherence, a process of emplotment which configures these actions into a meaningful, comprehensive interpretation.'[35] This book seeks to do just that as part of an unashamedly feminist historiography. It takes the materials and looks through the accretions of past histories, including the findings of neglected early feminist historians such as Rosamond Gilder and Lucyle Hook, in order to read against the grain, to form new patternings, new stories in the history of theatre women. This approach must, therefore, remain self-conscious about its twenty-first-century perspective. Moreover, this book carries an interest in relating this story to theatre women today – how they are perceived and how they perceive themselves in the light of the history they inherit. This means that we must look round to the present as urgently as we look back and, to return to

Bratton's argument, be aware of the sandbanks of nineteenth-century interests that we inherit.

Sex sells in the business of theatre

From the moment the professional actress was given licence to appear on the London public stage in 1660 she has been an object of fascination. She is both admired and derided, desired and vilified. Unlike the female playwright, she does not share her identity with her male counterpart – *only* a woman can claim the title of actress – suggesting a unique professional status not usually associated with women in seventeenth-century society. There were, of course, already actresses performing on the public stages of Europe and, as Susan Bassnett argues in her search for the performing woman's history, questions of respectability and virtue were never far away. In spite of these performers' creative successes and public popularity, 'the myth of the late arrival of the actress still prevails' in accounts of western theatre.[36] Stephen Orgel also considers actresses in Spain, Italy and France and draws attention to documentary evidence demonstrating payments to English female performers at a number of public entertainments in the early part of the seventeenth century. What has made the female performer at the Restoration into the 'first' actress of theatre histories?

The crucial shift in 1660 concerns the terms upon which performing women in England now appeared. Following the absence of any public theatre companies during the eighteen-year Puritan rule of the Interregnum, the royal warrant granting Killigrew and Davenant sole rights to produce theatrical performance for a paying public audience specified that women were to be part of that essentially commercial activity – not simply bought in for an occasional appearance but recruited as members of the company of players. They were rarely paid on the same basis as the actors, an issue I will return to in later chapters but, having been hired as part of the new money-making theatrical enterprise under a royal patent, they shared with actors some of the privileges and protection of being recognised as His Majesty's Servants. As Elizabeth Howe notes, the actresses were entitled to 'elaborate scarlet cloaks with crimson capes to be worn on state occasions. These liveries made them recognized servants of the king and meant most usefully that they could not be sued or arrested for debt without the express permission of the Lord Chamberlain of the Household.'[37] It is this participation in the public, commercial sphere that marks the establishment of the 'first' English actresses in Restoration theatre – and it is within the context of a newly invigorated commercial theatre, endorsed and protected by royal warrant, that I will reconsider their work and the alliances made with other women working in the business of theatre.

From this perspective, it is not difficult to see the how anxieties arising from women working in an openly commercial and wholly public sphere quickly led to parallels with prostitution, a link that has endured for generations in a patriarchal society employing the binaries of private/public, virgin/whore as its constructs of femininity. Restoration society was enthralled by the actress's craft on stage and simultaneously engrossed by the stories surrounding her sexual liaisons off stage. The elision between her public and private identity, the visual spectacle of her acting body on stage and the potential availability of her sexually active body off stage, created an ambiguous perspective so that, as Bassnett puts it, 'the actress came into being, the creature distinguished as much by her gender as by her skills as a performer'.[38] Such an approach has underpinned historiography for the last three hundred years.

Attitudes toward the female playwright are more complex but reveal a similar anxiety circulating around notions of women in the public sphere with the public/private binary working in similar ways. The presence of writing women in the rapidly growing print culture is treated quite differently from the appearance of their performed texts in the public arena of the playhouse.[39] The arrival of the first wave of professional female playwrights was fiercely resisted in some quarters and simultaneously exploited in others: one popular marketing ploy to attract a changing and sometimes diminishing London audience in the later years of the seventeenth century was to announce a new play 'by a young lady'. Teasing references to her sex in prologues and epilogues were matched by salacious stories surrounding her activity off stage in the satires and lampoons of the day – providing successive generations of biographers and theatre historians with a string of scandals to use as ammunition to discredit her personally and professionally, thus reinforcing her canonical exclusion from literature. Twentieth-century feminist historians and critics have done much to recover the lives and works of women occluded from traditional theatre histories. Biographies, annotated editions of forgotten plays, collections of critical and theoretical essays have all worked to recover and celebrate the silenced voices of our theatrical foremothers. A range of theoretical and methodological approaches has been employed by feminist revisionists as we pursue what is essentially a shared agenda: to establish the fact that women are and always have been contributors to cultural discourses, despite the patriarchal desire to erase their presence. In the first book of this series, *Women, Theatre and Performance: New Histories, New Historiographies*, the editors' introduction reinforces the ongoing nature of this work as it seeks to 'concretise the notion of a continuum in women's involvement in theatre, to demonstrate that absence from the histories is not an indication of absence from history'.[40]

The project is clear but, as Deborah Payne has argued, the process is fraught with difficulties. In a discussion which urgently draws attention to the potentially uncomfortable contradictions arising from the coexistence of the 'professional regard and sexual objectification'[41] of the actress, Payne suggests that: 'modern criticism reproduces this split, construing the Restoration actress as either reified object or an emergent professional. Clearly, these are radically different versions of the same story, but which one do we choose: an all too familiar tale of oppression or an equally tired romance of feminine skill triumphing against all odds?'[42] If, as Payne argues, the work of revisionist theatre history has been guilty of romanticising the first actresses, a criticism that can certainly be extended to include the recuperation of female playwrights, it is perhaps because we have attached a particularly twentieth-century glamour to women's public appearance in the playhouse, reflecting the mystique created by Hollywood rather more than the immediate fame/notoriety attached to the small world of the Restoration playhouse. We have underestimated the power of the Cinderella myth and the way it has been used to inform approaches to women in theatre history for three hundred years: the lower-class girl overcomes her exclusion from the world of male education and social privilege and gets to go to the ball, where she dances with the prince: Nell Gwynn is one example of a neat fit with this trope. This essentially reductive attitude towards women's participation in the theatre draws attention to the need not only to examine the current cultural framework in which we recover women's stories but also to acknowledge the extent to which we carry traces from the past which influence our story-telling.

Doing history differently

The temptation to claim individual women as the first, the outstanding, the most famous, or infamous, is at the root of that problem – but where does the impulse to reclaim the individual arise from and why is it potentially damaging in the recovery of women's work? The notion of the individual creative artist is central to patriarchal discourse and was firmly established in early critical practice by the Romantic insistence on the individual (male) genius and the creative outsider. Jonathan Bate's exploration of the ideological appropriation of Shakespeare in the eighteenth century draws attention to Romanticism's bid to establish the writer as the dominant and desirable focus of the theatre,[43] an approach that has been reinforced and enshrined within academic practice, in spite of the disruptive claims of cultural theories. In the current postmodern, post-everything atmosphere, there are even signs of a somewhat bashful turn to what we might call a post-Leavisite tradition in which we self-consciously return to the practices of 'close reading'. The emphasis on authorial intent and 'meaning' is particularly seductive as we work to argue for lost and neglected writing women. Fuelled by a determination to rewrite history and challenge the traditional canon, feminist recovery has, inevitably perhaps, bought in to the valorisation of the individual. But there is a further danger attached to the cult of the individual 'genius'. In our desire to identify our new-found heroines we have reinforced the traditional model of the artist or poet as divergent from the society in which she works, rather than a product of it. This particularly male imagery works to undermine the impact of writing and performing women in that it identifies them as 'different', unique individuals who are not representative of – or to be identified with – ordinary, 'normal' women at all. This in turn is reinforced by our impulse to compare women's works with those of their male contemporaries in order to justify the importance of their achievements.

Susan Bennett identifies this move as 'filiation',[44] a historiography that '"legitimises" a place, that of its production, by "including" others in a relation of filiation or of exteriority'.[45] It cannot be denied that we have been successful in challenging the literary dramatic canon but, as Bennett goes on to point out, that success has been won within the framework of our roles as 'dutiful daughters': 'in this setting, women's dramatic writing is almost never categorised as "unique" – I cannot think of a single example – but it is generally categorised only inasmuch as it meets – or charmingly fails – the criteria that men's plays and male-authored dramatic theory have laid down as exemplary for a given historical moment or for a particular trajectory of dramatic genre.'[46] Bennett argues for a historiography that moves to new territories, that draws on new notions, which she defines as being 'what history most fears: imagination'.[47] This is not, as the positivist backlash would have us believe, an excursion into the realms of romantic fantasy but an acknowledgement of the need to offer new contexts within which we might revisit the well-thumbed documentary evidence and reread it through the lens of new relationships – making new connections between theatre women.

Our understanding of the first actresses and female playwrights is impoverished if we treat their work as entirely *separate* spheres of activity. Theatre is essentially a collaborative act and the relatively recent work of drama and theatre scholarship has been crucial in establishing academic credibility for an approach which addresses the dramatic text from the alternative perspective of performance – but this is not yet fully reflected in feminist historiographical practice. There continues to be a steady stream of publications on the life and works of the early professional female playwrights, particularly Aphra Behn, but none of them makes more than a passing reference to the creative contribution of the actresses who performed her plays. The recently published six volumes of *Eighteenth-century Women Playwrights* usefully includes a short section on the 'Actors' *sic* [48] but, even in this collection of women's plays, the actresses' notable roles are usually attributed to parts created by male playwrights of the day and comments about their personal reputations outweigh observations on their stagecraft. Our enduring fascination with the off-stage life of the actress has also resulted in a rash of modern biographies on eighteenth- and nineteenth-century actresses, long forgotten on the stage but recalled to a modern audience for their connections with influential, even royal lovers.[49]

The emphasis on individual achievement, particularly of the female playwright, quickly leads to isolationism – a move that works to separate women in theatre not only from one another but also from themselves. If writing women have been seduced by the notion of the writer as individual genius, they are effectively alienating their work from their female selves – and that includes their reader/audience. Women's texts sit on bookshelves beside the work of their male contemporaries and, as in the case of the most commercially successful British female writer at the beginning of the twenty-first century, J.K. Rowling, there is nothing to immediately identify the work's female authorship. The work of the actress poses a more complex set of difficulties as she cannot be separated from her work in the same way. The tools of her craft are her body and it is through the public display of her body/self that her work enters the public sphere. The identity of the writing woman can remain, and largely has remained, distinct from her work (although stories of

Rowling, a single parent, huddling for warmth in a café while she created Harry Potter somehow seemed designed to justify the fact that she is now worth millions: a literary lottery winner). The identity of the acting woman, however, is automatically conflated with the identity she creates via the demonstration of her craft: Julie Andrews can no more escape the innocent nanny/nun label than Marilyn Monroe could escape her labelling as a breathy blonde sex-bomb.

The actress's body is the canvas/paper on which she creates, her use of movement, gesture and voice the colours she uses to demonstrate her skills, yet the objectification of her body has successfully deflected revisionist theatre histories from considering the actress's body as the essential tool of her craft. It is not by any means the intention of this book to romanticise or ignore the sexual(ised) identity of the actress, for at the heart of my argument is the notion that the actress *uses* her public, performed, identity in the representation of the female self. But this representation is stronger still when her work is conjoined with that of the female playwright – the written text of one woman embodied by the other, disrupting the stability of a phallocentric historiography.

Performing texts in context

This book explores the texts and context which mark the work of early theatre women on the public London stage. There are a number of ways in which this task might be pursued, not least by beginning with the many recently recovered plays by female playwrights of the period and using these to consider the work of the actresses who first created the central roles. But the move from text to the performance of the text implies a hierarchy of influence that my approach sets out to challenge. Instead, I have chosen another perspective, a different starting point for this story of influence and collaboration between theatre women: the perspective of the actress. An account of the entire history of the early actress is, of course, well beyond the scope of this book[50] and so I have focussed on the careers of two prominent early actresses: Elizabeth Barry and Anne Bracegirdle. These two women appear frequently in the annals of theatre history, and stories of their triumphs on stage and their conquests off stage are readily available: but less has been made of their undoubted influence and participation in the work of the first generation of female playwrights, especially in the creation and management of a new company that produced so many works by playwriting women.

Barry and Bracegirdle's story serves as a framework for my investigation – a case study – from which a wider picture of early theatre women may be built. This overarching narrative is divided into two parts: Part I comprises three chapters which deal with the context in which theatre women were operating in the middle of the seventeenth century. The shifts and changes in the company system into which Elizabeth Barry, Anne Bracegirdle and the 'first' female playwright appeared are discussed in the first two chapters. Other, largely unseen, theatre women operating outside the boundaries of the patent houses are also discussed. Chapter 3 moves on to consider the ways in which theatre women gained ground in the public sphere of the commercial theatre, and the rise of antagonistic voices against them. The construction of the actress' on-stage identity soon led to the publication of salacious gossip about her off-stage activities: public attacks that might make modern tabloid hacks blush. A study of the construction and exploitation of Barry's and Bracegirdle's public identities demonstrates the potency of these constructs and leads to a wider consideration of their influence on representations of women on the stage. Moves to limit their influence backfired on the management of the patent house, who soon found themselves facing fierce competition from a rival company.

In Part II, the focus on Barry and Bracegirdle tightens to reveal an unprecedented moment of activity by theatre women. Chapters 4 to 7 deal with this largely unexplored period of women's theatre history: a ten-year period between 1695 and 1705 when a new theatre company was granted a royal license to perform plays in a small abandoned theatre in Lincoln's Inn Fields. The company was formed on the basis of a players' co-operative, creating a conspicuously alternative model to the dictatorial management practices of the Theatre Royal Drury Lane at a time in which that theatre had enjoyed a thirteen-year monopoly on the performance of plays on the London stage. The Players' Company, as I have called it, took the unprecedented and radical step of allotting 'shares' – a take of the profit – to actresses as well as actors. The playing season at this time ran from September through to June or July with revivals playing as important a part in the economic success of the company as new plays. Most plays were considered successful if they ran for more than three nights, the third night being the point at which the playwright received payment. Many new plays failed, though some, discussed in later chapters, proved successful enough to become part of the seasonal offerings year after year. The Players' Company took few risks in its choice of revivals but, during the course of their ten-year run, it produced a number of new plays that have become part of the Restoration dramatic canon. Crucially to my argument, the company also premiered at least seventeen new plays written by five female playwrights, representing approximately one-quarter of all new dramatic works produced in London between 1695 and 1705.

There has only been one major study of this radical company in the twentieth century: Judith Milhous's *Thomas Betterton and the Management of Lincoln's Inn Fields 1695–1708.*[51] Published in 1979, Milhous's study is an excellent and thorough work of positivist theatre history; but one which, as its title suggests, conforms to the dominant story of the actor/manager as the leading figure in the creation and running of the company. Chapters 4 to 7 problematise that history and challenge its inherent assumptions, particularly in relation to the actresses, Elizabeth Barry and Anne Bracegirdle, who head the list of players named alongside Thomas Betterton on the licence for the new company. The Players' Company opened its first full season in 1695 with *She Ventures and He Wins*, a new play tantalisingly billed as written by the anonymous young lady 'Ariadne'. This was the first of many new plays by female playwrights to be performed by Barry and Bracegirdle during the Lincoln's Inn Fields decade. Here then is another history of women in theatre, a different story to be told.

The final chapter returns to wider questions raised in this introduction concerning the materials and methods feminist historiography might continue to develop and pursue. The desire to move beyond the perceived limitations of mere recovery of women's work has already resulted in new ways of telling a wider story: here, a detailed look at the work of two actresses, a case-study in which the connections between theatre women might usefully be considered. If we are to change the way that theatre women are included in today's stories, we must attend to how they have been marginalised in the stories of the past. How does the actress of today, who augments her professional income on stage by representing Nell Gwynn beneath the stage, perceive her own identity in light of the story she embodies and plays out each day of the contemporary Drury Lane theatre's backstage tour? The story of theatre women has many starting points: one of the earliest for the London stage begins in the 1660s, the first decade of the theatres re-opening following an eighteen-year ban on public performance. This then is the place from which I will begin to trace the connecting paths forged by early theatre women in the rise of the actress and the disputatious appearance of the 'first' professional female playwright.

Notes

1. Richard J. Evans, 'Prologue: *What Is History?* – Now', in *What Is History Now?* ed. David Cannadine (London: Macmillan, 2002), pp. 1–18, p. 10.
2. This account is taken from two tours in October 2004 but reflects my experience of several other visits with groups of students from Royal Holloway, University of London's Department of Drama & Theatre over the past three years.
3. The first building on the site of what is now the Theatre Royal Drury Lane burnt down in 1672. The second building, reputed to have been designed by Christopher Wren, opened in 1674. The theatre was renovated at various times but virtually demolished and rebuilt to Henry Holland's design in 1794. It burnt to the ground in 1809. The fourth building was erected in 1812, the portico added in 1820 and the colonnade in 1831. The interior underwent a number of changes during the twentieth century, with the last significant remodelling taking place in 1922.
4. Simon Verelst's portrait of Nell Gwynn c. 1680, National Portrait Gallery, London.
5. Evans, '*What Is History?* – Now', p. 10.
6. p. 12.
7. p. 11.
8. Ibid.
9. Richard Eyre, 'A World Like Any Other', *The Guardian*: Arts section, 21 August 2004, pp. 16–17.
10. p. 17.
11. p. 16.
12. Kirsten Pullen, *Actresses and Whores: On Stage and in Society* (Cambridge: Cambridge University Press, 2005), pp. 22–23.
13. Sophie Tomlinson, 'She that Plays the King: Henrietta Maria and the Threat of the Actress in Caroline Culture', in *The Politics of Tragicomedy: Shakespeare and After,* ed. Gordon McMullen and Jonathan Hope (London: Routledge, 1992), pp. 189–207, offers a convincing discussion that situates the anxiety surrounding performing women around the Queen's influence at court. Issues of xenophobia and the fear of a return to Roman Catholicism are explored and demonstrated as crucial to the invocation of the actress/whore trope in Caroline culture. Tomlinson makes a convincing argument for the contemporary use of 'actress' in reference to performing women, some thirty years before the first professional actress was admitted to the newly formed companies at the Restoration and some seventy years before the *Oxford English Dictionary* records the 'first' use of the name in 1700. For more on the actress in Caroline culture and the European stage in the two centuries prior to her 'arrival' on the Restoration stage see Gilli Bush-Bailey, 'Revolution, Legislation and Autonomy', in *The Cambridge*

Companion to the Actress, ed. Maggie B. Gale and John Stoke, forthcoming, Cambridge University Press.
14 See Tracy C. Davis, *Actresses as Working Women* (London and New York: Routledge, 1991) for a convincing refutation of the assumption of the actress/whore in Victorian theatre histories.
15 Evans, 'What Is History? – Now', p. 10.
16 See Tracy C. Davis, 'Questions for a Feminist Methodology in Theatre History', in *Interpreting the Theatrical Past*, ed. Thomas Postlewait and Bruce A. McConachie (Iowa: University of Iowa Press, 1989), pp. 59–81, for references to further reading in key texts relating to feminist literary studies and theatre studies.
17 *The Oxford Encyclopaedia of Theatre & Performance*, ed. Dennis Kennedy (Oxford: Oxford University Press, 2003), 2 vols, is among the number of new reference books in theatre history that seek to break from the exclusively western, Eurocentric history of theatre and performance.
18 Susan Bennett 'Decomposing History (Why Are There So Few Women in Theater History)', in *Theorizing Practice: Redefining Theatre History*, ed. W. B. Worthen with Peter Holland (Basingstoke: Palgrave Macmillan, 2003), pp. 71–87.
19 Tracy C. Davis, 'A Question of Context', *Theatre Survey* 45:2 (November 2004), pp. 203–209. This special edition is entitled *Theatre History in the New Millennium: A Forum* and invites contributors to respond to the question: 'What is the single most important thing we can do to bring theatre history into the new millennium' (p. 174).
20 p. 206.
21 See Chapter 7 below for further discussion on the terms by which women's theatre history has been established and through which new historical narratives have been formed.
22 Susan Bennett, *Theatre Audiences* (1997), 2nd edition (London: Routledge, 2003), p. 126.
23 p. 128.
24 The first theatre in Covent Garden was built by John Rich in 1732, some twenty-five years after the period dealt with in this book but, as the royal patent to perform had moved with Rich (from his current refurbished theatre in Lincoln's Inn Fields) and remained with Covent Garden and Drury Lane theatres until the introduction of the 1843 Theatres Act, both houses have tended to adopt the label of the oldest London theatre.
25 At the time of writing, the Theatre Museum is preparing to close its Reading Room, currently housed beneath the Museum's building in Covent Garden, in order to relocate the archives in Olympia, West London. The proposed move is intended to give researchers greater access to the many archival holdings (some of which have yet to be catalogued). Collections and individual items in the Theatre Museum's archive can be located via the Backstage Project, an electronic research resource which brings together

theatre holdings in a large number of British universities and museums at www.backstage.ac.uk.
26 The theatre licensing laws dictated that the performance of drama should be limited to the Theatres Royal, principally Drury Lane and Covent Garden (see n.24 above). Other 'illegitimate' theatres were granted performance licences but the content was strictly controlled to the performance of burletta and melodrama with the emphasis on music, dance and pantomime. This edict was not strictly adhered to by the illegitimate theatres but remained the law until the 1843 act which finally broke the monopoly of the patent houses.
27 Jacky Bratton, *New Readings in Theatre History* (Cambridge: Cambridge University Press, 2003), p. 16.
28 p. 10.
29 p. 90.
30 p. 16.
31 Mark Fortier, *Theory/Theatre: An Introduction* (1997), 2nd edition (London: Routledge, 2002), p. 164.
32 Simon Trussler (ed.), *The Cambridge Illustrated History of British Theatre* (Cambridge: Cambridge University Press, 1994). The entry for Restoration Theatre has a box with a caption reading 'the last "boys", the first Actress' (p. 123). The following chapter also carries a box dedicated to '"the female wits" and the drama of sensibility' which includes a portrait of Centlivre (p. 143).
33 Evans, 'What Is History? – Now', p. 11.
34 Thomas Postlewait, 'History, Hermeneutics, and Narrativity', *Critical Theory and Performance*, ed. Janelle G. Reinelt and Joseph R. Roach (Ann Arbor: University of Michigan Press, 1992), pp. 356–368, p. 361.
35 p. 361.
36 Susan Bassnett, 'Struggling with the Past: Women's Theatre in Search of a History', *New Theatre Quarterly*, 5: 18 (1989), pp. 107–112, p. 107.
37 Elizabeth Howe, *The First English Actresses* (Cambridge: Cambridge University Press, 1992), p. 27.
38 Bassnett. 'Struggling with the Past', p. 111.
39 See Chapter 1 for a more detailed account of attitudes to the female playwright. See also Paulina Kewes, *Authorship and Appropriation: Writing for the Stage in England, 1660–1710* (Oxford: Clarendon Press, 1998), for a full discussion of male and female playwrights writing for the English public stage.
40 Maggie B. Gale and Viv Gardner (ed.), *Women, Theatre and Performance: New Histories, New Historiographies* (Manchester: Manchester University Press, 2000), p. 5.
41 Deborah C. Payne, 'Reified Object or Emergent Professional? Retheorizing the Restoration Actress', in *Cultural Readings of Restoration and Eighteenth-century Theater*, ed. Douglas Canfield and Deborah C. Payne (Athens, G: University of Georgia Press, 1995), pp. 13–38, p. 15.

42 p. 16.
43 See Jonathan Bate, *The Genius of Shakespeare* (New York and Oxford: Oxford University Press, 1998), and Jacky Bratton's extrapolation of this argument in *New Readings,* pp. 83–91.
44 Susan Bennett, 'Theatre History, Historiography and Women's Dramatic Writing', in *Women, Theatre and Performance: New Histories, New Historiographies*, pp. 46–59, p. 50.
45 p. 50.
46 pp. 50–51.
47 Ibid.
48 Derek Hughes (ed.), *Eighteenth-century Women Playwrights* (London: Pickering & Chatto, 2001), 6 vols.
49 Paula Byrne, *Perdita: The Life of Mary Robinson* (London: Harper Perennial, 2005) is one of the most recent publications to demonstrate the popularity of historical biographies of the actress. This follows the success of Claire Tomalin's biography of actress Dora Jordan, *Mrs Jordan's Profession: The Story of a Great Actress and a Future King* (1994) republished London: Penguin Books, 1995.
50 See n. 13 above and Elizabeth Howe's *The First English Actresses,* which continues to be the most comprehensive study on the work of the early actresses. Howe's discussion is largely confined to the Restoration (c. 1660–1700) and she does not consider the female playwrights or the actresses' activity at Lincoln's Inn Fields after 1695 in any detail.
51 Judith Milhous, *Thomas Betterton and the Management of Lincoln's Inn Fields 1695–1708* (Carbondale: Southern Illinois University Press, 1979).

Part I
Background

1
IN THE COMPANY OF WOMEN

Thomas Killigrew opened the doors of the first purpose-built Theatre Royal in 1663 but neither was it the first Theatre Royal nor was he the only theatre manager to entertain the newly restored King and his subjects. On Charles II's return from exile in France in May 1660, a royal warrant was drawn up permitting two of the King's loyal courtiers sole rights to the public performance of plays – for profit. The commercial theatre was born and the rights to this potentially lucrative enterprise were held by two patentees: Killigrew, a playwright who had remained close to the King's court in exile, was one, the other was the Poet Laureate and theatrical impresario William Davenant. The 'stock' plays and the players that had survived the English Civil War and Cromwell's edicts against public performance were divided between the two patentees. Killigrew's King's Company gained the majority of the old plays and more experienced players, while Davenant's Duke's Company was expected to produce new work or modernised adaptations of the remaining stock plays. The companies were to recruit actresses and produce their plays in indoor playhouses, both innovations that had pleased the King during his exile in France and, more importantly perhaps, proved commercially successful.

Following the French model of converting indoor tennis-courts to indoor theatres, Killigrew hastily converted Gibbon's Tennis Court in Vere Street, opening its doors for business on 8 November 1660. Davenant took rather longer, but his conversion of Lisle's Tennis Court in Lincoln's Inn Fields offered the innovative spectacle of changeable scenery. When the Duke's Company opened its doors on 28 June 1661, the audience was greeted with a scenic stage that offered a range of scene changes via screens and shutters moved across the stage space behind the proscenium arch. A set of grooves running across the stage from a series of wing positions carried shutters that could be opened or closed on the action behind, or create a new vista further up the scenic stage. Little wonder that Killigrew swiftly set into motion a scheme to move to a bigger building in Bridges Street (the site of the first 'Drury Lane' theatre): the battle of the box-office had begun and, contrary to Drury Lane's current account of its history, Davenant and the Duke's Company at Lincoln's Inn Fields were soon leading the theatrical field.[1]

By 1682 the King's and Duke's companies merged to become the only company permitted to perform on the London stage; an audacious takeover of Drury Lane and its sister theatre in Dorset Gardens that is discussed in Chapter 2. For the first twenty-two years of commercial theatre in London, however, the King's and Duke's Company were in direct competition. Killigrew got the pick of the pre-Commonwealth actors, including leading players Charles Hart, Michael Mohun and Edward Kynaston. The appearance of the first actress on the public stage occurred within a month of Killigrew opening his theatre in Gibbon's Tennis Court to a paying public, albeit affordable only to the wealthiest and, initially at least, predominantly aristocratic audience. Elizabeth Howe names four women recruited into the newly formed King's Company – Katherine Corey, Anne Marshall, Mrs Eastland and Mrs Weaver – and suggests Ann Marshall as the most likely candidate for Desdemona in the production of *Othello* on 8 December 1660.[2] In 1665, Nell Gwynn was also among the growing number of actresses recruited to the King's Company but it is at the lesser-known Duke's Company in Lincoln's Inn Fields that the trail can be picked up that leads not only to the appearance of some notable early actresses but also to the production of plays written by the 'first' female playwright – and all this in a theatre operating under a female manager.

In the long list of 'Patent holders, Lessees and Managers' named on the plaque displayed in the foyer of the Theatre Royal Drury Lane, there is only one woman. Janet Holmes à Court took control of the theatre in 1990, following the death of her husband, Robert, Chairman of then powerful Stoll Moss Theatre group. Some three hundred years earlier another widow, Lady Mary Davenant, took control of the Duke's Company at Lincoln's Inn Fields, following her husband's death in 1668.[3] Theatre histories generally fail to comment on the fact that William Davenant managed the Duke's Company for only eight years. He had recruited and established the original company, including the first actresses who, initially at least, lived in a wing of the house adjoining the playhouse, which he had built as part of his successful conversion of the former tennis court. Following Davenant's death, most histories suggest that managerial control of the company was placed in the hands of the Duke's Company's two leading actors, Thomas Betterton and Henry Harris. But Jacqueline Pearson is among several historians to assert that his widow 'Lady Davenant was a working manager ... and not merely a figurehead'.[4] Pearson supports her claim with evidence from a lawsuit of 1677 in which Lady Davenant 'testified that she "had, used or exercised the sole Government of the said Theaters ... & the appointment of Treasurers and Receivers, making Dividends and ordering of affairs'".[5] *A Biographical Dictionary* is also assertive about Lady Davenant's managerial leadership, particularly over financial matters. 'She was a shrewd and sensible businesswoman ... [who] guided her husband's collected *Works* into print ... took a particular interest in the company accounts, seeing to it that most if not all the payments for plays done before royalty were routed through her.'[6] There was another scheme of her late husband's which she also saw brought to fruition – the completion of a new purpose-built theatre which stood near the river, south of Fleet Street. When Dorset Gardens opened in 1671, three years after Davenant's death, the Duke's Company came into even closer competition with its rivals at Drury Lane. The new theatre must have been impressive, as Killigrew employed the same architect, Sir Christopher Wren, to design a new theatre at Drury Lane, following the catastrophic fire at the first theatre in 1672. As leading actor/manager for the Duke's Company, Thomas Betterton is usually credited with the creation of Dorset Gardens but Lady Davenant held the purse-strings. There is also evidence that she fought and won the right to establish a Nursery for training young actors in the Barbican and, even after direct control of the company passed to her sons, she insisted on her rights to the income from the fruit concession at Dorset Gardens.[7] Lady Davenant was evidently interested in performing more than a caretaking role in her late husband's interests but she is rarely credited as a theatrical entrepreneur. It was, however, during Lady Davenant's management of the Duke's Company that Aphra Behn, the 'first' professional female playwright, had a new play performed on the public stage. Over the next twelve years the Duke's Company at Lincoln's Inn Fields was the exclusive producing house for twelve plays by Behn. As Pearson puts it, 'the period's most distinguished female dramatist was perhaps attracted to this company ... by the presence of the period's most distinguished female manager'.[8]

Introducing Aphra

Aphra Behn has been the subject of numerous biographies and critical studies, especially at the end of the twentieth century where Janet Todd appears to have virtually cornered the market with the simultaneous publication in 1996 of *The Works of Aphra Behn* (in seven volumes), *Aphra Behn Studies* (a collection of critical studies) and a five-hundred page biography, *The Secret Life of Aphra Behn*.[9] Behn's recent biographers all grapple with the lack of hard evidence concerning her birth, her marriage, indeed most of the details concerning her private life, and dismiss the sensational stories that have peppered the largely censorious historical accounts of her life and work, but even the most hardened cultural critics cannot resist speculating about Behn's adventures in the colony of Surinam, her work as spy for the court of Charles II and her frustrated amorous relations with the bisexual lawyer John Hoyle.[10] Many of these stories have worked to reinforce the conventional theatre woman/whore trope but also, by focusing on the *literary* value of her work – Behn following and vociferously claiming her place beneath the literary banner of the dramatic poet – feminist critical revision of her plays has isolated her, presenting Behn as unique in her heroic status as the only (known) female playwright between 1670 and her death in 1689. This emphasis, which has effectively dominated the recovery of Behn's dramatic works, misses an exploration of Behn's crucial attachment and involvement with the work of other professional theatre women operating successfully within the playhouse.

    A piece of living theatre is never the result of one individual's work (the utterance of one poetic genius) and yet the development of Behn's work *in performance*, within the social and cultural context of the playhouse – the living space in which her dramatic voice is first heard – has received little critical attention. There were other women around writing plays for performance, even if, as Virginia Woolf so famously claimed, 'all women together ought to let flowers fall upon the tomb of Aphra Behn ... for it was she who earned them the right to speak their minds'.[11] But what of the other theatre women – the actresses through whom Behn's female characters found their voice? In the introduction to her lengthy biography of Behn, Janet Todd rightly argues that 'the story of Aphra Behn *must* ... be constructed from the works'.[12] But in order to understand the full impact of her dramatic works, they also *must* be recovered in the context of the playhouse and the actresses who performed them.

    The stories around Behn's entry into the theatrical community are as varied as the accounts of her origins and early life. Many modern biographers, including Angeline Goreau and Janet Todd, quote from a contemporary source, Elizabeth Cottington's letter to a relative[13] describing her visit to London in the Spring of 1669: 'Ther is a bowld woman hath oferd one [a play]: my cosen Aston can give you a better account of her then I can. Some verses I have seen which ar not ill; that is commendation enouf: she will think so too, I believe, when it comes upon the stage. I shall tremble for the poor woman exposed among the criticks. She stands need to be strongly fortified agenst them.'[14] For Goreau, the image of Behn 'at the door of the theater with a play' is irresistible and she quickly concludes that 'it seems quite likely that she was in fact the "bold woman" Elizabeth Cottington is referring to'.[15] There were (at least) two other aspiring female playwrights, Frances Boothby and Elizabeth Polwhele, who might well have been the bold woman in question, as Goreau notes, but she interprets their limited success (each woman has only one performed play attributed to her) as a 'tribute to [Behn's] courage, perseverance and force of character'.[16] Janet Todd also presents an engaging version of the story and seems equally reluctant to deconstruct this romanticised image of Behn in the main body of her text, preferring to reserve her true opinion for a footnote: 'Cottington was probably referring directly to Boothby ... the first woman to write an *original* play for the English public stage. *Marcelia* was performed by the King's Company and licensed for publication in October 1669.'[17] What is clear is that Goreau and Todd *want* to present Behn as the lone heroic female in the all male world of the Restoration theatre: 'For one reason or another, Behn had no female fellows.'[18] In order to establish Behn's pre-eminence as a female playwright Todd is among critics and biographers who feel it necessary to separate her from other women – theatrical or literary.

> In her period of intense theatre-going, Behn made new, play-writing friends, but few could have been women. Katherine Philips was dead. A Frances Boothby had put on *Marcelia* to little acclaim and then, along with the shadowy Elizabeth Polwhele who wrote *The Faithful Virgins*, died or simply disappeared. If, as seems unlikely, Margaret Cavendish *had* written the play performed under her husband's name in 1667, she did not repeat the experiment.[19]

Behn is known to have encouraged favourable comparisons between herself and the aristocratic Katherine Philips – dubbed by her contemporaries as 'The Matchless Orinda'. Whether she intended it or not,[20] Philips's translation of Corneille's *Pompey* (1662) was performed successfully at the newly constructed theatre in Smock Alley in Dublin and, according to Gerard Langbaine's *Account of the English Dramatic Poets* (1691), was revived on the London stage as late as 1678. Frances Boothby and Elizabeth Polwhele may have had only limited success with their plays, but they *were* publicly performed by the King's and Duke's companies respectively not more than two years before Behn's first production.

As for Margaret Cavendish, the Duchess of Newcastle, at least one contemporary commentator thought Cavendish also had her play publicly performed.

In his *Diary* entry for 11 April 1667, the avid theatregoer Samuel Pepys records an event at the playhouse which excited the talk of the town and the diarist, even though he apparently missed the occasion having expected the lady to appear at court.

> The whole story of this Lady is a romance, and all she doth is romantic. Her footman in velvet coats, and herself in an antique dress, as they say; and was the other day at her own play, *The Humorous Lovers*; the most ridiculous thing that ever was wrote, but yet she and her Lord mightily pleased with it, and she at the end made her respect to the players from her box and did give them thanks.[21]

Whether Pepys rightly attributes the play to Margaret Cavendish or not, it is interesting to note that she is seen as a 'romantic', if somewhat eccentric figure. Pepys registers no degree of alarm at the idea of a female playwright although he confirms contemporary prejudice against the writing woman in his observation that the play was 'a ridiculous thing'. So why is Todd so adamant in her dismissal of Cavendish's dramatic credentials and so certain that 'Katherine Philips would be no real role model for Aphra Behn working for "Bread" and negotiating the sexuality of the Restoration'?[22]

In the drive to prove precedence, Behn as 'first' and 'best', feminist historiography unconsciously replicates male hierarchies and legitimises Behn's dramatic writing by separating her from other writing women while seeking alliances and comparisons with the dominant, male playwrights of her age. Whether Behn had *direct* contact with any of these writing women seems to me to be immaterial. The point is that they, among others, were already there and active within the social and cultural milieu that Behn participated in. A more interesting question perhaps is posed by Dawn Lewcock: 'Almost all Behn's early writing was for the theatre. How and why she chose this route to attempt to support herself is merely another teasing question mark in the many that surround that enigmatic woman.'[23] The numerous books and articles on Behn testify to the fact that this fundamental question – how and why she chose to make a living in the theatre – has not yet been fully answered. If we move the focus away from the model of the artist-as-individual, we can begin to consider other patterns, new ways of describing cultural and social relationships around the theatre, and new directions for understanding Behn's theatrical work.

Paula Backsheider suggests that at the Restoration 'Charles II attempted to use theater in its broadest sense to help establish his concept of monarchy and its prerogatives'.[24] Backsheider makes a strong case for the argument that, through public spectacle and pageantry, Charles excited the people's desire for entertainment and frivolity while re-establishing the glamour and power of the King and his court. Many Royalist sympathisers received rewards for their loyalty during the Interregnum, including, of course, William Davenant and Thomas Killigrew. The newly constructed, indoor public theatres that housed the Duke's and King's companies enjoyed the direct patronage and, for the first time, the *presence* of the King and his followers; an unprecedented social attraction in itself. If the King used spectacle and pageantry to re-establish monarchical authority, the playhouse afforded another kind of spectacular opportunity for emerging social groups to reinforce, or challenge, that hegemonic project. As Backsheider observes: '[Behn] and her generation of nonaristocratic – male and female – writers were actively and self-consciously experimenting with ways to enter and influence public discourse on the great national questions as well as on pressing domestic concerns.'[25] As the widow of a merchant, a single woman with no apparent material wealth to buy into high ranking society through an advantageous marriage, even if she had wanted one, Behn had no obvious access to the aristocratic society she supported in her overt advocacy of Tory politics. The playhouse was a new social space, offering the potential for a new social and cultural discourse. Behn was among many that recognised this potential and it does not seem surprising to find that she set about using it as a means of making her way in society – and even less surprising that she should take her plays to the company which was under the control of another independent woman, a widow like herself, Lady Mary Davenant.

Female fellows

As impressive as Lady Davenant was, there were other women, other 'female fellows', who made up the Duke's Company. By 1670 the first generation of English actresses had been professional theatre practitioners for nearly a decade. Mary Betterton and Mrs Jennings were two of the original actresses signed to the Duke's Company in 1660 and both appear in Behn's first play, *The Forc'd Marriage* (1670). It was in the company of these women that Behn's plays were first produced and through their voices that her voice was realised. Mary Betterton is a particularly important figure in the history of theatre women. The weight of traditional histories has effectively occluded the extent of her influence by placing her firmly in the shadow of her husband, the Duke's Company's leading actor/manager and playwright, Thomas Betterton. She has also come to represent an early alternative to the actress/whore trope through another, equally potent binary that underpins constructs of femininity. In contrast to the assumptions of sexual profligacy attached to lives of most of her contemporaries, Mary Betterton is applauded for her stainless reputation; an equally reductive construct that defines her as 'virtuous wife' to her more famous husband and, interestingly, is extended to describe her professional work: 'All contemporaries agree that she was an honourable and generous woman, and even the most licentious libellers have nothing to say against her. Appropriately, she usually played the roles of good women.'[26] Rosamond Gilder, one of the early and greatly underrated female theatre historians of the twentieth century, devotes an entire chapter to Mary Betterton. Although Gilder adopts some of the censorious tone favoured by her male contemporaries, she is interested in demonstrating the crucial link between the first English actresses and the long line of theatre women already established as actress/managers in other European countries. Gilder's history was written between the two world wars and the tone of her writing reflects the desire to reinforce the moral certainties of the period but her emphasis on Mary Betterton's moral example to other Restoration actresses is matched by the refreshing and unusual emphasis she places on Mary's considerable professional achievements:

> We have an actual record of sixty different roles which she performed between 1661 and 1694, and this does not by any means cover her entire repertory ... She created in all some twenty-five original roles during her years of active service, ranging through the whole gamut of Restoration comedy and tragedy, farce and opera ... [she] had all the versatility and technical equipment which made her an invaluable member of the company.[27]

Mary Betterton is known to have extended her work to include the training of younger women. Her gifts as a teacher are remarked on in most references to her work[28] and it is hard to avoid the extension of the virtuous wife and its maternal connection with woman as 'natural' nurturer. But Mary had no children of her own and in some biographical histories this has been used to explain her involvement in the training of younger players; a substitute for thwarted maternal instincts and, latterly, a fading personal career rather than an extension of her professional activity. 'She had a flair for teaching, however, and an interest in playing foster mother to young actresses ... [her] interest in helping others continued long after her own acting career ended, for after the turn of the century her chief function in the theatre was training the younger performers.'[29] Gilder is among the earliest, possibly even the first, theatre historian to suggest a more radical creative influence between Mary Betterton and female playwright, Aphra Behn: 'Ianthe and Astrea flourished side by side ... [actresses] were soon re-enforced by the advent of playwrights of their own sex'.[30]

This story makes direct connections between theatre women and reads directly against the grain of the histories we have received and which have been adopted by revisionist histories, even though their agenda has been to increase awareness of women's place in theatre history. Ellen Donkin's *Getting into the Act* (1995) is an example of a revisionist project which, none the less, adopts the traditional assumption that Behn's entry to the playhouse was due to the beneficence of Thomas Betterton, and her success a result of his instructions concerning theatrical conventions and stage-craft.

> Women could, under Betterton, join the club and mix freely with male counterparts in order to learn about theatre. How else were they to familiarize themselves with the actors for whom they wrote, with the stage machinery that would dictate the rhythm and speed of scene changes, with the tastes of the audience, except by mingling, talking, observing, and asking questions?[31]

The point that Gilder makes, and which is worth pursuing further here, is that there were *female* contemporaries from whom Behn could and *did* learn. Much of the critical work around Behn's dramatic writing focuses on her female characters; parts written for and created by actresses whose creative work is largely ignored. This is not to deny the undoubted influence of actors and contemporary male playwrights, but to move Behn from the peripheral position of a lone woman allowed to 'join the [male] club' in the disreputable world of the theatre and reconsider her work alongside that of other theatre women. To rework Gilder: the first actresses and the first female playwright flourish because they reinforce each other's work. The conflation of the actress/whore writer/whore trope, so keenly felt in the vituperative attacks aimed specifically at Behn's dramatic writing, works to justify the argument for the conjoining of Behn's written texts with the physical text of the actress. Accusations of immorality and 'bawdy' can be seen as attempts to suppress a female discourse worked out in the very public sphere of the playhouse; a female discourse that, at times, openly challenged the male hierarchies in theatre companies and, in a broader context, questioned constructs of femininity.

A female audience

The argument for the playhouse as a site of an emerging female discourse is posited on the notion not that this was the *only* expression of resistance to the dominant social hegemony but that the playhouse participated in a unique way in a wider discussion on the position of women in society. The presence of writing and performing women in matched by presence of women in the audience. Recent historical research has rejected the earlier insistence on the Restoration audience as a purely aristocratic coterie, accepting the inclusion of servants and, most significantly, the growing mercantile class as a significant presence in the playhouse. David Roberts's *The Ladies: Female Patronage of Restoration Drama* (1989) pays particular attention to Samuel Pepys's playgoing records in which he notes one hundred and ninety-eight visits to the theatre made by his wife Elizabeth, many of which were made without him. Elizabeth's theatre visits were frequently made in the company of other women and, as Pepys's wealth increased, also included her maid. Roberts concludes that during the nine years covered by Pepys's *Diary*, 'the total female audience could be swollen significantly by the presence of maids and companions, whom it was apparently normal for affluent families to treat to a play in the afternoon'.[32] It is unfortunate that Pepys's last entry in his *Diary* predates the performance of Behn's first play by some eighteen months; however, it does not seem unreasonable to assume that the pattern of theatregoing he records for himself, his wife and her female servant can be used as an indication of the continued playgoing habits of their social peers.

Women now had unprecedented access to new representations and ideas and their presence on the stage and in the auditorium constitutes a radical form of social interaction. As female playwrights, players and audience members they participated in an essentially public debate on the position of women in Restoration society. In the conjoining of two female voices, Behn's written text and the actress's physical text, the female audience were not only *hearing* arguments against the inequalities in matters of love and marriage, they were also *seeing* women controlling the action and, to some extent, their own lives; together they were *experiencing* the debate as it was worked out in the public sphere of the playhouse. It is not possible, however tempting it may be, to claim that the stability of the patriarchy was seriously threatened by the advent of such a strong female presence but the accusations of indecency and immodesty hurled at theatre women suggest that their work, at the very least, touched the nerves of the patriarchal hegemony.

In spite of Behn's repeated claims that her plays were no more guilty of bawdy than her contemporary male playwrights and that she, more than others, advocated virtue in both men and women, the main weapon used against her was that her plays offended 'the Ladys' in the audience. The fact that her critics directed their attacks against her dramatic works with a ferocity that her prose writing escaped reinforces the notion that it is in the fusion of the written text and the physical text of the actress – the word made flesh – that the dissident female voice is fully recognised. Behn complicates such a reading of her work in her much-quoted demand for the 'Priviledge for [her] Masculine Part', and the assertion that she is not merely 'content to write for a Third day (money) only [valuing] Fame as much as if [she] had been born a *Hero*'.[33] This claim to the laurels of the male dramatic poet has been used by critics and celebrants alike to establish Behn as an aberrant, unnatural woman on the one hand and an exceptional, unique woman on the other. One modern critic, Frances M. Kavenik, suggests that Behn was '"one of the boys", so to speak, in her forthright presentation of the perils and delights of unleashed sexuality'.[34] Kavenik goes some way toward aligning the playwright with the actress by arguing that Behn, like the many female characters she created, is playing the breeches role.[35] The attendant and disappointingly conventional suggestion is that Behn is, ultimately, a woman imitating a man in order to get what she wants. Jessicca Munns, however, argues convincingly against this perspective:

> Rather than cross-dressing, Behn double-dresses and insists that her audience/readers accept her female gender and her right to a freedom of expression and range of topics hitherto limited to male literary production ... It is the doubleness of her claims and the doubleness of her vision that characterizes not merely Behn's 'feminism' but her creation of a new sexual space from which to speak ... she marks out a territory from which to operate.[36]

In some ways, the territory of the playhouse had already been marked out by the actresses; the new sexual space had been created by theatre women and their audience. But with the advent of Behn's voice through the dramatic text, that sexual space took on a new power and authority; a double-act created and performed with the company of actresses in Mary Davenant's Duke's Company.

Who were they and how was it done?

None of Behn's critics and biographers offers an explanation for what Dawn Lewcock describes as the 'sheer professionalism Behn's plays show' and her 'unusually acute feel for the visual opportunities the stage offered'.[37] All agree with Todd, who says that she 'must have haunted the theatre',[38] seeming to assume that her knowledge was gained from merely sitting in the auditorium. Yet the intimate knowledge of theatre practice that even Behn's early plays show suggests that she must have experienced the *process* of production as well as the moment of performance. In the twelve-year period of Behn's exclusive association with the Duke's Company (1670–1682) twelve plays are directly attributed to her, with three more attributed to a possible writing partnership with Thomas Betterton. A different patterning of Behn's dramatic work can be seen in the following table, which lists eleven actresses from the Duke's Company and puts them together with sixteen Behn plays produced between 1670 and 1682. Where records exist for the cast list at the play's first performance, the play and character are recorded in bold. There are also a number of plays attributed to Behn for which there are no extant records of the cast. These are identified by italics and include suggested castings for the main female characters based upon the actresses available to Behn in the company at that time. These suggestions have been arrived at by drawing together accounts from several sources (identified in the accompanying notes). The table is, of course, partially speculative but is intended to suggest hitherto unexplored aspects of Behn's dramatic work within the network of actresses in the Duke's Company.

The table can be read in two ways: firstly, it offers a striking visual image of Behn's prolific dramatic output within a twelve year period showing, for example, that there were occasions when she had several new plays produced within the same year. Secondly, it offers a visual representation, a map, of the connections between the actresses, and between them and the dramatist as they bought their individual and collective experience to their working relationship with the 'first' female playwright. Setting aside for a moment my conjectural cast lists for some Behn plays listed here, the recorded cast lists demonstrate that the actresses frequently worked together on new Behn plays. Working mainly from Howe's list of 'Major actresses and their roles in new plays'[39] we can see that Mary Betterton and Mary Lee (Slingsby) worked together on at least twenty-one new plays between 1670 and 1682, two of which were known to be Behn plays. In the first six years of Elizabeth Barry's long career she appeared in eight new plays with Mary Betterton and eleven with Mary Lee (Slingsby). These three women began their creative partnership in Behn's *Abdelazar* (1676). The casting patterns for these actresses suggests that there is the potential for further research in tracing the trajectory of playing partnerships and, alongside that, of the development of characters by playwrights aware of the strengths and popularity of the players they wrote for – a winning combination that ensured the place of the play in the repertoire of Restoration companies. This will be discussed further in later chapters but it is worth pausing here a moment to consider an example of what might, conjecturally, be extrapolated from this mapping of interactions by taking the case of Elizabeth Currer, first recorded in a major role in Behn's *The Counterfeit Bridegroom* (1677) but who may well have appeared much earlier.

Elizabeth (Betty) Currer is thought to have joined the Duke's Company in 1674. She probably played minor roles before her first recorded appearance in Elkanah Settle's *The Conquest of China* (1675) but her first notable success was as Betty Frisque in John Crowne's *The Countrey Wit* (1675). Elizabeth Howe suggests that this 'first whore role in comedy' was one that Nell Gwynn had made popular for the King's Company and that soon 'the skilled comedienne Elizabeth Currer began to specialise in such roles'.[40] Howe further suggests that Currer may have played Betty Flauntit in Behn's *The Town Fopp* (1676), noting that 'Currer was a "Betty" herself and the repetition of this Christian name in Behn's play surely makes the possibility that she played Flauntit more likely'.[41]

It is interesting here to consider the extent to which Behn capitalised on Currer's success in Crowne's play and tailored Flauntit to exploit Currer's talents and the audience's expectation – made clear by using the familiar 'Betty' to reinforce the point. Currer's next two roles in Behn plays build on her comic gifts and evidently play into the mistress/whore roles she had made her own. In *The Counterfeit Bridegroom* (1677) Currer appears in the first of many breeches roles and is also named as the prologue speaker, a sure sign of her growing status in the company.

The company of women: Aphra Behn's plays perfo[rmed]

	1670	1671	1673	1676	1676	1677	1677	167[7]
	The Forc'd Marriage	The Amorous Prince	The Dutch Lover	Abdelazar	The Town Fopp	The Debauchee	The Rover (Part 1)	Count[ess of] Bridegr[oom]
Elizabeth Barry[e]				Leonora (girl)			Hellena (girl)	
Mary Betterton	Erminia (wife)	Clarina (wife)	Euphemia (woman)	Florella (wife)		Lady T (wife)	Florinda (virtuous)	
Charlotte Butler[f]					Diana (girl)			
Elizabeth Currer[g]					Betty Flauntit			Mrs Ha[...] & Prol[ogue]
Mrs Gibbs[h]								Clar[a]
Mrs Jennings[i]	Princess Galatea (girl)							
Elinor Leigh[j]		Cloris (girl)	Cleonte (girl)			Crostill (widow)	Moretta	
Mrs Norris[k]		Lucia (maid)	Olinda (maid)			Betty (maid)	Callis	Old L[ady] Sant[...]
Margaret Osborn[l]				Elvira	Bawd	Alitia (wife)		Wid[ow] Land[...]
Anne Quin (Gwin)[m]						Phebe (maid)	Angelica Bianca	
Mary (Lee) Slingsby[n]	Olinda (girl)	Ismena (girl)	Hippolyta (girl)	Isabella (villainess)	Celinda (girl)	Clara (girl)		

actresses in the Duke's Company 1670–1682[a]

	1679	1679	1680	1681	1681	1681/2	1682
nt :y	The Feign'd Curtezans	The Young King[c]	The Revenge	The Rover (Part 2)	The False Count	The Roundheads[d]	The City Heiress
	Cornelia (young woman)	Urania (young woman) Epilogue	Corina (whore)	La Nuche (Courtizan) Epilogue	Epilogue	Lambert (wife)	Lady Galliard (passionate mistress) Prologue
lla ɔus)							
			Marinda (mistress)			Desbro (wife)	Charlot & Epilogue
y :y	Marcella & Prologue			Ariadne	Isabella		Diana
ɪdy							
			Mrs Dashit (wife)			Cromwell (wife)	Mrs Closet
	Phillipa		Mrs Dunwell (Bawd)	Petronella Eleanora		Gilliflower (maid)	Mrs Clacket
					Jacinta		
y ⱱell ʒue						Fleet-wood (wife)	
	Laura Lucretia	Cleomena (Amazon)					

Notes for Table 1.

a   This table deals only with the plays performed between 1670 and 1682 when Behn's plays were produced exclusively by the Duke's Company either in their original theatre at Lincoln's Inn Fields or in the newly built theatre at Dorset Gardens. I have drawn on various sources in creating this table, my principal sources being *A Biographical Dictionary* (1973) and *The London Stage 1660–1800: A Calendar of Plays, Entertainments and Afterpieces Together with Casts, Box-receipts and Contemporary Comment Compiled from the Playbills, Newspapers and Theatrical Diaries of the Period*, part 1, *1660–1700*, ed. William Van Lennep (Carbondale: Southern Illinois University Press, 1965), from here on referred to as *The London Stage*. I have made some use of J. H. Wilson's *All the King's Ladies* (1958) but much more of Elizabeth Howe's *The First English Actresses* (1992). The detailed list of the leading actresses' credits contained in her book and the additional character 'types' suggested for each role have been repeated or adapted in this table.

b   Janet Todd does not include *The Counterfeit Bridegroom* in *Works* (1996), probably because it is an adaptation of Middleton's *No Wit, No Help, Like a Woman's*. Todd does acknowledge the attribution to Behn, possibly in collaboration with Betterton. I include the play here as it is recorded for this season in *The London Stage*.

c   *The Young King* was not successful in performance and was not published until 1683. *The London Stage* only identifies Barry as epilogue speaker; the other casting suggestions are mentioned in Todd, *Works* (1996), vol. 7, p. 82.

d   There is evidence for another Behn play performed shortly after *The Roundheads*. *Like Father, Like Son* was never published and although *The London Stage* records a first performance around March 1682 there is no record of a cast list. J. H. Wilson (1958) suggests that Charlotte Butler was the Prologue speaker for the play and that Elizabeth Currer was also among the cast. As there is such scant information I have not included it in this table.

e   Elizabeth Barry's first recorded performance for the company is in 1675 when she played the maid Draxilla in Otway's *Alcibiades*.

f   Charlotte Butler joined the company in the season of 1673/4. It is, therefore, highly likely that she appeared in a Behn play before 1680 when her name is first included in the cast list.

g   Elizabeth (Betty) Currer also joined the company in the season of 1673/4. It seems unlikely that the role recorded for her in *The Counterfeit Bridegroom* was her first appearance in a Behn play, as I shall discuss below.

h   Although listed as a minor player, Mrs Gibbs played a number of significant supporting roles between 1676 and 1678.

i   Mrs Jennings was one of the first actresses to join the company between 1660 and 1661. She left the company in 1670 and is possibly best remembered as one of the actresses who, as Downes recorded, 'by force of love were Erept the stage', Downes (1708), p. 35.

j   Elinor Leigh joined the company in the season of 1670/1. She left the stage (possibly to have a child) the following year but is recorded in cast lists from 1676. She may well have appeared in Behn's first two plays and it is more than likely that she later appeared in other Behn plays. Elinor Leigh continued playing with the United Company and also joined the breakaway company in 1695 where she played leading character roles and was also one of the first actress/sharers in that company.

k   Mrs Norris was one of the original eight actresses in the company and continued to be recorded in cast lists through to 1683.

l   Margaret Osborn was another minor player who joined the company in 1672 and continued through to the United Company, disappearing from the records in 1691.

m Anne Quin was one of the first actresses in the King's Company under her maiden name of Marshall. After a brief absence she returned to that company in 1667 but the following year had an argument with the management. There is then a ten year gap when her movements are not recorded. She joined the Duke's Company in 1677. She is not recorded in cast lists after 1682.

n   Mary Lee joined the company in 1670, playing as Lady Slingsby following her second marriage in 1680 to Sir Charles (or possibly Sir Arthur) Slingsby. In spite of her now elevated social position she seems to have performed consistently through to 1685. Again, it is highly likely that she played more roles than are recorded for her in Behn's plays.

As the adulterous Lady Fancy in Behn's *Sir Patient Fancy* (1678) the playwright and her leading comedienne extended the comic possibilities by pairing her with actor Anthony Leigh as the cuckolded husband in what Howe describes as 'another comic case of thwarted desire'.[42] Interestingly, the comic couple, Currer and Leigh, went on to repeat this success when they were cast in similar roles: first by Thomas Otway in the comic sub-plot to *Venice Preserved* (1682) and later by Nahum Tate in *A Duke and No Duke* (1684). Howe notes both these plays but does not comment on the fact that Behn was the first to establish Currer in the comic-couple territory.

The working relationship between Behn and Currer continues to develop in the creation of Marcella in *The Feign'd Curtezans* (1679). Here Currer is paired with a younger woman, played by Elizabeth Barry, as they embark on a reckless sexual adventure in an attempt to avoid a future that holds marriage for one and a convent life for the other. Disguised as courtesans they follow a plot that swings from light comedy to outright farce in a play that Behn wittily dedicated to the King's mistress, Nell Gwynn. Once again, Currer is also named as the prologue speaker. The point is that whether Behn exploited Currer's growing popularity as a comedienne, or Currer developed the 'types' she made her own in Behn's plays, they worked in a creative partnership that had benefits for the whole company – not least in ticket receipts. Currer is paired with Barry in two further Behn plays and it seems likely that she appeared in more than the seven plays that have a record of the full cast list. Elizabeth Currer's last known role is as the comic and wholly novel Widow Ranter in the play of the same name posthumously produced by the United Company in 1689. It seems fitting that the comedienne who began by realising Behn's string of gutsy mistresses, courtesans and widows should end her career by creating a woman who finds herself alone in the 'new world' of the colonies, far from the restraints imposed on women by civilised society, who smokes, drinks and curses like a man and wears breeches so that she can fight like a man too. As Margarete Rubik puts it: 'Mrs Ranter, her name reminiscent of a religious sect suspected of political and social insubordination, is loud, vulgar, free-minded and splendidly vigorous and comic, the complete match for the daredevil lieutenant she woos, and as such a unique figure in the comedy of the time.'[43] Whether Behn wrote this character to suit Currer's particular talents and her move into character parts cannot be known but it is the last part recorded in Currer's fifteen year career on the London stage.

Further patterns of development between female playwright and performers might be traced in the table above. Of course, as the leading actresses in the company, these women had little choice but to work together; but that very necessity reinforces the notion of collaborative, ensemble work developed over an extensive period of time – a working environment that is almost unimaginable in modern theatre companies. A similar map for the actors appearing in Behn's plays might also reveal an interesting set of patternings and casting. Betterton, Nokes and Leigh all created notable characters for Behn. But creative collaboration between playwrights and actors, many of whom went on to write their own plays, has long been established in theatre histories. The purpose here is to draw attention to the first moment at which women dramatists and actresses had the opportunity to represent women on the public stage and the way in which that opportunity was fully exploited, not least by the female playwright.

Given the doubts that have been cast upon the competence of women in the Restoration playhouse, even some of the most ardent advocates of Behn's work have questioned whether she would have been in a position to work actively and closely with the actresses. In her discussion of Behn's first play, *The Forc'd Marriage* (1670), Janet Todd refers to the fact that authors 'were frequently in charge of the actors' at rehearsals, but asks 'how far this would be true of Behn as a novice and a woman'.[44] If, as suggested earlier, the company's manager Lady Davenant took the decision to perform Behn's first play it is as likely that she, possibly in consultation with the most senior actress in the company, Mary Betterton, would have advised Behn over casting. Downes's reference to the production is frequently quoted in relation to the playwright Thomas Otway's disastrous debut as an actor, and Downes seems quite clear that the responsibility for casting Otway lay with Behn: 'Mrs *Bhen* gave him the King in the Play, for a Probation Part.'[45] Todd comments on the fact that Thomas Betterton appears not to have insisted on any changes to the play, a prerogative that he frequently took advantage of, going on to suggest that playwrights 'needed to know the members of the company intimately' and that Behn 'tailored the [leading] parts' to Mary and Thomas Betterton's skills.[46] Behn appears to have the confidence of the whole company and with a cast of experienced players, and the debut of a new company member Mary Lee (Slingsby), Otway's failure in the role of the King appears to have had little effect on the overall reception of the play, which ran for six nights: a considerable success. But it was to be Behn's third play, *Abdelazar* (1676), which provided a less than auspicious start for the young actress who would eventually contribute to, and gain most from, a long and successful association with Aphra Behn.

Introducing Elizabeth Barry

Elizabeth Barry was in her early teens when Behn joined the company – she was not an overnight success. She is recorded in the cast list for eight of Behn's plays but it is likely that she too appeared in others, sometimes in the favoured position of prologue or epilogue speaker, as in *The False Count* (1681). The stories surrounding Barry's entrance to the theatre stem from contemporary writing concerning her initial failure as an actress. Colley Cibber argues that her later success serves as 'particular Proof of the Difficulty there is in judging with Certainty from their first Trials, whether young People will ever make any great Figure on a Theatre'.[47] In *A Brief Supplement to Colley Cibber* Anthony Aston remarks that 'Lord Rochester took her on the Stage; where for some Time they could make nothing of her'.[48] Barry's private connections with Rochester are well, if not always accurately, documented and it is certain that she bore his child in 1677. However, the notion that Rochester was instrumental in launching her professional career becomes detailed 'fact' by 1741 when Curll reports the episode in his *History of the English Stage*.[49] Barry's story has been repeated and embellished through the centuries and this is how it is told in Todd's biography of Behn.

> The story goes that Rochester and his cronies saw [Barry's] performance and found it so appalling that the Earl, a natural actor and steeped in the theatre, struck an improbable wager: that he would in six months make Barry the most convincing actress in the theatre. He then set about training her, making her rehearse repeatedly on stage and in costume. Although she had no talent for mimicry, the usual basis of acting, Barry was intelligent and, where she could not learn lines and remember how to say them, she could enter into feelings, becoming another person when inspired. Rochester developed her potential power from September until July of the next year, when Behn was flattered to be asked to give her friend the small part of Leonora in *Abdelazar*.[50]

As the adopted daughter of Sir William and Lady Davenant the young Barry was brought up in a household that revolved around the activities of the playhouse; the Davenants occupied a house attached to the theatre in Lincoln's Inn Fields. Their social connections would have included members of the court and others in the higher ranks of society as well as close contact with the players in the Duke's Company.

The relationship between aristocratic patrons and the 'King's Servants' in the playhouse is complex and peppered with examples of abusive as well as advantageous sexual and social liaisons between actresses and their admirers. However, the notion that Barry's theatrical training was entirely in the hands of Rochester seems at best the result of male boasting and at worst yet another example of the appropriation of women's work to male control. So how might we read against the grain of that historiography? With Mary Betterton's proven skills as a teacher is it fanciful to suggest that Lady Davenant might place her ward's potential career in the hands of this experienced actress? Why would Behn be 'flattered to give her friend' a part when she was, above all things, concerned with the commercial success of her work? After the Otway incident, it seems unlikely that she would knowingly risk another disastrous performance. There is evidence that Behn and Elizabeth Barry were firm friends from an early stage, notably in Behn's 'A Ballad on Mr J. H. to Amoret, asking why I was so sad' (c. 1670s) where it is commonly accepted among literary critics that 'Amoret' was the young Barry, receiving a warning from the more experienced speaker on the pain of love and sexual passion. So if we look for an alternative pattern of influence, it is possible to suggest that Barry's success in *Abdelazar,* performed in July 1676, followed by another in Behn's *Rover (Part One)* the following year, was as much to do with the playwright's direction and encouragement to the young actress as any contribution Rochester may have made. Janet Todd also refers to the creative relationship between Behn and Barry in the production of *The Rover* in which she notes that Barry proved herself to be a 'notable comedienne ... whom Behn could coach in precisely the gestures she wanted for her heroines'[51] – a direct contradiction to the assertion that Barry had no skills in mimicry. As in *Abdelazar*, the cast for *The Rover* included Mary Betterton who was now joined by two other experienced actresses, Anne Quinn (Gwin)[52] and Elinor Leigh. From this perspective we might conclude that the pragmatic Behn deliberately surrounded her talented but relatively inexperienced leading actress with the most experienced actresses available.

Over the next twelve years political changes, both inside and outside the theatrical community, created new opportunities and brought new pressures to bear on the company of women with whom Behn can be so closely identified. It seems extraordinary that no other female playwright is recorded as having written, or having attempted to write, during these or the following twelve years. Considering the commercial success of Behn's work, it seems even more extraordinary that the rival King's Company appears to have made no attempt to produce a female playwright of its own. As the two patent companies moved toward the theatrical monopoly of 1682, Behn's dramatic output was at its peak and yet within the next seven years, until her death in 1689, she had only two more new plays produced. The union between the King's Company and Duke's Company may not have resulted in the appearance of a bevy of new writing women – that was to come later – but it did provide a fertile ground for the development of that other group of theatre women: the company of actresses.

Notes

1. For more on the tennis-court theatre see David Thomas's video documentary *From Tennis Court to Playhouse* (Warwick: University of Warwick, 1996) in which Thomas argues that Christopher Wren's design for Drury Lane was inspired by Davenant's scenic playhouse at Lincoln's Inn Fields.
2. Howe, *The First English Actress*, p. 24.
3. The *Oxford Dictionary of National Biography* records the little that is known about Mary Davenant in the entry for her husband, William Davenant. Henrietta Maria du Tremblay was William's third and last wife, returning to England with him following a visit to France in 1665. The *DNB* notes that she 'was a capable business partner during his years as a theatre manager, a role she continued after his death'. See www.oxforddnb.com/view/article/7197 p. 6.
4. Jacqueline Pearson, *The Prostituted Muse: Images of Women and Women Dramatists 1642–1737* (Hemel Hempstead: Harvester Wheatsheaf, 1988), p. 32.
5. p. 32.
6. *A Biographical Dictionary of Actors, Actresses, Musicians, Dancers, Managers & Other Stage Personnel in London 1660–1800*, ed. Philip H. Highfill (Carbondale: Southern Illinois University Press, 1973), 16 vols, vol. 4, p. 167.
7. Vol. 4, p. 168, cites the Lord Chamberlain's accounts as the source for details on Lady Davenant's altercation with John Perin over the creation of the Barbican actors' nursery.
8. Pearson, *Prostituted Muse*, p. 32.
9. Janet Todd, *The Secret Life of Aphra Behn* (London: André Deutsch, 1996) *The Works of Aphra Behn*, ed. Janet Todd (London: William Pickering, 1996) 7 vols. *Aphra Behn Studies* ed. Janet Todd (Cambridge: Cambridge University Press, 1996), from here on identified as Todd, *Life*, *Works* and *Studies*.
10. The anonymous 'An Account of the Life of the Incomparable Mrs Behn', placed as a foreword to the posthumous publication of *The Younger Brother*

(1696), is generally attributed to Charles Gildon, who compiled Behn's unpublished works after her death in April 1689. 'Memoirs of the Life of Mrs Behn', published in the same year and attached to *All the Histories and Novels written by the Late Ingenious Mrs Behn, entire in one Volume ... etc.* (London: Samuel Briscoe, 1696), is also anonymous, claiming authenticity only in that it was written by "one of the Fair Sex". It is likely that the author was once again Behn's opportunistic editor, Charles Gildon. Montague Summers (ed.), *The Works of Aphra Behn*, 6 vols (1915), also includes a memoir drawing on Gildon's history of her life. Even recent critical readings on Behn's work, such as Heidi Hutner (ed.), *Rereading Aphra Behn* (Charlottesville: University Press of Virginia, 1993), choose to include some of the more sensational stories about Behn's life.
11 Virginia Woolf, *A Room of One's Own* (1928), reprinted London: Penguin Books, 1945, p. 66.
12 Todd, *Life*, Introduction, p. 1.
13 Todd identifies the recipient of the letter as an uncle, while Angeline Goreau, *Reconstructing Aphra* (Oxford: Oxford University Press, 1980), states that Elizabeth Cottington was 'writing to her cousin', p. 115.
14 Todd, *Life* (1996), p. 135. Todd cites her source as *The Tixall Letters; or, The correspondence of the Aston Family, and their Friends, during the Seventeenth Century,* ed. A. Clifford (Edinburgh, 1815), vol. 2, pp. 59–61.
15 Goreau, *Reconstructing Aphra* p. 115.
16 p. 116.
17 Todd, *Life*, p. 461, n.3.
18 p. 136.
19 p. 136.
20 Philips's virtuous reputation rests largely on the notion that she wrote 'privately', for herself and a few friends, repeatedly resisting publication of her work. When her collected poems were placed in the hands of a publisher she is said to have insisted that her anonymity be preserved. Given the relatively small readership of London at this time, and the numerous eulogies that were written following her death in 1664, it is arguable that Philips deliberately colluded with the construction of the 'virtuous' anonymous female writer as an effective marketing ploy.
21 Samuel Pepys, *The Diary of Samuel Pepys,* eds Robert Latham and William Matthews (London: G. Bell and Sons, 1970–1983), 11 vols. From here on I shall identify this text as Pepys's *Diary*. As the *Diary* is also available in concise editions I shall refer to the date of the entry as a more secure means of reference.
22 Todd, *Life*, p. 128.
23 Dawn Lewcock, 'More for Seeing than Hearing: Behn and the Use of Theatre' in Todd, *Studies*, pp. 66–83, p. 66.
24 Paula Backsheider, *Spectacular Politics* (Baltimore and London: Johns Hopkins University Press, 1993), Introduction, p. xiii.

25 p. 70.
26 J. H. Wilson, *All the King's Ladies – Actresses of the Restoration* (Chicago: University of Chicago Press, 1958), pp. 118–120.
27 Rosamond Gilder, *Enter the Actress* (London: George G. Harrap, 1931), pp. 157–159.
28 Most references to Mary Betterton refer to her training the Princesses Mary and Anne (both later Queens of England) for the court masque *Calisto* performed in March 1675. Queen Anne later granted Mary a pension – although it appears that this was never paid.
29 *A Biographical Dictionary*, vol. 2, p. 97.
30 Gilder, *Enter the Actress*, p. 173. 'Ianthe' was the nickname given to Mary Betterton by Pepys, who first saw her performing this role in Davenant's *Siege of Rhodes* (1661). 'Astrea' was first used by Behn when writing from abroad (when she is thought to have been working as a spy) and appears in various references to her thereafter.
31 Ellen Donkin, *Getting into the Act* (London: Routledge, 1995), p. 23.
32 David Roberts, *The Ladies: Female Patronage of Restoration Drama 1660–1700* (Oxford: Clarendon Press, 1989), p. 64.
33 Behn, *The Lucky Chance* (London: W. Canning, 1687), Preface.
34 Frances M. Kavenik, 'Aphra Behn: The Playwright as "Breeches Part,"' in *Curtain Calls: British and American Women and the Theater, 1660–1820*, eds Mary Anne Schofield and Cecilia Macheski (Athens: Ohio University Press, 1991), pp. 177–191, p. 179.
35 The term 'breeches role' is generally applied to female characters in a play who adopt male disguise. This is a dramatic device frequently employed on the Restoration stage and used by Behn in several of her own plays.
36 Jessica Munns, '"I by a double right thy bounties claim": Aphra Behn and Sexual Space' in *Curtain Calls*, pp. 193–210, p. 195.
37 Lewcock, 'More for seeing than Hearing', pp. 67–68.
38 Todd, *Life*, p. 133.
39 Howe, *The First English Actresses*, Appendix 1, pp. 178–189.
40 p. 78.
41 p. 79.
42 p. 101.
43 Margerete Rubik, *Early Women Dramatists 1550–1800* (London: Macmillan Press, 1998), p. 39. The play was not a success and barely made the third day benefit.
44 Todd, *Life*, p. 142.
45 Downes *Roscius Anglicanus: A New Edition*, ed. Judith Milhous and Ribert Hume (Society for Theatre Research, 1987), p. 72. All quotations from Downes are from this edition unless otherwise specified. Downes goes on to say that Otway, 'being not us'd to the stage; the full house put him to such a Sweat and Tremendous, Agony, being dash't, spoilt him for an Actor'.
46 Todd, *Life*, p. 142.

47 Colley Cibber, *An Apology for the Life of Mr Colley Cibber* (c. 1740), with notes and supplement by Robert W. Lowe in 2 vols. (London: John C. Nimmo, 1889), vol. 1, p. 159.
48 Anthony Aston, *A Brief Supplement to Colley Cibber Esq.* (c. 1769) in Cibber, ed. Lowe (1889), vol. 2, pp. 297–318, p. 303.
49 Thomas Betterton, *The History of the English Stage* (London: E. Curll, 1741). This is usually attributed to the publisher Edmund Curll who, with William Oldys, compiled the material from Thomas Betterton's notes. As Betterton died on 2 May 1710 it is likely that Curll and Oldys made some additions, even if they were *based* upon Betterton's notes. In the case of Elizabeth Barry's training for the stage, it seems to strain credulity that a theatre practitioner of Betterton's standing and influence would attribute Barry's success purely to Rochester's instructions.
50 Todd, *Life*, p. 192.
51 Todd, *Life*, p. 213.
52 Anne Marshall was with the King's Company, but following her marriage to the actor Peter Quin (Gwin) seems absent from the stage until she joins the Duke's Company in 1677. Various spellings of her name have contributed toward the confusion between roles played by Anne and those played by Nell Gwynn.

2
United we stand

The events of the 1680s reveal something of the social anxiety surrounding shifts in political power in both country and playhouse. This was a decade of political change in British society, signalling a departure from the triumphant libertine monarchism of the Restoration to the constitutional reforms introduced by the 'Glorious Revolution' of 1688/9.[1] In the playhouse, the dramatic texts of this decade largely continue to support the Restoration values of the monarchy but there were also fundamental changes afoot in the day-to-day management of the two theatres at Drury Lane and Dorset Gardens. The accounts of this period in theatre history follow a conventional top-down approach, tracing the failure of the two-company patent system, granted by Charles II to Killigrew and Davenant and inherited by their respective sons, Charles Killigrew and Charles Davenant, and the creation of the United Company under the artistic management of the principal actor of the day, Thomas Betterton. In the previous chapter, this straight-forward story of inheritance, merger and artistic delegation was problematised by identifying Lady Davenant's role in the creative and managerial processes of the Duke's Company. This chapter moves on to look at the events that led to the formation of the United Company and the creation of a theatrical monopoly of theatre in London that was to last for thirteen years. By pursuing a bottom-up approach to the power shifts in the company and considering afresh the position of the players and their response to changes in company practice, the actress can be seen to occupy a visible presence and emerging power in the economics of the playhouse.

The demise of the King's Company

The King's Company had begun to experience financial difficulties from as early as the 1677/8 season. It is quite likely that this was mainly due to the constant disputes between the now aged patentee, Thomas Killigrew, and almost everyone else involved in the company, including his son, Charles, who finally wrested control from his father in 1677.[2] Judith Milhous offers a concise summary of the final years of the King's Company, concluding that Thomas Killigrew's handling of events serves 'as an object lesson in how not to operate a theatre company'.[3] In spite of their new theatre buildings, both companies had experienced depleted box-office receipts. The most pertinent details of the 'Articles of Union', drawn up between Charles Killigrew and Charles Davenant at the point of union on 4 May 1682, are usefully summarised by Milhous and Hume:

> Charles Killigrew will dissolve the King's Company within six days; will deliver the stock of playbooks and other possessions (scenery excepted) to Charles Davenant; and will yield tenancy of the Drury Lane theatre. In return, Charles Davenant engages to pay £3 for the use of Drury Lane every time *either* theatre is used and to grant Charles Killigrew 3/20 of the profits of the joint acting company.[4]

Far from the gentle merger of traditional historiography, the terms of this agreement suggest an out-and-out commercial takeover: the King's Company was to be 'dissolved', with Charles Davenant and the Duke's Company emerging as the victors. The first and most obvious advantage in creating a United Company was that there was now a genuine theatrical monopoly but the players from the former Duke's Company undoubtedly benefited most from the reorganisation. As Judith Milhous notes: 'An obvious problem created by the union was the surplus of actors it gave the United Company. A few, like Coysh and Disney, left London, and some women were squeezed out, but accommodation was made for as many performers as possible, perhaps as a means of ensuring acquiescence.'[5] As with any commercial take-over, there were some who found themselves surplus to requirements. Many of the veteran actors from the King's Company had begun to hand their parts to younger players, or were about to, yet not all it seems retired as gracefully as others, and not all who continued to play with the new company were entirely happy with the conditions they were offered. As the prompter John Downes puts it: 'Upon this Union, Mr Hart being the Heart of the Company under Mr Killigrew's Patent never Acted more, by reason of his Malady; being Afflicted with the Stone and Gravel, of which he dy'd some time after. Having a sallary of 40 shillings a week to the Day of his Death.'[6] This frequently quoted passage from Downes masks Hart's sense of disaffection behind ill health, which forced his retirement from the stage and follows this observation with a list of the 'remnant of that company', eight actors and three actresses from the King's Company who now merged with their rivals.[7] Interestingly, Milhous and Hume's heavily annotated edition of Downes includes an extensive footnote which continues to insist on the more benevolent interpretation of the merger of the two companies: 'Something is missing from Downes' text here – evidently a statement to the effect that these actors *joined* the United Company' (my emphasis).[8] The fact is that with the dissolution of the King's Company their players were effectively out of work and the implication is that they had to *apply* to join the new company. Milhous and Hume go on to provide convincing evidence that some of the late King's Company were paid *not* to play, others played occasionally and there are large gaps in the records for some players who may have found work outside London.[9] Milhous and Hume conclude that 'though the United Company may technically have agreed to accept all of them, several did not get full-time work with the company'.[10]

The Duke's Company now had access to all the old plays assigned to Thomas Killigrew under the 1660 patent, all the new plays written for the company since that time and, crucially, access to the Theatre Royal in Drury Lane. It is not difficult to imagine the relish with which the Duke's players engaged with the treasure chest of stock plays and parts that had previously been the property of their rivals. For the more seasoned players it would present the opportunity to offer new interpretations of roles which, until this point, had been associated with their former rivals. Under the two-company system a part would inevitably take on the character of the actor or actress playing it and, even if the role was passed to a younger player, it is highly likely that there would be traces of the earlier performance, if not an actual reproduction of the part as created by the original player. The availability of a wide range of stock plays and proven successes was particularly advantageous for the actresses. Parts created for the first time by actresses in the King's Company were now available to a new company of women and, more importantly, to a new generation of actresses. Already gaining a growing reputation as the leading actress of her generation, Elizabeth Barry had most to gain from the leading female characters now available to her.

In an unpublished work from 1945, which appears to have been completely ignored by contemporary or subsequent histories, Lucyle Hook, once a theatre practitioner herself, expresses a delightful and unashamedly subjective view of the actress' appetite for parts previously beyond her reach: 'One can almost hear [Mrs Barry] smack her lips over the parts which inevitably fell to her share'.[11] Within three years of the union it was this actress, a player from the Duke's Company, who secured the first benefit performance for an individual player. Although barred by her sex from owning a 'share' in the company profits, Elizabeth Barry's popularity and influence carried serious financial weight. As Elizabeth Howe notes, 'one benefit could increase her yearly income to more than [Thomas] Betterton's'.[12] Howe also recognises that Barry moves from being the Duke's Company's main draw in the late 1670s to a position which gave her 'some authority over her fellow players', although she appears to be somewhat mystified as to how, or why, 'Barry's power within the company seems to have slowly increased during the 1680s'.[13] Lucyle Hook's account presents Barry as a more proactive figure within the new company structure, suggesting that she deliberately exploited the unique conditions created by the monopoly to extend her creative range as an actress and, as a direct consequence of her success, gained in public popularity. Hook lists eleven stock plays in which Barry re-created the leading female role for the United Company between 1682 and 1688, concluding that: 'By the time she was twenty-eight … Mrs Barry had played all the existing great roles in English drama and could look forward to another fifteen years of even greater activity.'[14] The opportunity for Barry and other theatre women to engage in greater activity within the company system came about through changes in the balance of power within the world of the public playhouse. It is in the gaps and fissures, the lacunae created when dominant forces shift and renegotiate power structures, that women's work can be seen most clearly. It is also in such moments that they become most vulnerable to attack by their contemporaries and, as the dominant force regroups, to erasure by the makers of our hegemonic histories.

The playwright versus the players

The atmosphere of heightened political tension was considerably calmer between 1682 and Charles II's death in 1685 but the storm clouds surrounding the succession were still looming on the horizon, with mounting opposition to Charles's openly Catholic brother, James, taking the throne. This undoubtedly contributed to the company's decision to concentrate on revivals, rather than risk politically sensitive new plays and the inevitable censure, not to mention the decline in box-office receipts, already experienced during the Exclusion Crisis in 1679.[15] But another emphasis is possible here, one that goes against the flow of theatre histories. The focus of the company at this moment is on the players, not the playwrights, and it is this focus that reveals a rather different balance of power at work in the structure of the United Company.

In the early days of the two-company system, the King's and Duke's companies competed for new works by courtiers such as Rochester and Etherege, and later sought agreements with the new breed of professional playwrights, Dryden, Otway, Lee and, of course, Aphra Behn. The wit and popularity of the playwright was as important to box-office success as the skills and popularity of the players. Soon after the union, the company shifts its focus, concentrating largely on revivals, plays already tried, tested and effectively owned by the United Company, the novelty for the audience was less in who had written the play and rather more in *how* the play was performed and by whom.[16] The playwright had already received his/her garland and the most to be hoped for would be a good 'third day'.[17] In the season of revival, the play now serves as a vehicle to demonstrate the talents of the players, especially if it is the first time they have played an established role. It is evident from some contemporary writings that there were those who objected violently to the growing power of the players and the decline in status for the playwright: a cry echoed in the long line of theatre histories that privileges text over performance, writer over player.

Robert Gould, a minor playwright, was among those who used the satirical lampoon to vent his frustration at the power wielded by the leading players in the United Company. Apart from putting his name to various 'Satyrs', in the collection of his *Works*, edited and prepared for publication by the author in 1709, he is known to have had only one play, *The Rival Sisters* or *The Violence of Love*, performed at Drury Lane in 1696. Ten years earlier *The Play-House, A Satyr* (1685) sees the frustrated would-be playwright appealing to all writers to join him in a vituperative attack against the players:

> Then turn your chiefest strength against the *Stage*,
> Which you have made the *Nuisance* of the Age;
> Strive that judicious way to get applause,
> And remedy some of the ills you cause:
> Lash the lewd *Actors* – but first stop your *nose*,
> It is a *stinking Theme*, may discompose
> All but your selves – almost as bad as those.
> Let this thought screw you to the highest pitch;
> They keep you *poor*, and you have made them *rich*;
> Toil'd night and day t'encrease their ill got store,
> And who do they despise and laugh at more?
> But make you dance attendance, Cap in hand,
> That once, like *Spaniels*, were at your Command;

> Wou'd cringe and fawn, and who so kind as they,
> If you but promis'd they should have their *Play*
> But since *Hart* dy'd, and the *two Houses* join'd
> What get ye? What *incouragement* d'ye find?
> Yet still you write and sacrifice your ease;
> Your *Plays* too shall be acted, if they please.[18]

The references to Hart's death and the union of the companies suggests that this lampoon was in circulation shortly after the United Company was first established, earlier perhaps than the 1685 date on the manuscript held by the British Library. The inevitable reference to the players' lewdness serves as an introduction to a less usual string of complaints and accusations which are worthy of closer examination.

The assertion that the players are actively exploiting the writers reveals Gould's perception of the extent to which the power relations between the player and the writer had been reversed. This is most clearly expressed in the image of the player as the once obedient 'spaniel' who is now the master upon whom the writer must 'dance attendance, Cap in hand'. Gould's attack expresses a wider anxiety about the social mobility of the players of both sexes, but what is most interesting here is the assumption that the playwright assumes a higher worth for his work as the creator of text. The binary of text and performance, text-maker over performance-maker that has so influenced the making of theatre histories is clearly at work here.

Gould's attack is implicitly aimed at Thomas Betterton and Elizabeth Barry. Although the first printed edition of his satire in 1685 refrained from actually naming names, he rectified this in his amended edition of 1709, making Barry a clear and obvious target.[19] The anonymous writer of *A Satyr on the Players* (c. 1682–1685), takes a rather different approach. Not only does his lampoon vilify both actors and actresses by clearly spelling out the extent of each supposed sexual proclivity and action, it also takes delight in naming each player in turn. By comparing the list of players with the sometimes incomplete company rosters in *The London Stage*, the list of names can be tied in more precisely to the 1682–83 season in which the United Company was launched. As lampoons depended upon the topicality of their satire, this earlier date for publication is more likely.

The first half of the satire is directed against the actors. The author humiliates each victim by drawing attention to his physical appearance, his sexual activity – or lack of it – his drunkenness and, that familiar target, his bad acting. The second half is reserved for the actresses where the focus remains firmly on the well-worn actress/whore trope. The body of the actress is the target for the usual tirade of sexual abuse and her presumed exploitation of her body is at the heart of the main complaint: the actress's personal wealth and her social aspirations and status. The full version of the satire is included here and is, to my knowledge, the first time that it has been fully reproduced in print. Montague Summers published a heavily edited and bowdlerised version as an appendix to his edition of Downes's *Roscius Anglicanus* in 1928 which has, until now, been considered as a full transcription.[20]

A Satyr on the Players[21]

The Censuring World perhaps may not Esteem	
A Satyr on so Scandalous a Theam	
As a Stage Ape, yet meerly for the sake	
Of Novelty, I'll once a tryal make	
For who can hold to see the Foppish Town	5
Admire so bad a wretch as *Betterton*	
Is't for his legs, his Shoulders, or his face	
His formal stiffness or his awkward Grace	
A shop for him had been the fittest place	
But Brawny *Tom*: the Playhouse needs must choose	10
The Villains Refuge & Hells' Rendevous	
Where being chief, each playing Drab to Swive	
He takes it as his just Perogative	
Methinks I see him mounted, hear him Roar	
And foaming Cry; God's blood you little whore	15
Zounds how I fuck; I fuck like any Moor.	
Then in comes *Smith* who Murders every shape	
The crying Lover & the squinting Ape	
So very dull in both that you may see	
Sorrow turn'd Mirth, & Mirth turn'd Tragedy	20
Passion he ridicules, so whines & cryes	
That you would swear he something more than Dyes	
Then by his Antick postures men of sense	
Do say he plays Jack Pudding; not a Prince	
Since it is so we'll e'en in time be wise	25
Stick to thy Bottle, there thy Talent lyes	
But for the Stage conceited Malepart	
Thou'rt worse than Scolding Coysh, or strutting Burt	
You smockfac'd lads secure your gentle Bums	
For full of Lust & fury see he comes	30

'Tis Buggering *Nokes* whose damn'd unweildy Tarse
Weeps to be buried in his Foreman's Arse
Unnatural Sinner, Letcher without sense
To leave off Cunt, to dye in Excrements.
    Roaring mad *Cave* is the reproach o'th'Age   35
Scandal to all but the lewd shameless Stage
The Coffee-houses & the Taverns Scum
Drunk every night; The Looby tumbling home
Alarms the Watch; his chiefest Eloquence
Does lye in many Oaths & little Sense   40
E'gad he'd make a swinging Evidence
    But the new Character of one you'll read
Who has strove the Fool so long to be believ'd
That at the last he is a Fool indeed.
Witness his bantering nonsense & his Noise   45
Stealing from Stalls & fooling with the boys
If still thou plays't these Tricks the world shall see
The Difference betwixt Jack Sparks & Tony Lee.
Which is the Silliest cur the Dog or she.
    Goodman the Theif swears 'tis all women's lotts   50
To be in Love with ugliness and Pox
Many by Common Puncks have been mislead
But to be Jilted by a Sily Maid
Is a damn'd thing; *Wiltshire* I'd be asham'd
At last among the Cuckolds to be nam'd   55
Thou'dst better still kept on thy whoring life
Than to be Curs'd with Poverty & wife
    The next might e'en have Acquiesc'd but *He*
Big with the hopes of Popularity
Must play again although it was decreed   60
The wise prophetick should his Omen read
When first he strutted on Farce I was there
Whose here cry'd all, a Puppet not a Player
But when he nam'd a God, the Sparks did fear
The very Fop would make a God appear   65
For God's to him no more than Bottle beer.
    Jevorn's chief business is to swear & Eat
He'd turn procurer for a dish of meat
Else the poor Hungry Ruffian must I fear
Feed on grey pease & Salt for half a year   70
    The rest tho' moving in a lower Sphere
Yet no less Villains than their Masters are
So sharping & so infamous a Crew
Long as old Tyburn stood, it never knew,

But fame does say their Equals you may find 75
Of the other Sex, so lewd in Every kind
You'd swear that Rogue & Whore has both combin'd.
 Imprimis *Slingsby*[22] hath the fatal curse
To have Ladies Honour with a Players Purse
Tho' now she is so plaguy haughty grown 80
Yet 'Gad my Lady; I the time have known
When a dull Whiggish Poet would go down.
That Scene's now chang'd yet prithee dandy beast
Think nor thyself an Actress in the least
For sure thy Figure ne'er was seen before 85
Such Arse like breasts; stiff neck; with all thy store
Are certain Antidotes against a Whore.
 But Antiquated *Shadwell*[23] swears in Rage
She knows not what's the lewdness of the Age
And I believe her now her days are past 90
Who'd tempt a witch that on meer force is chaste
Yet in her youth none was a greater Whore
Her lumpish Husband Ogg can tell you more.
There's one (Heaven bless us) by her curs'd pride
Thinks from the World her brutish lust to hide 95
But will that pass in one whose only sense
Does lye in Whoring, Cheats & Impudence
One that is Pox'd all o'er *Barry's* her name
That mercenary prostituting Dame
Whose nauceous Cunt like Tony's tap does run 100
Unpittied Arse that can't their Ulcer shun
Tho' like a Hackney Jade just try'd before
And all her little fulsome stocks run o'er
Tho' faces are distortur'd with meer pain
And that wry mouth ne'er since came right again 105
Yet more she'll bear ten times for slavish Gain.
 Impudent *Sarah*[24] thinks she's prais'd by all
 Mistaken Drab back to thy Mother's stall,
And let true Savin whom thou hast prov'd so well
'Tis a rare thing that belly will not Swell 110
Tho' fuck't & fuck't and as debauch'd as Hell.
 And *Butler's*[25] wiles are now so common grown
That by each feather's Cully they are known
So that at least to save her tottering Fame
At Musick Clubs she strives to get a name 115
But mony is the Siren's cheifest aim.
At treats her Squeamish stomach cannot bear
What Amorous Sparks provide with cost and Care

But if she's hungry faith I must be blunt
She'll foe a dish of Cuttlets shew her Cunt.   120
    What a pox is't makes *Petty*[26] seem to be
Of such demure pretended Modesty
When 'tis apparent she'll in private prove
As Impudent as any Punk in Love
Strangers she fears so cares not much to roam   125
Whilst she can have a Sharer's prick at home
    Corey's[27] 'tis time thou wert to Ireland gone
Thy utmost Price is here but half a Crown
Ask *Turner*[28] if thou art not fulsom grown
    Su: Percivall[29] so long has known the Stage   130
She grows in lewdness faster than in Age
From eight or Nine she there has frigging been
So counts that natural which is counted Sin
Her Coffee Father[30] too so basely poor
And such a hireling that he'll hold the door   135
Be pimp himself that she may play the Whore.
Once *Twyford*[31] had some Modesty, but she
Her Husband being close in Custody
Would be unkind to see him famish there
So fucks for Gunea to provide him fare.   140
    But *Osborne*[32] moves in a Religious strain
She'll pray & fuck & fuck & pray again
Sure now her fucking praying days are o'er
Who'd have an ugly old yet Zealous whore.
    Then *Norris*[33] & her daughter pleasant are   145
One's very young the other desperate fair
A very well proportion'd equal pair.
    Yet *Hall's*[34] of use, faith as the matter goes
For she must fuck to get her Father cloaths

Chorus.[35] If you bugger says Cunt, I shall beg my bread   150
    If I swive you says Prick, I shall hazard my head
    I'll swive you says Bollocks tho' God strike me dead
    God damn you says Arse hole that's very well said.
I've pleas'd myself, now Critick do thy worst
I value not thy Mallice, nor thy Curse.   155

The reasons for providing a full transcript of this lampoon are twofold. Firstly, small sections of the Montague Summers's version frequently appear in theatre histories and biographies and, as the footnotes indicate, Summers's version contains errors and omissions which have been integrated into theatre history and are long overdue for revision. Secondly, the extracts quoted in biographies and theatre histories are always used in relation to *individual* players and, most frequently, work to reinforce the actress/whore trope.[36] What is so striking about this satirical attack is that it is aimed at the *entire* theatrical community, both male and female members of the company at, or near the point of, the union. Beneath the endless tirade of sexual abuse hurled at both sexes there is, however, a distinction between the first half (lines 1–70) directed at the seven actors, and the second half (lines 71–150) concerning the *eleven* named actresses; predictably, this is one of the few occasions when the actresses are seen to out number the actors in a company.

The company system in the Restoration inherited traces of traditional company hierarchies; made by men, run by men and including only male players. With the advent of the actress, who was quickly recognised as an indispensable part of the theatrical company, the internal dynamic of the theatre company was irreversibly changed and the influence and power wielded by some actresses within the company bitterly resented. *A Satyr on the Players* clearly demonstrates that both actors and actresses were, as Kristina Straub puts it, 'sexual suspects'[37] but, whereas the social mobility of the actor was largely tolerated, the same move for the actress was vigorously opposed. Sarah Burton offers a straightforward, and convincing, explanation for this fundamental inequality between the sexes: 'It was, after all, men who were writing the court satires; whilst male actors were to some extent on the margins of male society, they *were*, as actresses *were not*, part of the male hegemonic "we".'[38] Although the writer of *A Satyr on the Players* uses every kind of ammunition available to discredit the actors, when it comes to the actresses, the writer's rage at *her* presumption rises to a frenzy. As Burton rightly notes, the actor, however near the edges of society in his social standing, is still male subject, 'part of the hegemonic "we"' whereas the woman, whatever her material or social position may be, is still Other. The natural dominance of the male is revealed in the bridge between the two parts of the lampoon: 'The rest tho' moving in a *lower* Sphere / Yet no less Villains than their *Masters* are' (lines 71 and 72, my emphasis).

The force of the salacious and overt sexual abuse of the actress should not distract the reader from the underlying expression of anxiety running through a society that is attempting to renegotiate social relationships in a climate of social instability. The potential financial independence and, therefore, social mobility of this new group of professional women, the actresses, issues a challenge to the most basic of social relations in this and any historical period; the relationship between the sexes. It is one thing to see rivals amongst your own kind – men – rise in society, quite another to see an inferior group – women/other – rise above you. The most effective way to control and undercut these women was to first attach them to the 'oldest' profession and then cite their commercially driven sexual activity as the means by which they have raised their social status: the actress/whore trope at work. The lengthiest attack of some thirteen lines is reserved for Barry and the emphasis on her 'mercenary' nature is a reaction to her personal popularity and, more importantly, her status as an independent, unmarried woman of personal wealth; wealth gained through the very public activity of a professional actress. If the anonymous author of *A Satyr on the Players* intended to fire a warning shot across the bows of the ambitious actress, he clearly failed and, like Robert Gould, may well have paid the price for underestimating the actress's influence.

The benefits of money

The most conclusive evidence for the actresses' growing position of power within the company structure is, as always, revealed through the financial arrangements. In 1685, three years after the union became effective, Elizabeth Barry renegotiated the financial terms for her services as the leading actress with the United Company. Colley Cibber's reference to Mrs Barry as the 'first Person whose Merit was distinguish'd by the Indulgence of having an annual Benefit-Play, which was granted to her alone'[39] recognises the pre-eminence of Barry's position within the company. Robert Hume rightly notes that the principle of the benefit payment was originally intended 'as a means of compensating playwrights for their work'[40] with the 'third night' payment representing the profits from the performance – after the house charges had been deducted. Hume's rigorous but wholly positivist study traces the history of the benefit performance as it was extended to compensate groups of players, noting that there were occasions when a group of actresses or young players had been permitted to play for their own benefit in the past, usually in the summer when the patent houses were between seasons. Hume acknowledges that Elizabeth Barry was the first actress to negotiate this for *any* individual player, and his surprise that a woman might earn a weekly salary of 50s, equal to that of the leading actors, which when combined with an annual benefit 'guaranteed [Barry] £70 over and above her salary' is barely disguised as he concludes that 'this astonishing arrangement must have been the envy of the other performers'.[41] The other well-worn trope of female competition, especially between actresses, is implicit as Hume goes on to discuss Anne Bracegirdle's failed attempt to negotiate similar terms in 1694 – a curious argument as in 1685 she was not yet even a member of the company.

Hume goes to extraordinary lengths to represent Barry's arrangement as a separate model from the benefit payments made to actors after 1695 which, as Colley Cibber notes, 'became not common to others 'till the Division of this Company after the death of King William's Queen Mary'.[42] Although Hume acknowledges that Barry 'rivalled the principal male actors in importance for the success of the whole company',[43] he does not recognise that her negotiation of an additional payment in the form of the benefit represents a fundamental shift in power relations within the company system itself. Barry's benefit payment reveals a recognition of the fact that a successful play has as much to do with the skills of the actress or actor as it does with the skills of the playwright who, until this point, was the only recipient of the benefit payment. Hume concludes that:

> The appeal of the benefit to the actors was rooted in psychology. The performer could hope for a big take, and could bestir him or herself to peddle tickets and urge friends to turn out for the occasion. The results were sometimes disappointing, but the benefit was an opportunity to demonstrate popularity, to make an effort in one's own behalf, and perhaps, just perhaps, to make a profit far beyond what could be earned in many weeks of salaried work.[44]

I entirely agree with Hume's notion that 'the appeal of the benefit was rooted in psychology', but my conclusions are quite different. Just as the playwright began to demand the box-office takings of the sixth night as well as the third, in recognition of the success of her/his endeavour, so the benefit payment to the player acknowledged her part in a successful season and provided a suitable financial reward.

The actress's demand for a benefit payment was a highly pragmatic move, rooted firmly in the desire to be better paid. Banned by her sex from being a sharer, the actress was increasingly aware of her share in the company's success which was not adequately reflected in her annual salary. If we read against the grain here, the introduction of the benefit becomes less about the player peddling tickets and rather more about reflecting the position a player held within the company – a position demonstrated by their popularity with the audience who paid to see them. Elizabeth Barry was the first to identify this potential in the mid-1680s and seized the opportunity afforded through the theatrical monopoly to press her advantage home. Her successful negotiation for an annual benefit, on top of her weekly salary, signals, for the first time, the potential power of the actress within the company system.

Theatre women outside the patent houses

Although Aphra Behn was still, at this point, the only known female playwright to have her plays produced by the patent company, there is another interesting episode concerning the activity of theatre women outside the patent system. The importance of theatrical production at Bartholomew Fair is dealt with by Jacky Bratton, who draws attention to this site of performance which has been 'ignored by modern theatre scholars' as being 'neither rustic nor the property of an authentically industrial working class'.[45] The annual fair took place in August, a time when the patent houses were closed or given over to young, inexperienced players as most theatregoers had left the summer heat and stench of the city. The theatrical booths set up at Bartholomew Fair offered an array of entertainments and provided the opportunity for some leading players, especially comics, to augment their annual income. This story concerns a woman who was looking for a way to extend her theatrical activity by gaining access to the patent house. It is surprising to find that the following incident is recorded in Hotson's overarching history of the period but has been widely ignored in more recent theatre historians.[46] It is less surprising to find that Hotson's interest is in the plight of the abused playwright, Elkanah Settle, rather than the woman with whom he entered into an agreement: the actress and booth operator Elizabeth Leigh.[47] The incident concerns the plot and dramatic scenario for a new play and it is one of only a few extant records that demonstrate the active presence of women as managers of public entertainment in the period. Hotson notes that this is the 'earliest transaction of its kind that I know'[48] and his discussion of the financial details, based on his reading of the documentary evidence, is worth reconsidering.

A Chancery suit, brought by the playwright Settle in response to Elizabeth Leigh's legal actions against him, reveals the details of this interesting agreement.

> on 13 October, 1681, she gave Settle 'the Theme, Subject, and design of the said Play with what she had written thereof'. He thereupon entered

into a bond to her of £40, conditioned for the payment of £20 on or before 1 June, 1682 ('towards the design and subject of the said Stage Play'). Mrs. Leigh insists that this £20 was to be paid whether the play was acted or not. Further, she says that on the same thirteenth of October Settle entered into a second bond (this time of £100 penalty).[49]

Put simply: Settle was to write a new play on a subject and plot-line Elizabeth Leigh had developed and given to the playwright. Settle agreed to pay Leigh £20 when the play was produced against which he gave her a bond of £40. Further, he agreed that if the profits from acting, dedications, printing and publishing should exceed £40 he would share half the additional sum, to which end he gave Leigh a further bond of £100. Leigh had him arrested several times for non-payment of the first bond as she maintained that he had not fulfilled his undertaking to write the play in the time agreed and, therefore, had not presented it to the King's Company, resulting in the play not being performed by the date agreed. On this basis, Leigh was demanding immediate payment of £20 plus costs and the right to prosecute Settle for payment of the second £100 bond as well. Settle's defence was that he *had* delivered the play as agreed to the King's Company but its own internal disagreements, culminating in the dissolution of the company, had prevented the play from being produced; in other words it was out of his hands and he couldn't be expected to pay Leigh for a play that had never been produced. Hotson can find no evidence concerning how this dispute was resolved, but comments that:

> Since she [Leigh] admits that the play has never been acted and consequently has brought the unfortunate Settle no profit, Mrs. Leigh, in demanding both her bonds, seems very much the female Shylock ... no doubt the litigants came to a compromise; for we are told that, as late as 1716, Settle was writing drolls for Mrs Mynn [Elizabeth Leigh's mother] ... It has been said, too, that Settle had an 'annual salary from Mrs Mynn and her daughter, Mrs. Leigh, for writing Drolls'.[50]

Hotson's sympathy for Settle, and obvious antipathy toward Elizabeth Leigh, leads him to ignore the most interesting aspect of this documentary evidence. It is not only, as Hotson rightly points out, that this is a 'record of a sale of a dramatic plot for a sum which should equal half of all the proceeds of the production'[51] but also, this is a record of a detailed plot for a new play provided, in writing, by a woman which was handed over to a male playwright. Hotson quotes directly from Mrs Leigh's reply to Settle's action in which it is clearly stated that she:

'designed the Subject and story of a tragedy or stage Play and having composed and reduced part of the Story into writing, and the Complainant *having notice thereof and pretending himself skilful in poetry and in the composing and finishing Stage Plays*' (my emphasis).[52] Far from Settle being the hard-done-by writer represented by Hotson's account, he might be re-viewed as something of a con-man. It appears that Settle approached Mrs Leigh and persuaded her to let him complete the play, probably using his reputation and contacts with the patent company as an assurance of an early production – which he failed to deliver. From the plot description provided in the Leigh/Settle documents Hotson cites the play in question as *The Ambitious Slave, or A Generous Revenge*, which he goes on to describe as: 'a weak tragedy by Settle, in blank verse. Being at length acted and damned in 1694, it was published in the same year, and Settle's epistle dedicatory speaks of "the severity of this poor Play's Fortune." Even Mrs Barry's acting in the role of Celestina, the "Beautiful Scythian of unknown Birth" who causes all the trouble, could not save it.'[53] The weight of a historiography which privileges the writer is clearly visible here. Having uncovered the origin of the play and noted that Settle went on to receive direct commissions from Elizabeth Leigh in the future, Hotson makes no comment on her creative involvement, except to infer that the 'unfortunate' Settle was the inevitable victim of a bad arrangement with a mercenary woman. It does not seem to occur to Hotson to pursue the notion that, at best, Settle might simply not have made a very good job of scripting a workable and, according to Mrs Leigh, a detailed scenario for a play or, at worst, Settle took Mrs Leigh's money – and dramatic plot – on false pretences.

In the terms established by theatre histories, the work of theatre women is rendered even more invisible by her presence outside the patent system and her participation in the abjected performance site of Bartholomew Fair. The arrangement between an established playwright and a female theatre practitioner, especially one operating *outside* the patent company system, raises a number of further questions. How many other women entrusted established, or aspiring male playwrights, with plots and themes for stage plays? How many plays attributed to male playwrights had material, written or otherwise, created by women? The agreement between Settle and Mrs Leigh suggests the possibility of similar arrangements which did not result in recourse to the law and thus leave no documentary evidence of women's written contribution to the creation of dramatic works. It also suggests that if a woman outside the patent company was contributing to the writing of stage plays then women *within* the patent theatrical community, especially the actresses, may well have made creative contributions that extended beyond their acting talents.

Presence and influence

There has been much speculative writing around the actress's relationship with the male playwright. Often a romantic attachment is implied but more usually a sexual relationship is assumed. If the Restoration actress appears to reject his romantic/sexual advances, the virtuous label that would be attached to any other kind of woman is replaced by a label reading 'dishonourable ingratitude'. The most popular story of this kind revolves round Elizabeth Barry's cruel treatment of the besotted playwright Otway who, according to most accounts, having 'made her the gift of his talent, was only tormented by her indifference'.[54] There are frequent references to the outstanding roles Otway wrote for Barry and the inference is always that her popularity as a great tragedienne is indebted to his writing. Conversely, the success of Behn's career as a playwright is frequently credited to the skills of the actors and yet, as we have seen in the previous chapter, historians have generally failed to explore the collaborative contribution of the actress. The problem goes deeper than playwright and player; it is to do with the presence and influence of theatre women at all.

Elizabeth Howe's revisionist history does more than most to shift the focus from the actor to the actress, particularly in relation to the importance of the actress in the playwriting process:

> The Restoration theatre has been called an 'actor's' theatre. As we have seen, almost all dramatists wrote their plays for one specific company, tailoring roles in accordance with the 'lines' of the players within that company. Casting was something that happened before rather than after a play was written, and so the presence, and the disappearance, of popular and talented actresses changed and shaped the course of the drama to a degree which has gone unrecognised.[55]

Howe places the actress at the centre of the dramatic creative process but she also undercuts her position by assenting to a dominant historiography which privileges the playwright over the performer. Howe places great emphasis on the 'lines', or types of part associated with individual actresses which suggests a far more limited acting range than was actually the case but she does go on to argue that the actress's presence has a far greater effect on the drama of the period than traditional histories have allowed: 'the history of Restoration drama must be seen as partly the history of its female players. Such drama can never be properly understood unless we take account of which actresses were available at each and every stage of its development.'[56] If the theatrical monopoly enjoyed by the United Company drew attention to the rise of the actress, it also highlighted the presence of the female playwright – who also found herself under attack for her presumption and similarly tarred with the whorish brush.

When Aphra Behn's new play *The Lucky Chance* or *An Alderman's Bargain* was performed at Drury Lane in April 1686, there were a number of new actresses now available to her who had previously been members of the King's Company. Behn's biographers make much of the fact that this was her first play for four years but there is nothing to suggest that she was entirely absent from the playhouse, or the court of her royal patrons. *The London Stage* records that Behn wrote a new prologue for a court production of the late Earl of Rochester's adaptation of Fletcher's *Valentinian*,[57] performed on 11 February 1684, and Behn's *Rover* was revived in January 1685, prior to the closure of the theatres between February and April 1685 for a period of mourning following Charles II's death. James, Duke of York, was now King and, initially, royal patronage continued in much the same way as it always had with James enjoying weekly performances at court as well as visiting the playhouse. *The Lucky Chance* was one of the few new plays to be performed in the 1680s and, unlike some of Behn's earlier works of adaptation, it is considered by critics to be a genuinely new play.

There are three central leading roles for women, the best of which was played by Elizabeth Barry, who continued her working relationship with Behn by creating the passionate Lady (Julia) Fulbank; interestingly described in the cast list as 'honest and generous'.[58] The 'young and virtuous' Letticia was played by Sarah Cooke, an experienced actress from the King's Company who was noted for playing romantic roles,[59] and the equally virtuous Diana was played by the nineteen-year-old Susannah Mountfort.[60]

In this play Behn returns to her favourite political issues: women as the objects of transaction, female sexual desire and the restrictions of forced marriage to old men. Behn's satiric characterisation of the amorous old City gentlemen, the aptly named Alderman Sir Feeble Fainwou'd, and the banker Sir Cautious Fulbank is matched by the creation of their adversaries in love, the dashing young cavaliers Bellmour and Gayman. The lustful ambitions of the old men drive the central plot and the comedy revolves round their fear of being cuckolded –

which of course they are. This lively comedy did well at the box-office and Behn inevitably faced opposition posited on the grounds of her sex, a position she hotly defends in this much quoted extract from her preface to the published edition:

> If I must not, because of my Sex, have this Freedom [to write], but that you will usurp all to yourselves; I lay down my Quill, and you shall hear no more of me, no, not so much as to make Comparisons, because I will be kinder to my Brothers of the Pen, than they have been to a defenceless Woman; for I am not content to write for a Third day only. I value Fame as much as if I had been born a *Hero*; and if you rob me of that, I can retire from the ungrateful World, and scorn its fickle favours.[61]

Behn's use of 'Fame' here is not of course the kind of celebrity status we associate with the word today but is being used in the contemporary understanding of 'reputation' and further, of moral reputation. Behn equates fame, the unquestioned morally virtuous reputation, with notions of unimpeachable male honour associated with 'Hero'. But S.J. Wiseman argues that Behn's Preface plays with this understanding, deliberately working to exploit her gender while simultaneously demanding equal recognition for herself as a playwright on equal terms with her male contemporaries: 'The image of a woman dramatist is positively fetishized ... her sex is constantly referred to as part of a sales pitch in prologues, epilogues, and prefaces, offering the reader the frisson of an almost forbidden commodity – a sexual-political comedy, by a woman.[62] Wiseman goes on to note that this Preface was a response to 'a particular moment when the debates on female authorship and on female spectatorship coincided'[63] but her literary interests obscure the importance of the physical performance – the female bodies that female spectators saw on the stage. The combined effect of writing and acting women represents a disrupting political presence which flowed out from the confines of the playhouse along with the female spectators who were an increasingly significant part of the audience. In the playhouse the sexual-political debate has a physical immediacy, moving from the comparative safety of the written text to the more dangerous territory of the public stage where sexual-politics are worked out in the text of the actress's body to be judged and received by the female audience. The debate that starts at this point of performance might well ignite male authored anxiety and cries that is 'unfit for the Ladys'. But Behn's riposte suggests that, once again, it is an anxiety around economic power rather than moral power:

> The Poets I heartily excuse, since there is a sort of Self-Interest in their Malice, which I shou'd rather call a Witty Way they have in this Age, of Railing at every thing *they find with pain successful,* and never to shew good Nature and speak well of any thing; but when they are sure 'tis damn'd, then they afford it that worse Scandal, their Pity. *And nothing makes them so through-sticht an Enemy as a full Third Day, that's Crime enough to load it with all manner of Infamy;* and when they can no other way prevail with the Town, they charge it with the old never failing Scandal – That 'tis not fit for the Ladys.[64] (my emphasis)

For Behn it is male jealousy, not female immorality, that motivates the attacks launched against her and her play. She goes on to argue that:

> the first Copy of this Play was read by several Ladys of very great Quality, and unquestioned Fame, and received their most favourable Opinion, not one charging it with the Crime, that some have been pleas'd to find in the Acting. Other Ladys who saw it more than once, whose Quality and Vertue can sufficiently justifie any thing they design to favour, were pleas'd to say, they found an Entertainment in it very far from scandalous.[65]

New writers frequently sought the recommendation of an outside sponsor with connections in the playhouse but Behn clearly does not fit into this category. New plays by established playwrights were usually given to the leading players to read and recommend to the company – if there was a good part for them, the recommendation was probably all the more secure. This practice is documented in many theatre histories but, predictably, assumed to apply only to male members of the company.[66] Behn's reference to readers of 'unquestioned fame' suggests to me a rather tongue-in-cheek pointer to the most likely group of 'Ladys' to have read her play prior to production – the leading actresses.

Notes

1. The fears surrounding Catholicism were exacerbated when James, Charles II's brother and heir to the throne, converted to the Catholic faith. In 1673 an act was passed to prevent Catholics from holding government office and in 1678 the Popish Plot, so called because it was supposedly a Catholic plot to assassinate the King, resulted in further disquiet about the future of the Protestant monarchy. King Charles died in 1685 and the Catholic James acceded in 1685. He was deposed in 1688 and fled into exile in France. His Protestant daughter, Mary and her husband William of Orange, a member

of the Dutch royal family, were invited to take the throne in 1689 in what is known as 'the Glorious Revolution'. Many of the events surrounding these political upheavals were represented in plays of the time as the playhouses struggled to maintain commercial viability in the face of moments of extreme political and social instability.

2 The details of the protracted disagreements between Thomas Killigrew and his son Charles, who finally threatened a court action against his father in order to obtain control of the King's Company, are examined by Leslie Hotson, *The Commonwealth and Restoration Stage* (Cambridge MA: Harvard University Press, 1928), pp. 259–263. The elder Killigrew also surrendered to his son his role as Master of the Revels, a position he had held since 1673.

3 Milhous, *Thomas Betterton*, p. 31.

4 Downes, *Roscius Anglicanus,* eds Milhous and Hume, p. 81, n. 255.

5 Milhous, *Thomas Betterton*, p. 41.

6 Downes, *Roscius Anglicanus*, p. 39.

7 Downes includes Katherine Corey, one of the first actresses recruited by the King's Company, Elizabeth (Betty) Boutell, Sarah Cooke and Susannah Mountfort (née Percival), but oddly fails to include Frances Maria Knight, who joined the King's Company c. 1676, worked continually through the union and stayed on with the Patent Company after 1695 when she took over as leading tragedienne from Elizabeth Barry.

8 Downes, *Roscius Anglicanus,* eds Milhous and Hume, p. 82, n. 260.

9 Mr Watson certainly appeared in Dublin between 1684 and 1686, and Elizabeth (Betty) Boutell does not appear in any play records until 1688.

10 Downes, ed. Milhous and Hume, p. 82, n. 260.

11 Lucyle Hook, "Mrs. Elizabeth Barry and Mrs. Anne Bracegirdle, Actresses: Their Careers from 1672 to 1695; A Study in Influence', unpublished PhD dissertation, New York University, 1945, Ann Arbor: UMI Dissertation Services, 1999, p. 160.

12 Howe, *The First English Actresses*, p. 28. See n. 39 below for the reference to Colley Cibber's contemporary account of Barry's benefit payments.

13 Ibid.

14 Hook, 'Mrs. Elizabeth Barry and Mrs. Anne Bracegirdle', p. 161.

15 The Bill of Exclusion was brought before Parliament in 1679 in an attempt to prevent the Roman Catholic James from succeeding to the throne.

16 *The London Stage*, part 1, p. 341, introduces the calendar for the 1685/6 season by noting the lack of new plays performed in this and the preceding two seasons.

17 The playwright's income depended on the play surviving to the third day of performance at which point he or she received a cut of the box-office receipts. Many plays did not reach the third day and few ran beyond six. The playwright might also reap some reward from the publication of a successful play if it was dedicated to someone of influence who would then make a gift to the author.

18 Robert Gould, *The Playhouse, A Satyr* (1685), British Library MS, Add., 30492, pp. 23–24. This manuscript is followed by a printed edition which bears the date 1685. It is possible that the original was in circulation a little earlier.
19 In *The Works of Mr Robert Gould* (London: W. Lewis, 1709) 2 vols, the author makes a number of amendments to this satire, making direct references to Elizabeth Barry as well as other actresses. He also includes an 'advertisement' in which he acknowledges that Barry and Betterton were 'incensed' by his satire and that all his efforts to appease them had been rebuffed.
20 Montague Summers (ed.), Downes, *Roscius Anglicanus* (London: Fortune Press, [1928]). Summers not only omitted the more offensive words in the satire, he also omitted the final 'chorus'.
21 *A Satyr on The Players* (c. 1682), MS 'Satyrs and Lampoons', British Library, Harley 7317, pp. 96–100. The manuscript is one in a collection of satires and lampoons dated between 1678 and 1690. *A Satyr on The Players* comes in the middle of the collection corresponding with the accepted date of c. 1682–1685. The line numbering is my own.
22 Mary Lee became Lady Slingsby on her marriage in 1680. Biographical details on Mary Lee/Slingsby and other players have been largely informed by Highfill, *A Biographical Dictionary*.
23 Anne (Gibbs) Shadwell was one of the first actresses in the Duke's Company. She married the playwright Thomas Shadwell in 1667 and her last recorded role was in 1681, when it is assumed that she retired.
24 This is most likely to be Sarah Cooke, a member of the King's Company since 1677, who acted in the United Company until her early death in 1688. The MS includes an additional note reading 'Mrs Cook' on the right margin.
25 Charlotte Butler joined the Duke's Company around 1673/4 where she was a popular actress, singer and dancer. She continued to play with the United Company until 1692, when records show that her request for a rise in salary was rejected. She accepted an offer to join the Smock Alley company in Dublin for the season of 1694/5 and does not seem to have appeared again on the London stage.
26 Mrs Petty joined the Duke's Company in 1676 and is recorded on the cast list in the United Company until 1683.
27 Montague Summers's transcription has 'Currer' here, whereas the MS has 'Corey'. Elizabeth (Betty) Currer joined the Duke's Company in 1674 and played with the United Company until 1689. As there are no records of her performances between 1684 and 1689 it is thought that she did indeed join the Dublin company. There is far more evidence to suggest that Summers was mistaken here and that the actress referred to is Katherine Corey, one of the first actresses in the King's Company, often better known as 'Doll Common' through the pages of Samuel Pepys's *Diary*. Corey was among a group of players who became exasperated with the mismanagement of the King's Company in the late 1670s and so joined a company in Edinburgh for a year. There are no records

of her performances in London until 1682, when she rejoined the King's Company just before the union. *A Biographical Dictionary* (1973) describes Corey as 'an amply-built woman' who played 'nurses, serving women, governesses, mothers, scolds, and bawds. Her flair was for comedy', vol. 3, p. 494.

28 *A Biographical Dictionary* (1973) discusses the possible identity of this 'Turner', concluding that the satire may be referring to one of two actors, Robert Turner or Henry Turner, both of whom would have known Corey.

29 Susannah Percival joined the King's Company in 1681 when she was around fourteen years old. In 1686 she married the actor William Mountfort, also a member of the United Company. Two years after his untimely death in 1692, Susannah married the actor John Verbruggen. There is an additional note which reads 'now married to Montford a new player' in the right-hand margin of the MS, p. 101.

30 The context for this reference to Mr Percival is unclear but it seems obvious that the reference aims to upbraid the father for living off the income of his actress/whore daughter and spending the proceeds in the coffee houses. Mr Percival was arrested for 'clipping coins' and condemned to death in the autumn of 1693. Following his daughter's appeal to the Queen his sentence was reduced to transportation but he died en route to the convict ship.

31 Mrs Twyford was a minor player with the Duke's Company from 1676 and later continued acting with the United Company until around 1686.

32 Margaret Osborn was a supporting player with the Duke's Company from 1672 (see previous chapter Table 1, for details of her work in Behn plays) and later continued acting with the United Company until around 1691 when her name disappears from cast lists. She was listed as member of the breakaway company of 1695 and it is possible that she continued to play small parts there.

33 Mrs Norris was one of the first actresses recruited by the Duke's Company in 1660/1. She was married to a hireling actor, Henry Norris, and the daughter referred to in this lampoon appeared with her in Behn's *The Rover II* in 1681 at Dorset Gardens. She may have appeared briefly with the United Company, but her name does not appear in cast lists after 1683.

34 In Montague Summers's version this line reads 'The girl's of use …', p. 59. It is most likely that the 'Hall' referred to in the MS is the actress Elizabeth Hall, recruited by the King's Company in 1664. As a small-part player Hall's name is unlikely to appear in cast lists. The only known reference to her is in Pepys's *Diary* entry for 19 December 1668 in which the diarist identifies her as the mistress of Sir Philip Howard, adding that she was 'a mighty pretty wench'.

35 This sexually explicit 'chorus' is entirely omitted from Montague Summers's transcript, which picks the text up again for the closing rhyming couplet.

36 *A Biographical Dictionary* includes relevant sections of Summers's version of this lampoon in all the entries for the individual actors and actresses named there. J. H. Wilson, *All the King's Ladies,* uses sections of the text in his biographical notes on the actresses, and Elizabeth Howe, *The First English Actress,*

also makes several references to the lampoon and includes extracts from Summers's text in her discussion of the actresses.
37 Kristina Straub coins this phrase in the title of her book *Sexual Suspects: Eighteenth-century Players and Sexual Ideology* (Princeton: Princeton University Press, 1992).
38 Sarah Burton, 'The Public Woman: An Investigation into the Actress-whore Connexion', unpublished PhD dissertation, University of London, 1998, pp. 351–352.
39 Cibber, *Apology* (1740), ed. Lowe (1889), vol. 1, p. 161.
40 Robert D. Hume, 'The Origins of the Actor Benefit in London', *Theatre Research International*, 9:2 (1981), pp. 99–111, p. 100.
41 p. 102. Calculating the value of money in modern terms is, of course, an inexact science. There are some useful web sites in calculating cost of living and comparing the price of daily consumable items, such as: www.ex.ac.uk/~RDavies/arian/current/howmuch.html visited 30/04/0530 April 2005, which offers prices in the first half of the seventeenth century Lisa Picard, *Restoration London* (London: Wiedenfeld and Nicolson, 1997), cites the *Abstract of British Historical Statistics, the Schumpeter-Gilboy Price Indices* (Cambridge, 1962) as her source for some interesting calculations which also refer to Pepys's accounts in the *Diary* relating to household expenditure. Picard notes that '40s bought seven pairs of women's white gloves, six plain, one embroidered' while '£50 bought two carriage horses or a coach' and that '£7 a month covered Samuel [Pepys]'s housekeeping bills' (pp. 144–147). Pepys's rise in fortune is documented in his *Diary* but it seems clear that Elizabeth Barry's earnings did bring her into the realms of the more comfortable classes in her society.
42 Cibber, *Apology*, ed. Lowe, vol. 1, p. 161.
43 Hume, "Origins of the Actor Benefit", p. 101.
44 p. 109.
45 Bratton, *New Readings* pp. 142–145, p. 142.
46 Peter Holland, *The Ornament of Action* (Cambridge: Cambridge University Press, 1979), p. 72 includes a shortened version of Hotson's account.
47 The similarity in names between Elizabeth Leigh and the Dukes' Company actress Elinor Leigh has led to some confusion. Elizabeth Leigh was the daughter of Mrs Minn and worked with her mother operating a theatrical booth in the seasonal Bartholomew and Smithfields Fairs in London. Although outside the Patent Company system, women such as Elizabeth Leigh were, nevertheless, part of the growing number of women involved in theatrical entertainment.
48 Hotson, *Commonwealth and Restoration Stage*, p. 274.
49 p. 275.
50 p. 276. Hotson cites three sources for this information. In one, Baker's *Biographia Dramatica*, 1782, the entry for Settle reads: 'In the latter part of his life he was so reduced as to attend a booth in Bartholomew Fair, kept by Mrs. Minns and her daughter Mrs. Leigh, and received a salary from them for

writing drolls, which generally were approved of. He also was obliged to appear in his old age as a performer in these wretched theatrical exhibitions, and, in a farce called *St George for England*, acted a dragon enclosed in a case of green leather of his own invention', vol. 1, p. 398.
51 Hotson, *Commonwealth and Restoration Stage*, p. 276.
52 p. 275. Hotson does not provide a footnoted source for each part of the document he quotes from. An earlier footnote on p. 280 relating to the Chancery suit of 21 April 1687, offers only 'No. 54' in identification of the source.
53 p. 276.
54 *A Biographical Dictionary*, vol. 1, p. 316. Barry's rejection of the playwright is referred to in almost all accounts of the actress's life and career in which she is represented as heartless and uncaring, reinforcing contemporary lampoons and satires which continually referred to her mercenary and whorish character.
55 Howe, *First English Actress*, p. 66.
56 p. 90.
57 John Wilmot, Earl of Rochester, both friend and patron to Aphra, died in July 1680.
58 Aphra Behn, *The Lucky Chance*, "Actors' Names".
59 Sarah Cooke was another actress reputed to have been introduced to the theatre by John Wilmot, Earl of Rochester. *A Biographical Dictionary*, vol. 3, pp. 473–474, gives a full account of events leading to her first appearance at Drury Lane in 1677. Apart from the usual suggestion that she was another of Rochester's sexual conquests who (according to a reference from Rochester's *Memoirs*) had more in the way of looks than talent, the entry for Mrs Cooke provides some interesting material pertaining to her public stage appearances prior to her recruitment by the King's Company. An appearance in Edinburgh, and touring experience with John Coysh's company of strolling players, suggest that she had some experience of stagecraft before joining the company in Drury Lane.
60 Susannah (Percival) Mountfort had also been appearing on the stage at Drury Lane for some time and was already a popular young actress.
61 Behn, *The Lucky Chance*, Preface.
62 S. J. Wiseman, *Aphra Behn: Writers and Their Work* (Plymouth: Northcote House, 1996), p. 59.
63 p. 59.
64 Behn, *The Lucky Chance*, Preface.
65 Preface.
66 See *The London Stage*, part 1, pp. cxlix–clii, for details of how new plays were presented to the company. In some cases it is noted that the playwright read their own work to the assembled company but there are no records suggesting that this was, or was not, the case when Behn presented new work for production.

3
CONTROL AND INFLUENCE ON THE LATE STUART STAGE

The theatrical season of 1688/9 is marked by political upheavals which brought about fundamental changes in the government of both the country and the United Company. In November 1688, James II was finally deposed in the 'Glorious Revolution' and the throne passed to his Protestant daughter, Mary II and her husband William III. William and Mary did not share the passionate interest in the theatre expressed by Charles and James and there is a gradual, but marked, shift away from plays that dealt largely with subjects and characters familiar to the inner court circle. Many of the stalwart royalist playwrights were dead. Thomas Otway had died in poverty in 1685 and William Wycherley was in prison for debt until 1686 when King James was among those who came to his aid with a small annuity that ended with his flight into exile. Aphra Behn also died in poverty in April 1689 while some, like Dryden, found that their loyalty to the Roman Catholic faith now precluded them from public office under William and Mary's Protestant rule. This is not to suggest that Restoration drama, as the period has been defined in the literary canon, disappeared overnight; plays by Congreve, Vanbrugh and Farquhar had not yet been written, let alone performed. There were, however, further changes in the management and composition of the United Company that lead me to suggest that the Restoration theatre, so closely identified with and patronised by Charles II and his brother James II, was coming to an end. As Shepherd and Womack put it, 'Fairly abruptly as these things go, theatre ceased to be even residually a part of Court culture, and had to find its place in a dynamic city which was the capital at once of a landed oligarchy and of a commercial empire.'[1]

The players were still officially known as 'Their Majesties' Servants' but the prologues and epilogues of the time testify to the fact that the 'Cits', the influential merchant class, were the new audience the playhouse sought to attract and, increasingly, needed to appease. The move away from the libertinism of Restoration drama and toward the Sentimental drama which dominates the eighteenth century reflects the growing influence of what we might now call the middle-class audience, although the transition from court to city culture continues to be worked out well into the early decades of the eighteenth century.[2] The ascendancy of the Protestant merchant class had continued from the time of the Commonwealth but under William and Mary's reign it flourished and sought to establish its own identity and power within the social hegemony. Although marginalised, the Puritan voice had not been wholly silenced during the Restoration. The playhouse, with its direct connection to an old-style monarch and court patronage, was an obvious target for those anxious to expunge the perceived excesses of the Restoration. As the nineteenth-century theatre historian Percy Fitzgerald puts it, 'the influence of the stage was, during this era, a powerful element in the corruption of society'.[3] In his own contribution to moves that reinforce middle-class ownership of the theatre and its history, Fitzgerald points the finger at the female playwright for her part in the degeneracy of the stage: 'From the year 1671 to the end of the century, we shall find the sort of dramatic sewage that poured across the stage was swelled by diligent contributions from Mrs. Aphra Behn. A score of plays attest her unsavoury, unfeminine nature.'[4] It is not surprising to find that Fitzgerald supports the moves of the late seventeenth-century antitheatrical lobby (to be discussed later in Chapter 6) or that women, on stage, page and in the audience, are of concern in both seventeenth- and nineteenth-century discourse. There are parallels in the agenda in both periods: to establish social reforms which reflected the interests and moral perspective of what was essentially a patriarchal hegemony. Ownership of the public sphere in which the playhouse operated was on the way to becoming a central focus for contesting discourses.

Changing loyalties

The winds of commercial change were also blowing through the patent house as the family-controlled business of theatre attracted outside interest: after all, this was a profitable commercial concern. The move began with new dealings made by Alexander Davenant, Lady Mary's fourth son, who had acted as treasurer for the Duke's Company from 1675 and then the United Company until 1683. In May of 1687 Alexander began negotiations with his brother, Charles, and by August he had purchased his brother's shares in the United Company for a payment of £2,400. In spite of uneven audiences, the company continued to be profitable and it appears that the leading players were initially unperturbed by financial dealings within the Davenant family, who still seemed to be securely in control of the royal patent first granted in 1660. During Alexander's first full season as majority shareholder (1688/9), he took the curious decision to depose the actor/managers Betterton and Smith and hand the day-to-day management of the company to his inexperienced younger brother Thomas Davenant – presumably on the orders of the true shareholders. For it emerged later that £2,000 of the purchase price paid by Alexander to his older brother Charles was provided by an investment adventurer, Sir Thomas Skipwith, and that Alexander had sold his remaining shares to the lawyer Christopher Rich. As Alexander had recently made a good financial marriage, it was assumed that the money had been his, whereas in reality Alexander was merely farming the shares for Skipwith and Rich. The full implications of the loss of the controlling interest by the Davenants did not emerge until the 1690s but, in the short term, the power previously enjoyed by the players, particularly by Thomas Betterton, was clearly undermined.[5]

Anne Bracegirdle and the Late Stuart stage

It seems appropriate to seek to define this vital period in theatre history as more than just a period of transition between two apparent extremes: the bawdy excess of the Restoration and the restrained social sensibility of eighteenth-century Sentimental drama. I propose, therefore, to identify the period of twenty years between 1688–1708, which includes the accession of Queen Anne in 1702, as the Late Stuart stage: a period in which there is both innovative theatre that prefigures the cultural interests of the eighteenth century and reactionary theatre which seeks to invoke the perspective of Restoration social and cultural politics. The Late Stuart stage is characterised by the contradictions inherent in a theatre which seeks to represent contesting ideologies: on one hand its very existence advocates the social freedoms gained at the Restoration and yet, in order to survive, it must also appeal to the reformist politics of the merchant or middle class. Central to my definition of the Late Stuart stage is the powerful presence and participation of women in the life and development of the playhouse. Paradoxically, it is in the 1690s, when the presence and representation of women in the playhouse comes under renewed scrutiny, that there is an explosion of innovative work by theatre women. This chapter takes as its focus the rapid rise of the actress Anne Bracegirdle: the construction of her identity on and off stage, her collaborative partnership with Elizabeth Barry and their resistance to the disempowering moves of a new, commercial management team.

At the same time as Thomas Betterton was renegotiating his position in the United Company, his adopted daughter, Anne Bracegirdle, made her first recorded appearance as a full member of the company.[6] As with many actresses of the period there are conflicting dates given for Bracegirdle's birth and her first theatrical appearance, resulting in a discrepancy of some ten years. *A Biographical Dictionary* continues with the generally held assumption that she was born around 1663, unaware of, or simply ignoring, Lucyle Hook's convincing argument for a birth date of 1673, an argument begun in her unpublished doctoral thesis of 1945 and repeated with barely any changes in a subsequent article published in 1958.[7] The problem may simply arise from the difficulty some twentieth-century historians have with the notion of a six-year-old girl appearing on the public stage. An eighteenth century account states '[Anne Bracegirdle] had the good Fortune to be well placed, when an Infant, under the care of Mr Betterton and his wife, whose Tenderness she always acknowledges to have been Paternal, Nature formed her for the Stage, and it was to the Admiration of all Spectators that she performed the Page in *The Orphan*, at the Duke's Theatre in Dorset-Garden, before she was six Years old.'[8] Hook notes that this version was not doubted until the twentieth-century and presses home her point by arguing that:

> invariably girls made their first appearances in grown women's parts when they were only fourteen or fifteen years of age. If we believe that 'Nature formed her for the Stage', it is absurd to think that, brought up in the atmosphere of the theatre, reared by the foremost actor in England, and naturally inclined toward the stage, she should wait until she was twenty-five before taking a very small part in Shadwell's *Squire of Alsatia*.[9]

It seems quite likely that the twelve-or thirteen-year-old 'Miss Nanny' who played Clita in D'Urfey's *Commonwealth of Women* (1685) and also spoke the epilogue was the young Anne Bracegirdle. Finally Hook turns to Cibber, who records the details of the company as it was when he was recruited as a young actor in 1690: 'Mrs Bracegirdle was now, but just blooming to her Maturity; her Reputation, as an actress gradually rising with that of her Person'.[10] Hook compares Cibber's comments on Mrs Barry in the same year (1690) arguing that 'If Mrs Barry at thirty-two was "not a little past her youth", Mrs Bracegirdle at twenty-seven could hardly be "'just blooming to her Maturity'",[11] reinforcing her argument that Anne must have been around sixteen when she became a full member of the company in 1688.

The stories surrounding the arrival of Anne Bracegirdle to the United Company and her rise to prominence reveal the working out of another powerful binary, one that has been used to occlude the work of theatre women from considerations of the development of theatre practice and company structures. Although Elizabeth Barry was raised in the Davenant household, Anne Bracegirdle was one of the first successful leading actresses to be raised *directly* within the family of leading players in the patent company; a tradition that reached its zenith in the nineteenth century and still continues today.[12] To acknowledge this, of course, throws the actress/whore construction into question. The twentieth-century historian cannot hold the revered figure of Thomas Betterton aloft and, at the same time, pursue the actress/whore trope. In Anne Bracegirdle's case the logical conclusion of this approach renders the great actor/manager as little more than a pimp for a young woman in his household. An alternative to the whorish construction of the actress had to be found. In Chapter 1, I discussed the label of faithful and virtuous wife that was attached to Mary Betterton. Other actresses, notably Susannah Percival (Mountfort/Verbruggen), were known to have appeared as child players through familial connections with the playhouse but Bracegirdle was the first leading actress to enter the same company as her actress 'mother'. Although she never married, Anne Bracegirdle has been perceived as Mary Betterton's natural successor, not least by inheriting her 'virtuous' mantle.

The commercially driven playhouse was, much like television today, acutely aware of its need to renegotiate the relationship with a changing audience. As in every age, certain players capture the mood and imagination of a generation, and Anne Bracegirdle seems to have become the model of femininity for the Late Stuart stage, as demonstrated here in Colley Cibber's account of her career:

> never any Woman was in such general Favour of her spectators, which, to the last Scene of her Dramatick Life, she maintain'd by not being unguarded in her private Character. This Discretion contributed not a little to make her the *Cara*, the Darling of the Theatre: For it will be no extravagant thing to say, Scarce an Audience saw her that were less than half of them Lovers, without a suspected Favourite among them: And tho' she might be said to have been the Universal Passion, and under the highest Temptations, her constancy in resisting them served but to Increase the number of her Admirers: ... It was even a fashion among the Gay and Young to have a taste or *Tendre* for Mrs. *Bracegirdle*.[13]

What is interesting in this representation is that the 'virtuous' actress might be seen as a figure worthy of being *admired* from afar, rather than her appearance in the public sphere being a demonstration of her availability to the highest bidder. She may be tempted, indeed that is a great part of her attraction, with her resistance adding to her virtue and desirability. But Bracegirdle is still the object of male fantasy, with the added value that her public display of virtue is a reflection of her virtuous 'private character', not a veil to hide her true character.[14] It must be remembered that Cibber's essentially defensive autobiography was written toward the end of his life and consequently his recollections, albeit from the time of his own recruitment by the Patent Company in 1690, need to be treated with caution.[15] Another contemporary, the actor and sometime strolling player Anthony (Tony) Aston, contradicts many of Cibber's character studies of his fellow players but in this case they are corroborated by his representation of the virtuous Bracegirdle. He too testifies wholeheartedly to her steadfast rejection of a string of persistent lovers, including the playwright William Congreve, and reports fully on that other favourite demonstration of female virtue, Bracegirdle's charitable visits: 'going often into *Clare-Market*, and giving Money to the poor unemploy'd Basket-women, insomuch that she could not pass that Neighbourhood without the thankful Acclamations of People of all Degrees; so that if any Person had affronted her, they would have been in Danger of being kill'd directly; and yet this good Woman was an Actress'.[16] It is tempting to suggest that the power of the actress/whore myth was in some way being disrupted on the Late Stuart stage; but this is far from the case, as Aston's almost incredulous concluding remark makes clear. Later in her career, Bracegirdle's virtuous identity was used against her in stories that put into question her legendary chastity. The whorish/virtuous binary of our inherited historiography successfully maintains the focus on the sexual identity of the actress, the willing object of the male gaze and constructed by his social determination, rather than by her own creative and/or commercially successful work in the world of the playhouse.

The construction of Bracegirdle's virtuous public identity is in direct contrast to the reputation of the already established leading actress of the day, the 'mercenary' and 'whorish' Elizabeth Barry. Lucyle Hook suggests that:

> If Mrs. Barry had accomplished almost single handed the coup of changing the drama from male to female in 1680, Mrs. Bracegirdle accomplished almost single handed the feat of making it moral in 1690.

Mrs. Barry ... was of the old school of the theatre with her lovers and easy way of life. No illusion about her lurked in the minds of her auditors ... But there is a fascination in the strange, the unfamiliar, the unattainable ... it was Mrs. Bracegirdle's unimpeachable private life which gave a new fillip to play-going.[17]

What Hook misses here is the possibility that Elizabeth Barry's public reputation was as carefully constructed as Anne Bracegirdle's and the reality/illusion of Barry's whorish activity as potent as the reality/illusion of Bracegirdle's virtue. Furthermore, by representing their innovative contribution to theatre as 'single handed' accomplishments, there is little room to consider the power and influence of their collaborative work. The creation of contrasting female characters performed by actresses with contrasting public identities is a tried and tested model in contemporary film drama, and the Barry/Bracegirdle partnership offers an early example of that model. But it is how they exploited their public identity, what they *did* with their partnership, the way they used the creation of new characters *on* stage and fuelled new developments for theatre women *off* stage, that leads me to reconsider their work as a central feature of the Late Stuart stage.

The ladies of the audience

Lucyle Hook suggests that the presence of a 'sensible queen ruling quietly in her own right ... and the sure prospect of another queen [Mary's sister Anne] upon the throne as the next successor' contributed to the fact that by 'the early 1690s, the actual position of women in England had been changed, and in some ways, these changes were to be seen on stage'.[18] Hook is right to suggest that the dramatic texts produced in the first five years of the decade reveal marked changes in the representation of women but she is uncharacteristically naive here in suggesting that the 'position', or material circumstances, of *most* women's lives changed in the liberating sense her assertion suggests. For women in the playhouse, whether on stage or in the auditorium, the triumph of Protestantism resulted in the rise of the anti-theatrical lobby, culminating in Jeremy Collier's (in)famous attack in 1698. Jean Marsden offers a convincing summation of the direction in which the renewed expression of patriachal moral anxiety was moving:

> It is only in the late seventeenth century that attacks on the stage begin to focus directly and repeatedly upon the effect of theater on the audi-

ence, and in particular on the female members of the audience. Sexuality becomes the issue upon which this controversy pivots, both the sexuality of the female spectator and the sexuality of the female image that she watches. Specifically, the anti-theatrical writers express an unconcealed fear of the female gaze and its ramifications. How will women respond to what they see upon the stage – and how will their reaction affect family and state?[19]

The fear that the female spectator might in some way be contaminated or, worse still, positively influenced by what she sees on stage is a recurring preoccupation in contemporary writing. But there are levels of complexity contained within the female image here, layers of meaning attached to the woman on the public stage and her perception by her female audience that need further unpacking.

The actress not only transgresses boundaries between public and private spheres but also pulls into play questions of appearance and reality – a preoccupation worked out in a number of dramatic plots of the period. The conflation of the 'real' identity of the actress and the assumed identity of the character she plays combine to trouble the stability of the female construct. The female image performed and received in the playhouse is further problematised as it carries not only the social signs of the female character but also the sign of the actress who plays her. But what if we pursue the notion that both identities – character and actress, on stage and off – are performed identities and, arguably, not so far removed from the performative experience of all women negotiating the social constructs determined for them/us in different historical moments?

In the Restoration playhouse the female spectator was predominantly a member of the court coterie and the difference between the identity of the actress and the signs of the 'lady' she played were clear. By the 1690s the female spectator was more likely to be from the merchant class and in the business of appropriating signs for herself in order to display her rising position in society: a demonstrative display of upward mobility which was mirrored by the actress – especially in the case of the more successful ones. The signs that identify social difference were becoming more blurred and strategies are required to separate the wives and daughters of the rising and respectable merchant class from the women on public display in the playhouse. Inevitably, patriarchal concerns circulate around the question of sexuality and the attendant fear of female immorality: the ultimate threat to the stability of male inheritance. Jean Marsden argues that the defenders of the stage, predominantly the male playwrights, 'downplay any potential danger' and 'frequently ignore the female spectator altogether'[20] and yet the prologues and epilogues in this period repeatedly appeal to the 'Ladies'. Prologue speakers, often actresses, entreat the female spectator to be 'kind' to the play in a move that seeks to draw attention to and reinforce the moral intentions of the playwright. The public identity of the actress speaking, as it were, as 'herself' is an important part of this reassuring theatrical strategy – a strategy designed to fill the house and the pockets of the management, players and playwrights.

The attraction of opposites

The drive to attract new audiences resulted in renewed opportunities for playwrights and the players they wrote for: new products to attract new money. It is not unusual to find that the rise in popularity of a young actress, a new look, is accompanied by a gradual decline in the fortunes of the current favourites. Mary Betterton was one of several older actresses who gradually relinquished her parts to Mrs Barry before she finally retired from the stage.[21] Thomas Betterton, who had played opposite his wife throughout her career, saw no need to hand on his parts to a younger man though and, presumably, neither did his audience demand it. Betterton continued to play opposite the much younger Elizabeth Barry even when, by 1690, she too had dominated the London stage for nearly twenty years.

Following the creation of the United Company, there were at least three other rising actresses with the ability to challenge Barry's monopoly of the meatiest roles. Frances Maria Knight, who may well have begun her career as a child actress with the King's Company around 1676,[22] first appears in the cast list for Southerne's *The Disappointment* (1684). During the ten years that she and Elizabeth Barry were in the same company, there were only three occasions when they appeared in the same play, with Knight always reduced to a supporting role. It was only after 1695, following Elizabeth Barry's move to Lincoln's Inn Fields, that Knight became the patent company's chief tragic actress. Susannah Mountfort (also initially a King's Company player) was a versatile and increasingly popular comedienne who frequently played alongside Barry and Bracegirdle. With Charlotte Butler as an acclaimed singer and dancer, noted for her popularity in the spectacular operas of the period, it is evident that Barry's pre-eminent position was not without challengers; neither was the young Bracegirdle without able and ambitious competitors. If Bracegirdle was the fresh, virtuous, face of the moment, she needed a female foil to play against. In the seven years following Bracegirdle's debut she appeared with Frances

Maria Knight in at least twelve plays and yet their presence on stage together evidently did not suggest the kind of playing partnership established when Bracegirdle appeared with Elizabeth Barry. It is interesting to note that it was only after the Barry/Bracegirdle defection to Lincoln's Inn Fields that Knight was paired with a younger actress, Jane Rogers, in a direct attempt to emulate the extraordinary success created by the pairing of Barry and Bracegirdle.

The tradition of acting partnerships of this kind was not new. Mary Betterton and Mary Lee (Slingsby) also regularly appeared together during their years in the Duke's Company. Barry and Bracegirdle both shared personal and professional roots in the Duke's Company and this may well have contributed a great deal to the solidity and development of their acting partnership. Lucyle Hook makes little of this professional 'nursery', suggesting that Anne Bracegirdle's relationship with the Bettertons did little to advance her early acting career and yet the role chosen for her adult acting debut suggests that she was launched as carefully as any young starlet in the heyday of the Hollywood studio system.[23] As Antelina in *The Injur'd Lovers* (1688) she played a leading role in the first play by the actor/playwright William Mountfort where, as Elizabeth Howe notes, 'the part equals that of Oryala, her rival, who was played by Elizabeth Barry'.[24] With Bracegirdle as the gentle, suffering, innocent Antelina and Barry as the bold and passionate Oryala, the pattern for their partnership appears to have been established from the beginning of Bracegirdle's career but it would be another two years before it began to be fully exploited.

In the season of 1690/1 the Barry/Bracegirdle partnership was clearly proving successful at the box-office. Bancroft's tragedy *King Edward the Third* was performed early in the season and quickly followed by Settle's *Distress'd Innocence*. The genre of 'she-tragedy',[25] in which Barry had secured her dominance of the leading roles, was still hugely popular but with the arrival of Bracegirdle it began to take a different direction. Not only were the contrasts between Barry and Bracegirdle capturing the audiences' imagination, but also the 'she-tragedy' plot was increasingly resolved in a 'happy ending' with the young lovers, frequently played by Bracegirdle and the rising actor/playwright of the day, William Mountfort, ending in each other's arms. The contrast between Barry's passionate villainess and Bracegirdle's faithful suffering heroine became an established pattern which was repeated without much variation. As Elizabeth Howe observes: 'The two actresses did not swap types like Mary Betterton and Mary Lee. Although Barry played a wide spectrum of roles from evil to good, Bracegirdle always played the innocent virgin, whether she was cast as Barry's rival, friend or daughter.'[26] The trope of female competition, particularly between actresses, leads Howe to speculate on the grounds upon which this formidable female theatrical partnership was built: 'Personal friendship may have been one reason why such a balanced partnership existed between Barry and Bracegirdle from the very start of the latter's career. They were apparently always good friends; Barry did not feel threatened by her younger colleague, Bracegirdle had no wish to oust Barry from her position of tragic supremacy'.[27] In a bid to offer new insights and explanations for their working relationship, it is interesting to note that Howe turns to 'personal friendship' as a means to oppose professional competition. But how does this work as the fulcrum for the collaborative work of these two foremost theatre practitioners? Are there other explanations available to us in revising the story and do we need such explanations at all?

Both women had been adopted into, and raised in, the heart of the theatrical community. Working on Hook's calculations, there were fifteen years between these two women and Barry would surely have been aware of Bracegirdle's progress from child actress to fully fledged member of the company. In the same year that Anne Bracegirdle joined the main company Elizabeth Barry was absent due to illness. She collapsed with a fever during the premiere of Crowne's *Darius* in April 1688 and *A Biographical Dictionary* suggests that her illness coincided with the death of her daughter (most likely fathered by Rochester and of about twelve or thirteen years of age) noting that she was absent from the stage for the remainder of the season.[28] It is possible that the young Bracegirdle replaced the beloved lost daughter, although Barry's identity as a heartless, mercenary woman has failed to suggest the picture of maternal concern to her biographers. At a time when gay and lesbian histories are being recovered, might these two unmarried women be identified as lovers? But then the weight of the heteronormative assumptions around the image of Barry as the heartless prostitute or Bracegirdle as the virtuous object of male admiration might well resist such a radical rereading. My purpose here is not to advocate any one of these explanations but to point up the weight and importance given to stories surrounding the sexual activity and personal relationships of theatre women as part of the move to deflect attention from their theatre practice: an approach that would, at most, be an afterthought in a discussion on male collaborative practice. The age gap, again considered of more importance when discussing women's work, may partially account for the clear division in roles but it seems more likely that the prominence of their public identity ensured that Barry would always play dark passion to Bracegirdle's virtuous innocence. Perhaps the most cogent explanation for their enduring partnership is that it proved to be commercially successful. The two actresses appeared together in at least thirty new tragedies during the course of their careers.

The serious business of comedy

Barry and Bracegirdle were also successfully paired in at least twenty-two comedies but this has generally attracted less attention when considering their careers. From Colley Cibber's *Apology* to the *Dictionary of National Biography* the assessment of both actresses' careers focuses first on the quality of their work in tragedy. The definitions of serious drama and entertainment, high and low art, that have dominated our histories of theatre have worked to obscure the cultural importance of comedy in dramatic discourse. The notion of tragedy as a more noble, higher, dramatic form has extended to the work of the performer: the comedian may be well loved but the skill of the tragedian is more admired. The appropriation of the dramatic text as literary expression for private reception favours tragedy. Comedy lives in performance, in the life given by the performer, in the joke shared with the audience who in turn share it with one another. It is interesting though that modern revivals of plays from the period rarely, if ever, revive the tragedies. The handful of revived comedies, deemed to be 'good' plays and mostly written by male playwrights, reinforce the historiography of the Restoration as a time of witty writing and bawdy manners – on stage and off. But there are many comedies by men and women that did not make the canonical cut and it is through these that we may gain new insights into the cultural and social concerns of the historical past. In the 1690s Barry and Bracegirdle were paired in a number of new comedies produced by the United Company and, as Peter Holland argues, we can see the 'strong revival of a satiric comedy concerned with the actions of contemporary society'.[29] The strength of Restoration satire is fused with a new concern for social and moral reform and, as Holland points out, Southerne's *Wives Excuse* (1691) has not been given the full recognition it deserves as one of the early examples of reform comedy. There is, however, an earlier work which demonstrates the complex negotiation between the licentious comedy of the Restoration and the moves toward Sentimental comedy of the eighteenth century.

Shadwell's *The Scowrers* was recommended for production in the 1690/1 season by the comic Anthony Leigh and his wife Elinor, who played Lady Maggot. This was the first comedy to employ the Barry/Bracegirdle partnership with Barry as Eugenia, a predictably more adventurous woman than her gentler sister, Clara, played by Bracegirdle. The contrasting representation of female behaviour is not focused so much on the two sisters as on their relationship to their mother, the lustful Lady Maggot. This overbearing matriarch makes her entrance with a speech which anticipates the attitudes of the more famous Lady Wishfort in Congreve's *The Way of the World* (1700). In spite of all her efforts Lady Maggot has failed to attract male interest and bemoans the lack of gallants in Town:

> Are there no Gallants left? Poor gentle love is now neglected, and all mens heads lye towards Knavery and Business. I have walk'd the whole length of the Mall alone, on purpose for an amorous Adventure, and met none; nor have had any observe me except this old Red nos'd, batter'd Drunkard, and yet my shape and habit are enough inviting, besides some jewels which I seem to conceal, and yet take care to expose, shew my Wealth and Quality sufficiently.[30]

Apart from the obvious jibe at the lustful older woman who fails to recognise that she is past her prime, this speech extends the satire to target the rising merchant class, epitomised not only by Lady Maggot's flaunting of her wealth in the Mall – *the* place to be seen – but also by her husband's name: 'Sir Rich Maggot'. In an attempt to save younger women from the attentions of men, and save the attentions of men for herself, Lady Maggot keeps her daughters under the watchful eye of their governess, Priscilla, and wants them removed to the country and far away from the Town. But earlier in the same scene, Eugenia/Barry and Clara/Bracegirdle tell Priscilla/Katherine Corey[31] that they refuse to accept Lady Maggot's plans for their future:

Eugenia In short we are we are both resolv'd not to endure any longer the intolerable Yoke of Arbitary power, under which we have so long groan'd, if you will comply, one or both of us will provide for you.

then follow several comic exchanges in which the ineffectual governess Priscilla attempts to enforce Lady Maggot's authority but the young women are adamant.

> … we that are resolv'd to cast off my Mother's tyranny, will no longer suffer thy Insolence.
>
> Priscilla What will become of poor me?

Clara   We are true English women, Co-heirs of two thousand pounds a year and are resolv'd to assert our Liberty and Property.[32]

Far from being represented as 'disobedient daughters' these two sisters are presented as honourable, even patriotic heroines, demonstrated by their promise to provide for their foolish governess. The reform intentions of the play revolve around their attitudes and actions as, ultimately, they convince their lovers, Sir William (played by Mountfort and, in this play, cast opposite Barry) and Wildfire (played by Williams opposite Bracegirdle) to turn from their libertine ways and embrace domestic bliss:

Eugenia   The Pomps and all the Vanities of this wicked Town you must renounce
Clara   Wine, women and base Company.[33]

In spite of the rather draconian insistence that the men must prove their good intentions for a year before gaining their respective lovers, the men capitulate with remarkable ease:

Wildfire   Ladies your Charms a miracle have wrought,
And early us home to ourselves have brought;
No pow'r but Love could thus call back a stray,
From all the crooked Paths, to the right way.
Sir William   But where Wit, Beauty, Vertue keep the Field,
As Prisoners at discretion, all must yield,
Those Forces joyn'd, subdue all Vanities;
The most compendious way of being wise,
Is to be convert to a Ladies Eyes.
                                    Exeunt.[34]

This demonstrates the limitations imposed by reading, rather than seeing comedy in performance but my intention is to demonstrate that the play text places some emphasis on the potential power of women. Beneath the comedy there is a more serious discourse emerging, one that places the responsibility for male morality, especially sexual morality, on the woman; a construct that became even more firmly established in the course of the next two centuries and which, on stage and screen at least, was embodied by the actress.

The role of the actress

The drive to demonstrate the playwright as the architect of theatrical representation, the genius creator of character, star-maker even, has served to undermine the active participation of the actress in the exploitation of her own public identity. The slippage between the identity of the actress and the character she plays, the deliberate moves to exploit the conflation, or separation, of the player/character identity, was increasingly evident in the 1690s as Barry and Bracegirdle disrupted the 'typical' roles theatre historians have sought to confine them to. Through their on-stage partnership, Barry and Bracegirdle continually play with their public identity and popularity in certain roles; and this is clearly a much more complex manoeuvre than has generally been allowed.

D'Urfey's satirical comedy *The Marriage-Hater Match'd*, performed in 1692, offered new opportunities for the Barry/Bracegirdle partnership. Elizabeth Barry played the passionate Lady Subtle, described in the unusually detailed cast list as 'A Proud, high spirited Widow, who thinking her self affronted by Sir Philip, by his Intrigue with Phaebe, tho' she had ingag'd to Marry him, breaks off all, and takes another'. Anne Bracegirdle played the virtuous Phaebe: 'A pretty Innocent, well-natur'd Creature, who being in Love with Sir Philip, and debauch'd by him upon his promise of Marriage, puts her self into Boys Clothes, and manages his business against the Widow, underhand'.[35] As in the 'she-tragedy' partnership, Barry and Bracegirdle played women involved with the same man, Sir Philip Freewit, the titular marriage-hater, played by William Mountfort. Beginning the play as rivals, the two women are ultimately united in opposition to an abusive man and are successful in achieving the end they desire; Phaebe marries Sir Philip and Lady Subtle keeps her money and gains a foolish, but rich, husband into the bargain. Although apparently conforming to the typical Bracegirdle role, Phaebe is not the conventional passive heroine, spending most of the play devising and executing plots while disguised as a young man, Lovewell.

This was only Bracegirdle's second breeches role, and there is always a risk for any popular actress that her audience may not accept her in a part that presents her in a radically different light.[36] Bracegirdle appears to anticipate this in the prologue, where she plays directly into her virtuous public identity by reluctantly allowing Mountfort to persuade her to present herself in breeches:

> Mr. Monford[37] Enters, meets Mrs. Bracegirdle dressed in Boy's Cloaths, who seeing h[im],[38] Endeavours to go back, but he taking hold of her, Speaks:
> Nay, Madam, there's no turning back, alone;
> Now you are Enter'd, faith you must go on;
> And speak the Prologue, you for those are Fam'd
> And the Play's beginning[39]

This double-act prologue doubtless fuelled the rumours concerning Mountfort and Bracegirdle's off-stage relationship, especially as they are identified here by their real names. But the focus of the piece remains firmly on Bracegirdle's virtuous reputation, which is reinforced by her evident reluctance to appear in such unfeminine garb: 'Lord, I'm so ashamed.' After some reassuring references to the stability of her reputation, Mountfort persuades her to fulfil her duty and speak for the play:

> Well, Gentlemen, since then do what I can,
> Spite of myself, I must appear a Man;
> Pray let me beg ye not to like me less
> Than when you see me in my Maiden Dress;
> And free from rigorous Censure this one day
> For my sake spare the Poet and the Play.
> For to speak Truth in its incouragement,
> There is a Plot, and some good Humor in't:
> The Ladies too must needs approve the Matter,
> Because he punishes the Marriage-Hater.
> And if [it] bring good Humor, you shall Laugh.

Mountfort: Why, that's well said my Dear, and so lets off.   Exeunt.[40]

The success of this play suggests that Bracegirdle played the 'role' of the reluctant, innocent, actress, and all the inherent contradictions of that association, with as much skill as she played the character of Phaebe. The satirical comedies of the 1690s embrace the complex concerns with appearance and reality and, as Peter Holland puts it, 'character no longer has any meaning as a concept of *vraisemblance*; instead all forms of social activity are based on role-playing, the enacting of social set-pieces'.[41] The playhouse was the ultimate site of role-play, for performers on stage and those in the auditorium. Bracegirdle successfully played on the identity of the actress as sexually desirable and available, while reinforcing her own virtuous public identity. The deliberate sexually ambiguous tone of this prologue between Bracegirdle and Mountfort may have contributed to the off-stage events that culminated in Mountfort's death at the hands of one Captain Hill, an unsuccessful admirer of Bracegirdle's who, on following her home one night, found she was being escorted through the streets by Mountfort and so ran the actor through with his sword. Hill left the country, and the United Company lost a leading player.[42]

Colley Cibber records that 'Upon the unfortunate Death of Montfort, [the comic actor] Leigh fell ill of a Fever, and dy'd in a Week after him, in

December 1692'.[43] The company was mid-season and facing a seemingly endless catalogue of internal disasters. They had lost three of their leading actors (Nokes also died around this time), Elinor Leigh and Susannah Mountfort were now widowed and the playhouse audience was proving hard to please. Dwindling box-office receipts forced Thomas Betterton and other sharers to return to salary payments in order to survive. It was not until late February 1693 that Bracegirdle, Leigh and Susannah Mountfort returned to the playhouse to appear in Southerne's new comedy *The Maid's Last Prayer*.

Pleasing the audience

The drive to find new ways to attract their audience resulted in the inclusion of extraneous entertainments, prescient of the mixed bill that became the staple of theatrical entertainment in the following two centuries. The published editions of play texts throughout the 1690s contain several references to theatrical moments that had little or no relevance to the plot of the play: Mountfort's *The Successful Straingers* (1690) includes 'Mrs Butler's Dance' at the end of Act III and in the same year Southerne's *The Wives Excuse* also contains references to songs and dances which clearly stand alone – indicated by the direction 'after which' – the dance ended, the dialogue is picked up and the play proceeds.[44] Playwrights were evidently prepared to include any number of extra inducements and favour any genre in order to increase their audience.

Southerne's prologue to *The Maid's Last Prayer*, performed in February 1693, was spoken by Elizabeth Barry and demonstrates that knowing what makes a commercial success at the box-office was quite as difficult then as it is now:

> They who must write (for writing's a Disease)
> Shou'd make it their whole study how to please:
> And that's a thing our Author fain wou'd do;
> But wiser Men, than he, just tell me how:
> For you're so changeable, that every moon,
> Some upstart whimsie knocks the old ones down.
> Sometimes bluff Heroes please by dint of Arms:
> And sometimes tender Nonsense has its Charms:
> Now Love and Honour strut in buskin'd Verse:
> Then, at one leap, you stumble into Farce.[45]

Southerne's way to please was to revert to the full blooded comedy enjoyed at the height of the Restoration, adding a number of songs which are also included in the published text. In his dedicatory epistle Southerne is unusually frank about the commercial motives that led him to write for the theatre: 'Some Convenience, and a great deal of Pleasure, first carry'd me into this wanton way of Wickedness, (those old Seducers, Profit, and Pleasure) that have brought at last a great many of both Sexes, into the common Entertainment of the Town'.[46] *The Maid's Last Prayer* provides an unusual array of colourful characters for the company's leading actresses. Elinor Leigh plays the exotic Siam, while Mary Betterton is unusually cast as Wishwell, a bawd. Susannah Mountfort was heavily pregnant, which may explain her casting as Lady Susan Malepert, the maid of the title and a character part of a foolish old woman – probably a useful disguise to cover her pregnancy and accommodate any restriction of movement.[47] The Barry/Bracegirdle partnership again departs from the typical contrast. Barry plays to type in Lady Malepert, a passionate mistress who delights in cuckolding her foolish husband, while Bracegirdle plays the gambler, Lady Trickett, who uses her charms to pay off her debts. In the light of the recent scandal surrounding Mountfort's murder, this seems a potentially dangerous choice for Bracegirdle. Whether she considered her reputation to be irrevocably damaged, or simply exploited the moment of public notoriety, she took this opportunity to demonstrate the range of her ability as a comedienne. If this choice was in any way a gamble for the actress, it was one that evidently paid off, as Hook observes: 'It is a complete change of pace for Mrs. Bracegirdle – the change which is to bring her at last into her own as a *comedienne* with Congreve to write those parts which forever coupled their names. But it was Southerne who showed the talented young man the way.'[48] William Congreve was certainly Southerne's protégé. He contributed a song to *The Maid's Last Prayer* and a production of his first play followed a few weeks after Southerne's, but might it have been Anne Bracegirdle, not Southerne, who was instrumental in suggesting the line of comedy that Congreve wrote for her? Mountfort's death had robbed Bracegirdle not only of a leading man but also of his services as a playwright who had created some notable parts for her. It would not be surprising to find Bracegirdle encouraging a promising young playwright to create new parts which capitalised on her sympathetic reputation and exploited her comedic abilities.

Congreve and the actresses: a story of influence

It is not my intention to dwell on the strengths of Congreve's plays or his skill as a playwright – there are numerous works of literary criticism and biography devoted to that task already – but to offer a different perspective: one that repositions Congreve's work in the wider context of the Late Stuart stage and which, crucially, reviews his relationship to the company of players he wrote for – especially the actresses. Best known today for his comedies, Congreve's work appears to return to the old type of comedy favoured in the Restoration and yet, like Southerne and, to some extent, D'Urfey, there are innovations which belong entirely to the period in which he was writing: the Late Stuart stage. Lucyle Hook notes that in *The Old Batchelor* and his next play, *The Double Dealer*, performed later in the 1693/4 season, the plots surrounding 'cuckolding, woman chasing husbands and unfaithful wives' run alongside 'entirely new elements', including 'a clever use of the contemporary scene ... a smartness of repartee' depicting 'the eternal round which occupied fashionable London, and the many other futile occupations with which an idle society concerns itself'.[49] My intention here is not to question Congreve's skill as a playwright but to draw attention to the general move toward the middle-class 'comedy of manners' and situate Congreve's work as *part* of that move, rather than its sole creative force.

Congreve is undoubtedly an important figure in this period of theatre history but his canonical status as a playwright in the twentieth century has resulted in an unbalanced view of his influence at the time, both in his early days with the United Company and, as we shall see later, in the new company at Lincoln's Inn Fields. Congreve's first play, *The Old Batchelor* (1693), had been written some years before its first production and given to Dryden, who had made certain judicious alterations. Southerne recommended it to Thomas Davenant for production and persuaded the manager to break with usual practice by offering the young playwright the run of the playhouse *before* his first play was performed. It seems probable that Congreve was observing rehearsals and becoming more familiar with the individual talents of the company for some considerable time before they came to work on his play.[50] *The Old Batchelor*'s success relied heavily on the skills and experience of all the senior players. Their expertise in playing high comedy surely contributed as much to Congreve's first success as his evident facility for witty dialogue and comic set-pieces. In a footnote to a late nineteenth-century edition of Congreve's plays Alexander Ewald adds: 'It is said that when Mrs Barry, Mrs Bracegirdle, Mrs Mountford, and Mrs Bowman appeared together on the stage in the last act of *The Old Bachelor*, the audience were so struck with a group so beautiful, that they broke out into a fervour of applause.'[51] The play was framed with Anne Bracegirdle as prologue speaker and Elizabeth Barry as epilogue speaker, also working to ensure the play's warm reception. Barry chose the play for her annual benefit on 16 April 1694, while Bracegirdle is firmly identified with one of Congreve's later, and most memorable, female characters. The seeds of partnership between Congreve and the actresses may well have sown in the United Company years but Congreve's best-loved characters were yet to be created for, and by, the enduring success of the Barry/Bracegirdle partnership.

In the final two years of the United Company's monopoly of the London stage, the Barry/Bracegirdle partnership was seen in six new plays: three comedies and three tragedies. There were obvious advantages for both actresses: Barry consolidated her own position in the company, a position that might have been challenged had she entered into competition with the younger actress but which was evidently enhanced by their collaboration, while for Bracegirdle, the partnership not only worked to establish her own position in the company but also allowed her to develop the contrasts between their on- and off-stage identities to the full. Reading against the grain of actress-as-muse, Barry and Bracegirdle can be seen as actively promoting the potential of their partnership to the playwrights and the playwrights responding by writing female characters to exploit that partnership.

Cracks in the United Company front

In spite of the production of other successful plays, there continued to be ongoing problems in the management of the company which were aggravated by financial losses. By December 1693 the company was reeling from a series of internal disruptions. Alexander Davenant had fled abroad when the full extent of his fraudulent dealings had been made public. Control of the company had passed out of the Davenant family and into the hands of the lawyer Christopher Rich and the investment adventurer Thomas Skipwith. Thomas Davenant was quickly removed from his managerial position by the new patentees and Thomas Betterton was soon locked in numerous disputes with Rich and Skipwith. Most theatre histories place Betterton at the head of attempts to hold the company together, in spite of rebellious rumblings from other dissatisfied players. The company's comedian, Thomas Doggett, was the first to test the strength of the United Company's monopoly, leading a group of supporting players who wanted to form their own company. Betterton opposed the defection and finally persuaded the rebels to return to the patent house. As Betterton's chief modern supporter, Judith Milhous, admits, 'Betterton was very much the company man',[52] implying that, even though the rebels had good cause to defect, Betterton's loyalty, at this point at least, lay with the patentees. Although Milhous is adamant in her assertion that 'the idea that Betterton was "deposed" from management has been too readily accepted', she concedes that 'the 1693–1694 season was evidently spent in a power struggle between Rich and Betterton, which Betterton lost'.[53] Betterton was nearing sixty years old. He had recently suffered a large personal financial loss in an investment venture involving a cargo being transported from the East Indies.[54] When Rich made moves to further undermine his position as the leading actor in the company by suggesting cuts in salary, it is little wonder that he eventually joined other senior players in an act of open resistance.

When Colley Cibber joined the United Company in 1690 he recorded the names of the leading players as follows:

Of Men	Of Women
Mr. Betterton,	Mrs. Betterton,
Mr. Montfort,	Mrs. Barry,
Mr. Kynaston,	Mrs. Leigh,
Mr. Sandford,	Mrs. Butler,
Mr. Nokes,	Mrs. Montfort, *and*
Mr. Underhill, *and*	Mrs. Bracegirdle.
Mr. Leigh.[55]	

This visual sign of equality, the names in corresponding columns and almost of equal numbers, is reinforced by the fact that Cibber identifies both men and women as 'principal actors ... at the head' of the company. There are many ways he might have arranged this list but, as it is, this arrangement speaks of a perceived equality between the leading actors and actresses. In Cibber's account of the events leading to the formation of the breakaway company in 1695, he again places Elizabeth Barry in an equal position to Betterton – although this time it is as a target for Rich's high-handed tactics in attempting to return the company to profitability:

> To make this Project more feasible [the reduction in salaries] they propos'd to begin at the Head of 'em, rightly judging that if the Principals acquiesc'd, their Inferiors would murmer in vain. To bring this about with a better Grace, they, under Pretence of bringing younger Actors forward, order'd several of *Betterton's* and Mrs. *Barry's* chief Parts

to be given to young *Powel* and Mrs. *Bracegirdle* ... tho' the giddy Head of *Powel* accepted the Parts of *Betterton*, Mrs. *Bracegirdle* had a different way of thinking, and desir'd to be excus'd from those of Mrs. *Barry*; her good Sense was not to be misled by the insidious Favour of the Patentees; she knew the stage was wide enough for her Success, without entering into any such rash and invidious Competition with Mrs. *Barry*, and therefore wholly refus'd acting any Part that properly belong'd to her.[56]

Rich's policy of divide and rule seems aimed at forcing Betterton and Barry into retirement, and a cynical interpretation would be that he wanted to remove their influence over the younger, more malleable players. It is impossible to know exactly what Cibber understood when he suggests that Bracegirdle had 'a different way of thinking' but it is clear that she did not trust the patentees and ignored their attempts to create an atmosphere of competition between herself and Elizabeth Barry.

Cibber places Betterton at the head of the 1694 players' rebellion, and traditional theatre histories have not challenged this assumption. But documents relating to the move to form a breakaway company suggest that Barry and Bracegirdle were as instrumental in proceedings as Betterton. Judith Milhous usefully includes a full transcription of the 'Petition of the Players' and the 'Reply of the Patentees'[57] in a detailed discussion of the exchanges between the players and patentees which clearly places Barry and Bracegirdle at the forefront of the rebellion but which traditional historiography has failed to investigate. There are several key passages worth considering here as they highlight the strong position held by the actresses and cast light upon the nature of their objections to the current form of management.

Alongside her central position as leading player, Elizabeth Barry's strong financial position is confirmed by the revelation that Alexander Davenant had 'Couzen[ed] Mrs Barrey of 6 or 800*ll* & divers others of severall thousands'.[58] That Barry could afford to sustain a loss of that size without having made it public earlier is evidence of either her extreme personal wealth, her loyalty to the Davenant family or, of course, her embarrassment at having been defrauded in such a way. Apart from other references to Rich's attempts to renege on financial agreements made by the Davenants, including Barry's long standing agreement for an assured £70 from her benefit performance, the main complaints surround the patentees' disregard for the players' social standing: 'treateing us not as we were the King's and Queenes servants but the Claimer's slaves'.[59] The overall tone of the players' petition effectively threatens a strike if their grievances are not heard and that they are 'noe longer able to suffer & support themselves under the unjust oppressions & Violations of almost all the By lawes and Customes & usage that has been established among us from ye beginning.[60] The petition is signed by nine actors and the six leading actresses: Elizabeth Barry, Anne Bracegirdle, Susannah Verbruggen (formerly Mountfort), Elizabeth Bowman, Mary Betterton and Elinor Leigh.

As Milhous notes, the patentees could 'cite contractual obligations, and often precedent' in their reply to the charges against them; 'they were, however, at a political disadvantage. Betterton and the Lord Chamberlain had been friends for at least twenty years.'[61] But Barry and Bracegirdle also had powerful political friends (including Charles Sackville, the Lord Chamberlain) not least the playwrights who had benefited from their collaboration in the creation of new and popular characters. Milhous is determined to place Betterton, alone, at the centre of the dispute, asserting that 'obviously they [the patentees] regarded him as the ringleader of the rebellion.'[62] While I would agree that Betterton is the *figurehead* for the rebellion, a necessary strategy for such an audacious move in a firmly patriarchal society, the patentees evidently consider Elizabeth Barry an equal threat when it comes to refuting the players' claims: 'Nor doth Mr Betterton or Mrs Barry or any other person that we have heard of pretend to have any Mortgage or grant of ye said patent or those shares or any parte of them.'[63] Barry and Betterton are jointly mentioned in a number of other answers by the patentees, including a reference to the fact that, in response to their combined request, the patentees had raised Dogget's salary by 10s. The most obvious attack launched at both players is that they are simply past their prime. This is quite specific in Betterton's case:

> It is true Mr Betterton doth not think himselfe lessen'd in his Acting but ye Patentees & adventurers to their sad Experience find that a man at 60 is not able to doe That which he could at 30 or 40. He hath put himselfe into all great parts in most of ye Considerable plays Especially in ye tragedys & Yett when he Acts a great parte we must be forced to Act an Ordinary Play one or 2 dayes after as Scapin Monsieur Ragou & such like to Ease him & soe loose what wee got on ye day he played.[64]

Elizabeth Barry gets off lightly in comparison, but she too is accused of losing her once powerful box-office appeal to her younger partner. Intimations of her 'mercenary' character, as well as her inability to recognise her fading popularity, are offered as an explanation for her unwillingness to share her profits with Bracegirdle:

And wee Observing that although ye receipts of late had been lesse than usual yett ye Constant & incident Charges are higher & consequently needfull to be Retrencht … Itt was proposed that she would continue at her Usuall Sallary of 50s per Weeke & remitt one-third of ye proffitts of ye Days Play to Mrs Bracegirdle which we believed would be ye Addition of Mrs Bracegirdles ffriends so Increase ye Receipts as that Mrs Barry would not be a great looser.[65]

After this assault, there was little chance that the leading players would acquiesce and return to the patent company.

Plans for the breakaway company

Milhous is probably right in her suggestion that Rich would have welcomed the enforced retirement of the older players but was 'astonished and infuriated to discover that public and government sympathy lay with the rebels'.[66] The meeting with the Lord Chamberlain on 17 December produced no movement on either side, and within a week performances were cancelled as Queen Mary's illness was announced. Her death on 28 December resulted in a period of mourning and complete closure of the theatres until Easter Monday 1695. The rebels used the enforced cessation of public performance to negotiate a licence to perform and must have received assurances that they would be successful in their plans to create a new, rival company. By early February, plans to restore the theatre in Lincoln's Inn Fields were under way. In spite of a late attempt by the patentees to effect a reconciliation around 19 March, on 25 March the rebels received their licence.

The licence was granted by Charles [Sackville] Earl of Dorset and Middlesex, Lord Chamberlain of His Majesty's Household and was granted to 'Thomas Betterton, Elizabeth Barry, Anne Bracegirdle, John Bowman, Joseph Williams, Cave Underhill, Thomas Doggett, William Bowen, Susan Verbruggen, Elianoe Leigh, George Bright. His Majesties sworne servants and Comoedians … .And this Licence to continue untill further Order under my hand & seale.'[67] The order in which the names appear is not without significance. If Betterton *was* feeling the strain of his years, particularly in the demanding role of company manager, then the next most influential players were none other than Elizabeth Barry and Anne Bracegirdle. Some historians have included Congreve as a major player in the formation of the new company and, as I shall discuss in later chapters, his commitment to the company was certainly useful. At this point, however, it is evident that he would have been a fool *not* to throw his lot in with the actresses who had contributed so much to the success of his first two plays, and around whom he had already written his next. Lucyle Hook ends her extraordinary study on Barry and Bracegirdle at the very moment the full extent of their influence as theatre women really begins: in the management of a new company at Lincoln's Inn Fields. Barry and Bracegirdle were at the height of their public popularity and a new generation of female playwrights was about to burst on to the Late Stuart stage. To echo Hook, for the next five years Barry and Bracegirdle 'were in a position at last to dictate'.[68]

Notes

1 Simon Shepherd and Peter Womack, *English Drama: A Cultural History* (Oxford: Blackwell, 1996), pp. 150–151.
2 The definition of Sentimental drama, and especially Sentimental comedy, refers to the notion of characters exhibiting refined and elevated feelings rather than the witty ridiculing of social absurdities that is generally used to define the earlier Restoration comedy of manners. It is generally recognised that the Sentimental comedy reflects the interests of the growing middle-class audience rather than the aristocratic audience usually associated with the comedies of the Restoration.
3 Percy Fitzgerald, *A New History of the English Stage* (London: Tinsley Bros, 1882), 2 vols, vol. 1, p. 128. Fitzgerald makes many references to the immorality of the Restoration stage, the 'dramatic laxness of morals' (p. 108) that reflect widely-held views about Restoration plays and performance in nineteenth-century theatre histories and which are still visible in many twentieth-century accounts of the period.
4 p. 188.
5 Judith Milhous, *Thomas Betterton*, pp. 55–60, argues against the notion that Thomas Davenant's appointment as manager undermined Betterton's authority but, while I would agree that there may have been no immediate challenge to Betterton's artistic authority, there was now another layer of management with whom Betterton must negotiate. His position as 'consultant' to the inexperienced Thomas indicates, however subtly, that his rule as absolute authority in the day-to-day running of the company was over.
6 In referring to both Elizabeth Barry's adoption by the Davenant family and Bracegirdle's adoption by the Bettertons it must be noted that this was frequently a financially based arrangement to augment the family business, in this case the theatre. See John Gillis, *A World of Their Own Making* (Oxford: Oxford University Press, 1997) on the historical structuring of the family.
7 Lucyle Hook, 'Anne Bracegirdle's First Appearance', *Theatre Notebook*, 13 (1958), pp. 133–137.

8 Thomas Betterton, *The History of The English Stage*, ed. Curll (1741), p. 26. Also included in Hook, 'Mrs. Elizabeth Barry and Mrs. Anne Bracegirdle', p. 187.
9 pp. 188–189.
10 Cibber, *Apology*, ed. Lowe, vol. 1, p. 170.
11 Hook, 'Mrs. Elizabeth Barry and Mrs. Anne Bracegirdle', p. 192.
12 See Bratton, 'Claiming Kin: An Experiment in Genealogical Research, *New Readings*, pp. 171–199, for more on how we might reconsider the theatre family and especially the work of theatre women.
13 Cibber, *Apology*, ed. Lowe, vol. 1, pp. 170–172.
14 Cibber, *Apology*, ed. Lowe, vol. 1, p. 136 makes much of deriding another actress (probably Mrs Rogers) for professing virtue when her private life was far from beyond reproach.
15 It is probable that Anne Bracegirdle was still alive when Cibber was writing, although she died in the year of publication. Lowe, Cibber's late nineteenth-century editor is also cautious about Cibber's accuracy on certain points but limits his comments to footnotes rather than altering the first text. Lowe's decision to append Aston's biographies of the company, to Cibber's *Apology*, places some emphasis on the potential for alternative accounts of the players and their characters.
16 Anthony Aston, *A Brief Supplement to Colley Cibber* (c. 1769), in Cibber, *Apology* (ed.) Lowe, p. 306.
17 Hook, 'Mrs. Elizabeth Barry and Mrs. Anne Bracegirdle', pp. 226–227.
18 p. 225.
19 Jean I. Marsden, 'Female Spectatorship, Jeremy Collier and the Anti-theatrical Debate', *Journal of English Literary History*, 65 (1998), pp. 877–899, p. 877.
20 p. 878.
21 Although Cibber is almost boundless in his admiration for Barry's, he notes that she could not match Mary Betterton's portrayal of Lady Macbeth. See Cibber, *Apology*, ed. Lowe, vol. 1, p. 162.
22 Wilson, *All the King's Ladies*, p. 156, records appearances for Frances Maria Knight in 1676 and 1677 with the King's Company. He suggests a birth date of 'not later than 1662' which would make her twenty-two when she appeared in Southerne's *The Disappointment* (1684). As in the case of Anne Bracegirdle, it seems likely that Knight's appearances as a child were at a younger age than many theatre historians find comfortable. A birth date of 1666 would make her eighteen for her first appearance as a member of the United company and would explain the ease with which, at twenty-eight, she took on the mantle of leading tragic actress when Elizabeth Barry left for Lincoln's Inn Fields. If she did appear as a child player, a small part for a girl of ten or eleven years old would not be that remarkable, although it is also possible that the 'Knight' referred to was another small part player altogether.
23 Hook, 'Mrs. Elizabeth Barry and Mrs. Anne Bracegirdle', p. 230.
24 Howe, *The First English Actresses*, p. 156.

25 The 'she tragedy' is defined as a play in which the dramatic tragic plot focuses entirely on sexual love relationships rather than the concerns of honour, glory and power defined in the classical model of tragedy.
26 Howe, *The First English Actresses*, p. 157.
27 p. 156.
28 Other histories suggest Barry had a daughter by Etherege who settled a large sum for the child's upkeep but all the biographical accounts seem to agree that her daughter died around 1688/9 and that no child outlived her.
29 Holland, *The Ornament of Action*, p. 139.
30 Thomas Shadwell, *The Scowrers* (London: James Knapton, 1691), Act II, sc. i, p. 15.
31 Although Katherine Corey is named in the published edition of 1691 and known for her expertise in comedy playing nurses, governesses etc., *A Biographical Dictionary* does not include *The Scowrers* in her list of credits.
32 Act II, sc. i, p. 10. I have adjusted the layout for clarity and included the full name of the character speaking.
33 Act V, p. 52. The scenes are not numbered in this act, but this final scene is identified as taking place in 'Sir Humphrey Maggot's House'.
34 Act V, p. 53.
35 Thomas D'Urfey, *The Marriage-Hater Match'd* (London: Sam Briscoe, 1692). The published edition of this and D'Urfey's *The Richmond Heiress* (1693), also published by Samuel Briscoe, are unusual for the period in providing quite such a detailed breakdown of each character and their main plot line in the dramatis personae.
36 Semernia in Behn's *The Widdow Ranter* (1689) was Bracegirdle's first breeches role.
37 There is a great deal of variation in the spelling of players' names. I have not altered the spelling as it appears here but have adopted the conventional spelling elsewhere.
38 The published edition of 1692 reads 'her' but this is a scribal error. It is clear that the stage direction should read 'him' as, on seeing Mountfort, Bracegirdle attempts to leave the stage but is prevented from so doing.
39 D'Urfey, *Marriage-Hater Match'd*, Prologue.
40 Prologue.
41 Holland, *The Ornament of Action*, p. 151.
42 See the anonymous *The Player's Tragedy: or, A Fatal Love* (London: Randal Taylor, 1693) for a barely disguised and sensational account of events. Described as 'A New Novel', the author goes to great lengths to wring every ounce of romance out of this social scandal. The players are represented as wholly inferior to the 'gentlemen' and the author suggests that Hill's mistake was not in murdering Mountfort but in treating Bracegirdle as he would a Lady: 'you have all taken a wrong method, by imagining an Actress mov'd by those generous Principles that Women of Education and Honour do ... In short 'tis Money that must buy your satisfaction, if it center in a Player' (p. 40).

43 Cibber, *Apology*, ed. Lowe, vol. 1, p. 154.
44 Southerne, *The Maid's Last Prayer* or *Any Rather than Fail* (London: Bentley and Tonson, 1693). In the middle of Act I (p. 10), a song is announced as being 'by Major-General Sackvile' and printed in full. It is possible that Southerne paid Sackvile for the song but the less than inspiring lyrics might suggest that Southerne (or the company) were paid to include it.
45 Thomas Southerne, *The Maid's Last Prayer*, Prologue.
46 Dedicatory epistle.
47 It is probable that Susannah was carrying her fourth child by Mountfort. On 31 January 1694 Susannah married another actor in the company, John Verbruggen and from that point acted under her new husband's name.
48 Hook, 'Mrs. Elizabeth Barry and Mrs. Anne Bracegirdle', p. 333.
49 p. 331.
50 It is generally accepted that Congreve may have completed this play as early as 1689. In his dedication to Lord Clifford of Lanesborough (see William Congreve, *The Old Batchelor* (London: Peter Buck, 1693), Dedicatory epistle) Congreve writes of having 'four years experience', which suggests that he had been living in London and known to Dryden and Southerne some time before he received his first production. It is not possible to put a precise date on his introduction to the company but it seems plausible that it was some considerable time before his first play was produced.
51 Alexander C. Ewald (ed.), *Congreve: The Best Plays of the Old Dramatists* (London: Mermaid, 1887), p. 91, n.1.
52 Milhous, *Thomas Betterton*, p. 60.
53 pp. 58–59.
54 Sir Francis Watson had introduced Betterton to this investment opportunity which failed when, on its return from the Indies, the ship and its cargo was captured by the French. Watson died soon after and his daughter Elizabeth was taken into the Betterton household. She soon became an actress and later married fellow player John Bowman (see *A Biographical Dictionary*, entry for Elizabeth Bowman, vol. 2, p. 201).
55 Cibber, *Apology*, ed. Lowe, vol. 1, p. 98. A check against the first edition of Cibber's *Apology* reveals that Lowe has reproduced this list of names in exactly the same way as they appear in the original (see Colley Cibber, *An Apology for the Life of Mr. Colley Cibber* (London: John Watts, 1740), p. 59.
56 Cibber, *Apology*, ed. Lowe, vol. 1, p. 189.
57 Milhous, *Thomas Betterton*, Appendix A, pp. 225–229, source cited as P. R.O. LC 7/3 and Appendix B, pp. 230–245, from the same source. Milhous notes that there is no exact date for the first 'Petition of the Players' but the second, the reply from the patentees, carries an injunction to attend a meeting with the Lord Chamberlain (Charles Sackville, Earl of Dorset) on 'Munday 17 December 94 between 10 & 11 a clock'. Milhous provides the only thorough discussion of the exchanges between players and patentees in her chapter "Actors' Rebellion of 1694–1695", specifically pp. 62–68.

58 Appendix A, p. 226.
59 p. 227.
60 p. 225.
61 p. 62.
62 Ibid.
63 Appendix B, p. 233.
64 p. 240.
65 p. 239. It is not entirely clear whether this refers to any performance payment or, specifically, to the benefit payment Barry had negotiated some years before. I am inclined to conclude that this is direct reference to the benefit performance as these depended upon the support of the player's friends and admirers. In either case the point the patentees are making is clear; that Barry was less popular than the younger actress and could only benefit from the extra profits gained by the support of Bracegirdle's admirers.
66 p. 66.
67 p. 67. Milhous cites the source as P. R.O.LC 7/3. This licence differs from the sharing agreement (reproduced by Milhous in Appendix D, p. 249). Notably Susanna Verbruggen and Joseph Williams are missing from the list, while John Verbruggen is included but, in all the new documentation pertaining to the new company, Betterton's name is always immediately followed by Barry and Bracegirdle.
68 Hook, 'Mrs. Eizabeth Barry and Mrs. Anne Bracegirdle, p. 405.

Part II
The Players' Company at Lincoln's Inn Fields

4
New Moves, New Voices

The playhouse in Lincoln's Inn Fields had reverted to its original use as an indoor tennis court following the move of the Duke's Company into its own purpose-built theatre in Dorset Gardens in 1674. The first task facing the rebels was to convert it once again into a playhouse, and Edward Langhans is the only theatre historian to my knowledge to note the significance of the fact that the 'new' theatre the company decided to occupy was in fact the first playhouse created by Davenant in 1660.[1] The relevance of this connection is, surely, that the theatre at Lincoln's Inn Fields had an established theatrical identity as the first site of the Duke's Company, managed by the original patentee William and, later, Mary Davenant. From this perspective the *return* to Lincoln's Inn Fields reveals an interesting shift in the development of the Late Stuart stage – one that is both reactionary in its desire to invoke the values of traditional drama established in the early years of the Restoration and revolutionary as a site of unprecedented public activity by theatre women.

Theatre historians agree that the strength of the new company lay in the fact that it contained the most experienced and popular players of the day. It is worth noting at this point that of the thirty-four players listed in *The London Stage*,[2] twenty-two actors and twelve actresses, ten had begun their careers in the Duke's Company and eight of these are identified twice within the sharing agreement,[3] always appearing in the same order as well as being named as signatories: Thomas Betterton, Elizabeth Barry, Anne Bracegirdle,[4] John Verbruggen,[5] John Bowman, Cave Underhill, George Bright and Elinor Leigh. The most innovative aspect of this company is that it formed itself on the basis of a players' co-operative in which the actors and, for the first time, actresses were allocated shares. The sharing agreement makes no attempt to designate any one player as overall leader or manager, and even Milhous acknowledges that at its formation 'Lincoln's Inn Fields was not in any way officially "Betterton's" company, though contemporaries sometimes referred to it that way. Such a designation is misleading, and I have tried to avoid it.'[6] In the following paragraph, however, Milhous is more equivocal, asserting that 'Betterton became their leader only in the sense that he was the principal actor in London in 1695'. Within a few pages she slips a little further, suggesting that 'Betterton was presumably the first among equals, but initially he was given no formal authority at all'.[7] There is simply *nothing* in either the licence or the sharing agreement to suggest that Betterton or any other male player was the leader of this company – other than the considerable weight of traditional historiography which assumes such a hierarchy. The sharing agreement makes it clear that the company sought to form itself on lines that favoured the players of *both* sexes and so provides a conspicuously alternative model to the oppressive management practised by Rich and Skipwith in the Patent Company.

Sharing profits and responsibilities

The terms of the sharing agreement are striking in several ways. The licence to perform, with its attendant privileges and responsibilities, is shared by *all* the named players. References to the 'Extraordinary Charge and Expence' incurred by the sharers in converting the playhouse make it clear that by excluding the usual 'adventurers' from holding shares the company had to find an alternative funding source for the project. *A Comparison between the Two Stages* (1702) cynically suggests that there was a great deal of 'importuning and dunning … flattering, and … promising'[8] to various wealthy sponsors. Colley Cibber offers a more restrained account which states that 'many People of Quality came into a voluntary Subscription of twenty, and some of Forty Guineas a-piece'[9] in order to fund the alternative company. The agreement also makes specific financial provision for players who are prevented from performing through accident, illness, retirement, or death. But the evidence concerning the innovations of a company seeking to establish the rights of the players is passed over by Milhous in her pursuit of a more conventional model of male leadership: 'In many ways it is a humane and democratic document. But it betrays, first, a desperate lack of capital and, more important, a fatal vagueness about precisely who would set policy and make the company run.'[10] Milhous assumes that, because the documentary evidence does not include information about company hierarchies, the issue of leadership must have been left undecided – but this is far from the whole story.

The documents exchanged between the patentees and the players (discussed in the previous chapter) demonstrate that the Patent Company was quite aware that Barry's influence and position was as crucial as Betterton's. Even Milhous acknowledges that 'Mrs Barry's contribution was especially important in the search for new plays'[11] but chooses not to identify this proactive task as indicative of her managerial position. There is little doubt that Barry, Bracegirdle and Betterton were the moving force behind this company and, later, all three were accused of adopting a high-handed attitude in their management of company matters. Although there is no *direct* evidence in the sharing agreement to prove that Barry and Bracegirdle played a greater part in the day-to-day management of the company, there is some evidence to suggest that Betterton was no longer at the height of his powers. Betterton was now sixty years old – not a great age by today's standards but life expectancy was considerably shorter in the seventeenth century – the patentees had also clearly expressed doubts about his ability to play the full repertoire in his final season at Drury Lane. By contrast, Elizabeth Barry was thirty-seven and Anne Bracegirdle twenty-two years old. They were at the height of their acting partnership, appearing together in forty new plays during their decade at Lincoln's Inn Fields, at least a quarter of which were written by women. Whatever problems were to come – and they were many – the early years of the Players' Company are markedly more successful than those of their rivals in the Patent Company.[12] By reviewing the work of the Players' Company and reading against the historical assumption of Betterton's place at its head, the Players' Company success can be seen to depend on the powerful presence of the Barry/Bracegirdle partnership – on and off the stage.

Opening the doors to success

Announced as The New Theatre in Lincoln's Inn Fields, the company opened its first season with Congreve's *Love for Love* on 30 April 1695.[13] It was an outstanding success for the Players' Company and had an uninterrupted thirteen-day run; a success which contemporary accounts attribute to the popularity of the players as well as the playwright.

Ramble: You know the New-house opened with an extraordinary good comedy, the like has scarce been heard of.
Critick: I allow that Play contributed not a little to their reputation and Profit; it was the work of a popular Author; but that was not all, the Town was ingag'd in its favour, and in favour of the Actors long before the Play was Acted.[14]

Another contemporary report goes further by citing the appearance of the rebel players as the central attraction for the audience: 'This Play, tho' a very good Comedy in it self, had this Advantage, that it was Acted at the Opening of the New House, when the town was so prepossess'd in Favour of the very Actors, that before a word was spoke, each Actor was clapt for a considerable Time.'[15] The Players' Company had the sympathy and open support of their audience, not least of those 'Noble Persons' who had subscribed to the conversion of the new playhouse.

The gradual change of performance times from two-thirty in the afternoon at the Restoration to around four o'clock from 1695, moving to as late as six-thirty at the turn of the century, reflects the changing composition of a city-based audience who were not free from commercial activity until later in the day. The presence of the merchant classes was essential to box-office receipts but so too was the approbation of the aristocratic coterie:

Sullen: But the assistance they receiv'd from some Noble persons did 'em eminent Credit; and their appearance in the Boxes, gave the House as much Advantage as their Contributions.
Ramble: … and what the Quality approve, the lower sort take upon trust'.[16]

There is an unmistakable sense of elitism here but while the company was mindful of the old patronage system of the aristocracy, it was also mindful of its new, enterprising audience of merchants.

As a founder member of the Duke's Company, Betterton had triumphantly taken the stage at Drury Lane in 1682 to announce the opening performance of the United company. Thirteen years later Betterton reinforces the long theatrical credentials of the Players' Company by, once again, delivering the prologue for another new company's opening performance:

> The Husbandman in vain renews his Toil,
> To cultivate each Year a hungry Soil;
> And fondly hopes for *rich* and generous Fruit,
> When what should feed the Tree, devours the Root;
> …
> As Nature gave the World to Man's first age,
> So from your Bounty we receive this Stage;
> The Freedom Man was born to you've restor'd.
> And to our World, such Plenty you afford;
> It seems like Eden, fruitful of its own accord.[17]
> 			(my emphasis)

Few in the audience could miss the antagonism toward Christopher Rich and the implication that, by patronising the alternative house, they were part of a new 'Eden', where the creative fruits of the arts might be saved from the greed of the commercial investor. Keeping to its biblical and, therefore, righteous theme, the prologue goes on to refer to the defection of the actor Joseph Williams and the actress Susannah Verbruggen – 'one falling Adam, and one tempted Eve' – who had returned to the Patent Company before the new house opened following a disagreement over shares. Amid the swipes at the patent house, this prologue smacks of nostalgia, a desire to return to the somewhat idealised values of earlier theatre practice, with Betterton as on-stage husbandman and the audience as off-stage, noble, patrons: but in this new creative Eden the need for commercial success was of paramount importance.

Women on top

Congreve's decision to throw his lot in with the Players' Company must have been influenced by his dependence on Barry and Bracegirdle. They had created the leading female roles in his earlier works and there seems little doubt that they were essential to the success of *Love for Love*. Writing some considerable time after the play's outstanding success, Cibber gives an account of the negotiations surrounding the first production:

> This valuable Play had a narrow Escape from falling into the Hands of the Patentees; for before the Division of the Company it had been read and accepted at the Theatre-Royal: But while the Articles of Agreement for it were preparing, the rupture in the Theatrical State was so far advanced that the Author took time to pause before he sign'd them; when finding that all Hopes of Accommodation were impracticable, he thought it advisable to let it take its fortune with those Actors for whom he had first intended the Parts.[18]

Barry played Mrs Frail, 'a woman of the town', with Bracegirdle representing the virtuous heroine of the piece, Angelica. Bracegirdle was also the speaker of the all-important epilogue which picks up the biblical tone of the prologue by presenting the players as lost souls – righteous pilgrims – seeking a place of rest and refuge. The epilogue's appeal turns on Bracegirdle's plea to the audience to stay faithful and, more importantly, to continue to fill the house:

> I can't reflect without an aking Heart,
> How we should end in our Original, a Cart.
> But we can't fear, since your so good to save us
> That you have only set us up, to leave us.[19]

In stark contrast to this working of Bracegirdle's vulnerable and innocent identity, she is also named as the speaker for an alternative Prologue which is included in early editions of the published texts. 'Sent from an unknown Hand', the prologue is not assigned to Betterton but is 'propos'd to be spoken by Mrs. Bracegirdle in Man's Cloaths'.[20]

Although there is nothing unusual about an actress delivering the prologue in breeches, Anne Bracegirdle was yet to be strongly connected with the breeches role and neither was Angelica, her character in *Love for Love*, a breeches part.[21] There is a defiant tone to this prologue which, from the beginning, draws attention to gender constructs:

> Custom which everywhere bears mighty Sway,
> Brings me to act the Orator to Day:
> But Women, you will say, are ill at Speeches,
> 'Tis true, and therefore I appear in Breeches:
> Not for example to you City-Wives,   5
> That by Prescription's settled for your Lives.
> Was it for Gain the Husband first consented?
> O yes, their Gains are mightily augmented:
>   (*Making Horns with her Hands over her Head*)
> And yet, methinks, it must have cost some Strife: 10
> A Passive Husband, and an Active Wife!
> 'Tis awkward, very awkward, by my Life.

There is a disruptive force to this verse, a sense of active transgression where women not only appear disguised in men's clothes but operate outside the 'natural' passive modes of female behaviour. The prologue goes on to acknowledge the Players' debt to their patrons and moves to align issues of justice and national freedom with the rebel Players' own situation:

> A long Egyptian Bondage we endur'd,
> 'Till Freedom, by your Justice, we procur'd:
> Our Task-masters were grown such very Jews,   20
> We must at length have play'd in Wooden Shooes
> Had not your Bounty taught us to refuse.
> Freedom's of English Growth, I think, alone;
> What for lost English Freedom can attone?
> A Free-born Player loaths to be compell'd;   25
> Our Rulers Tyranniz'd, and We Rebell'd.
> Freedom! The Wise Man's Wish, the Poor Man's Wealth;
> Which you, and I, and most of us enjoy by Stealth;
> The Soul of Pleasure, and the Sweet of Life,
> The Woman's Charter,[22] Widow, Maid or Wife,   30
> This they'd have cancell'd, and thence grew the Strife.

The author knows the audience is sympathetic to the rebel players' cause and works to extend that sympathy to others struggling against tyrannical rule; specifically women. With Bracegirdle as the speaker, the clear implication is that any freedom enjoyed by women has to be gained by 'stealth' rather than afforded her as a right (line 28); physically demonstrated by Bracegirdle's appearance in men's clothes.

In what at first glance seems a curious move, the prologue then switches to the more conventional territory of the way the actress has used her sexual favours to gain the subscriptions needed to open the new playhouse:

>But you, perhaps, wou'd have me here confess
>How we obtain'd the Favour – Can't you guess?
>Why then I'll tell you, (for I hate a Lie)
>By Brib'ry, errant Brib'ry, let me die: 35
>I was their Agent, but by Jove I swear
>No honourable Member had a Share,
>Tho' young and able Members bid me Fair:
>I chose a wiser way to make you willing,
>Which has not cost the House a single Shilling; 40
>Now you suspect at least I went a Billing.
>You see I'm Young, and to that Air of youth,
>Some will add Beauty, and a little Truth;
>These pow'rful Charms, improv'd by pow'rful Arts,
>Prevail'd to captivate your op'ning Hearts. 45
>Thus furnish'd, I preferr'd my poor Petition,
>And brib'd you to commiserate our Condition:
>I laugh'd, and sigh'd, and sung, and leer'd upon ye,
>With roguish Looks, and that way won ye:
>The young Men kiss'd me, and the Old I kiss'd, 50
>And luringly I led them as I list.

Bracegirdle plays directly into the actress/whore trope, then makes a turn which demonstrates an awareness of her power to *use* her sexuality in order to achieve the end *she* desires (lines 42–46); the 'active' woman manipulating the 'passive' man (line 11). It is possible that the Players' Company chose to opt for the safer prologue spoken by Betterton, rather than this overt piece of female rhetoric but why then was it included in the early published editions? The weight of historiographical assumptions that place Betterton as leader of the company and Bracegirdle as the virtuous exception to the actress/whore trope must exclude the possibility that it was Betterton's prologue that was not given, or even that both were presented on the opening night. Nineteenth-century historians may well have baulked at the Bracegirdle prologue because she overtly serves herself up in a manner that links her sexualised identity with individual power.

It is, as Susan Bennett has argued, more convenient 'to forget'[23] that which troubles the perceived stability of our historical narratives or, at least, to edit that which offends the sensibilities of the historian and his/her reader. But to forget is to occlude and, ultimately, to erase. The process of forgetting is made easier in this case by the anonymity of the writer – the lack of hard evidence to link a specific identity to the 'unknown hand' who provided this prologue. It is here, in the gap created by the unidentified, disembodied voice, that I begin to respond to Bennett's central notion of 'decomposing history' – the re-making of a theatre history that 'will have us, fully and appropriately, remember'[24] But is it only, as Bennett seems to suggest, a case of remembering and reconfiguring the work of the writing woman? The call for 'more inclusive theatre histories' that interrogate the 'categories of organizing narratives'[25] reinforces an argument that seeks strategies to break the boundaries between text and performance, writer and player, in our historical narratives. The forgotten story of the Players' Company is one of collaboration between women – as actresses and playwrights. The story begins with the anonymous prologue, which was quickly followed with a new play by another anonymous playwright, identifying herself only as 'Ariadne'.

She Ventures

The conventional assumption would be to attribute the prologue discussed above to a male author, but the sympathetic treatment of the female perspective in the first half of the prologue, combined with the assertive image of female sexuality in the second half, suggests the possibility that this prologue was written by a woman. It is clear that whoever the author was, he or she wrote it for Anne Bracegirdle and designed much of the impact to be carried by Bracegirdle's appearance in breeches. The argument for female authorship, albeit speculative, is reinforced by the new play chosen to open the Players' Company's first full season in September 1695, in which Anne Bracegirdle plays the titular heroine, Charlotte: a breeches role.

She Ventures and He Wins[26] was written by 'a young lady', adopting the pseudonym of 'Ariadne' for the published edition of 1696. This was the first new play by a woman since the death of Aphra Behn in 1689 and marks the beginning of a period of extraordinary activity by a rising generation of female playwrights. *She Ventures and He Wins* is a conventional five-act comedy driven by two far from conventional female heroines in Charlotte, played by Anne Bracegirdle and Urania, played by Elizabeth Barry. In a departure from their traditional acting partnership, the Barry/Bracegirdle heroines are at the centre of their own dramatic plots which, although being brought together in the final scene, deal with quite different social worlds. The first plot concerns Charlotte/Bracegirdle, a wealthy heiress who determines to find a husband 'who loves [her] Person as well as Gold', and insists that she will 'please [her]self, not the World, in [her] choice'.[27] To this end she and her cousin Juliana, played by Elizabeth Bowman, disguise themselves as young gentlemen and set out in search of a suitable husband. Having found him in the form of a penniless young man, Lovewell, played by John Hudson, Charlotte devises a series of tests to prove his fidelity and honourable character. The second plot circulates around Urania/Barry, who is married to Freeman, a vintner with whom she runs a tavern. Urania/Barry finds herself fending off the unwelcome advances of one Squire Wouldbe, who has set out to seduce her. Determined to defend her virtue, prove her fidelity to her suspicious husband and expose her would-be despoiler, Urania forms a plan in which she pretends to respond to Wouldbe's advances by inviting him to meet her at the tavern disguised as a woman (in order to avoid detection by her husband who, although not entirely trusting of his wife, agrees to participate in the plot).

The themes of appearance and reality, honesty and duplicity are reminiscent of Behn plays, particularly *The Feign'd Curtezans* (1679) which may well have been revived by the company later in the season. Like Behn, 'Ariadne' presents a wholly female perspective on male duplicity and advocates a woman's right to determine her own future, particularly in the realm of love and marriage. 'Ariadne's' prologue is 'spoken by Mrs. Bowman in man's clothes' and immediately advertises the play's women-centred perspective. More importantly, the author situates herself within the tradition of writing women established by poet/playwright Katherine Philips (Orinda) and Aphra Behn:

> This is a Woman's Treat y'are like to find;
> Ladies, for Pity; Men, for Love, be kind;
> Else here I come, her Champion to oppose
> The two broadsides of dreadful Wits and Beaux:
> 'Tis odd indeed; but if my Sword won't do,   5
> I can produce another Weapon too, –

> But to my Task. – Our author hopes indeed,
> You will not think, though charming Aphra's dead,
> All Wit with her, and with Orinda's fled.
> We promised boldly we would do her Right,   10
> Not like the other House, who, out of spite
> Trump'd up a Play upon us in a night.
> And it was Scarcely thought on at the most,
> But Hey-Boys, Presto! Conjur'd on the Post.
> These Champions bragg'd they first appeared in Field,   15
> Then bid us tamely, *article and yield*;[28]

In the published edition, 'Aridane's' preface states that the author is 'altogether unacquainted with the stage and those dramatic rules, which others have with so much art and success observed'. The prologue alone contradicts this assertion as she clearly makes effective use of sexual innuendo in the cross-dressed player (line 6) and is also keenly aware of the bitter feud with the Patent Company (line 12).[29] Although the epilogue is clearly attributed to Mr Motteux there is no such attribution for the prologue, indicating that it is the work of the playwright herself.[30] The theatrical skill with which the prologue and the body of the play are constructed suggests that, despite her protestations, 'Ariadne' had a thorough working knowledge of theatre practice.

The two central plots interweave in such a way that the audience (or reader) never loses track of the developments in each woman's story. Charlotte/Bracegirdle sets increasingly trying tests for her new husband, Lovewell, while Urania/Barry hatches a plot to humiliate Wouldbe. This leads to some wonderful moments of high comedy, such as the scene in which the cross-dressed Wouldbe finds himself hiding first in a water cistern, then a barrel of feathers and being finally being carried off by 'devils' in an effort to avoid the wrath of Urania's husband – a gift for the comic actor Thomas Dogget who played the would-be lover. The carefully crafted comic set-pieces are sharpened by social satire, particularly in the characters of Dowdy, Wouldbe's wife, played by Betty Boutell, and her social climbing mother, Mrs Beldam/Elizabeth Leigh, who keeps the family stocked with fine things 'borrowed' from her pawn broking business. In many ways the strength of this play is in the creation of the characters, particularly the women, who are all, in one way or another, seeking to fulfil their own ambitions in a society run by, and designed for the benefit of, men. 'Ariadne' represents men as they are seen through women's eyes, revealing the way in which their character and behaviour is perceived by women and, more importantly, the way in which these quite different women *want* men to be.

In the opening scene of the play Charlotte asserts her independence and satirises male posturing in a speech which must have given Bracegirdle ample opportunity for some cruelly accurate impersonations:

> I'm not obliged to follow the World's dull Maxims, nor will I wait for the formal Address of some Ceremonious Coxcomb, with more Land than Brains, who would bargain for us as he would for his Horse, and talks of nothing but Taxes and hard Times, to make me a good Housewife; or else some gay young fluttering Thing, who calls himself a Beau, and wants my Fortune to maintain him in that Character: such an opinionated Animal who believes there needs no more to reach a Ladies Heart than a boon mien, fine Dress, the Perriwig well adjusted, the Hand well managed in taking Snuff, to shew the fine Diamond-Ring, if he's worth one; sometimes a conceited Laugh, with the Mouth stretch'd from one Ear t'other, to discover the white Teeth, with sneak and cringe in Affected tone, cries Damn me, Madam, if you are not the prettiest Creature my Eyes ere saw! 'Tis impossible for me to live if you are so cruel to deny me, with a world of such foolish stuff, which they talk all by rote.[31]

This overt attack on male behaviour is modified by Charlotte's intention to find a man who 'retains the Image Heaven made them in, Vertuous, and Just, Sincere and Brave' who will offer her true love; her optimism being undercut by Juliana who wonders 'If there's any such thing as real Love in that false Sex'.[32] The next scene plunges the audience into the middle of a heated dispute between Urania and her husband in which she defends her virtue and insists that her husband must 'Trust to [her] Honesty'.[33] Unusually it is the husband, Freeman, who is close to hysteria at the notion of being made a cuckold, while Urania, clearly the more intelligent of the two, forms a plan which will reassure her husband, discredit Wouldbe and vindicate her as an honourable and virtuous woman.

The way women manage their relationships with men is central to this play. Even Wouldbe's gullible wife Dowdy knows that the pawned objects given to Wouldbe by her mother 'makes him take Care to please me'.[34] At the play's conclusion the audiences know that Wouldbe will retain his wife, but be punished with the withdrawal of the material comforts provided by her mother. The two heroines get what they want. Urania's plan is successful, her virtue vindicated and she receives what is effectively a public apology from her husband who admits himself 'a Poor clownish fellow' who is grateful that his wife 'thinks me good enough for her'.[35] Charlotte proves Lovewell is honourable and in a delightfully sceptical response to his repeated protestations of enduring love observes that he is 'Wonderous zealous now, Pray Heaven it lasts'.

In a traditional historiography which has insisted on Thomas Betterton's leadership of the Players' Company, no one to my knowledge has drawn attention to his conspicuous absence from the production of *She Ventures and He Wins*. He is not named in the cast list and does not speak either the prologue or epilogue. Indeed his absence from a new play chosen to open the first full playing season may well be part of the reason that the play has frequently been written off as a failure – by which we must assume that, at the very least, it failed to reach the third day payment for the playwright, although there is no evidence for this assumption.[36] Furthermore, this play by an unknown female playwright was, as one contemporary report has it, 'brought in' by Elizabeth Barry.[37] If we pursue an alternative history that places Barry and Bracegirdle at the centre of the Player's company, sponsoring and playing in a new play by a new female playwright, we might consider the extent to which claims of failure operate as part of a historiographical strategy of 'forgetting'. The title and opening lines of the play tackle the issue of gender and power head on and, to an audience in the know, offers a warning that new-found authority will easily be discarded:

Juliana: Faith, Charlotte, the Breeches become you so well 'tis almost pity you should ever part with 'em.
Charlotte: Nor will I, till I can find one can make better use of them to bestow 'em on, and then I'll resign my Title to 'em for ever.
Juliana: 'Tis well if you find it so easy, for a Woman once vested in Authority, tho' 'tis by no other than her own making, does not willingly part with it.[38]

As an example of theatre women rebelling against the tyranny of the management of the Patent Company, participating in the moves to obtain a licence to perform, and receiving royal authority to exercise that licence – an authority that they were not willing to part with when called upon to do so later – *She Ventures and He Wins* marks a new departure for the actresses and heralds an unprecedented period of activity and output for a new generation of female playwrights writing for the Late Stuart stage.

Introducing Trotter, Manley and Pix

Three other named women, Catherine Trotter, Delarivier Manley and Mary Pix, all had plays performed on the public stage in the 1695/6 season. Some historians have suggested that 'the women in management and the women playwrights chose each other ... the playwrights could have written for either house; yet they chose the rebel's company'.[39] As appealing as this notion may be to the feminist historian it is not, at least initially, an accurate account. Trotter, Manley and Pix *all* had their first plays produced by the Patent Company in the 1695/6 season. They are known to have been closely associated with one another and it seems likely that, if 'Ariadne' had been one of them, they would have at some point have revealed her identity. As Constance Clark observes: 'It is peculiar, with all the excitement this event must have generated, that the author should have disappeared from the scene so abruptly. Even though the play failed, there must have been a buzz through the theatrical community as to who "Ariadne" was'.[40] Even though Clark accepts the failure story associated with the play, she does more than most to establish the author's true identity by comparing play-texts and concluding that the most likely candidate is Mary Pix.

Clark's argument is based on the fact that Pix was the only one of the three to be alive during Behn's lifetime and that, of the three contenders, Pix was the most successful in writing comedy, much of which is resonant of Behn's earlier work. She notes that the prologue to Pix's *Ibrahim*, performed at Drury Lane at the end of the same season, contains a similar apology for the writer's sex as that provided by 'Ariadne'. Following Clark's own argument, however, the 'apology' is also in the Behn tradition and does not provide sufficient evidence to attribute *She Ventures and He Wins* to Pix. Clark offers another possibility; that of Lady Lucy Wharton. This tentative suggestion is based on gossip concerning William Congreve's affair with Lucy Wharton, which is recorded in Manley's *The New Atlantis* (1709) and in which Manley uses 'Ariadne' as a pseudonym for Wharton. Clark, who considers Congreve to have been a 'mentor of both Pix and Trotter', wonders if 'Perhaps he also launched Lucy Wharton'.[41] The sheer theatricality of *She Ventures and He Wins* leads me to doubt that it was the creation of a 'Lady' unskilled in the business of theatre. Other critics have suggested that 'Ariadne' might have been a man, perhaps an actor or untried playwright, but the general suspicion toward the writing woman suggests there would be absolutely no advantage in a man assuming a female identity. It is equally unlikely that any established writer, least of all Congreve, would have been content to collaborate invisibly, let alone 'ghost-write' for a woman.

Clark's suggestion that Mary Pix was the author seems to appeal to most critics; Kendall glosses over the problem by simply mentioning the first production of *She Ventures and He Wins* and asserting that it is 'a play Mary Pix is now thought to have written'.[42] But this assumption needs further questioning. If Mary Pix had indeed written the play, why would she have taken her next two plays, *Ibrahim* and *The Spanish Wives*, to the rival Patent Company? It is arguable that the 'failure' of *She Ventures and He Wins* was sufficient reason for the playwright to approach the other company but, in a climate of such vehement competition, one might expect one or other of the companies to 'leak' her identity.

'Ariadne' unmasked

There is, of course, another group of women who have been completely ignored in the search for 'Ariadne's' identity: the actresses. The presence of the actor/writer is well established at this point in theatre history but curiously, albeit predictably, the move from player to playwright has not been considered for the actress. Susanna Centlivre is said to have been an actress for a short time before embarking upon her successful playwriting career, although she is generally considered not to have risen 'above the station of a country actress'.[43] Charlotte Charke appears to be the first actress from a legitimate Patent Company to be credited as a playwright with her satire on the manager of Drury Lane, *The Art of Management: or, Tragedy Expelled* (1735). There is no apparent reason to exclude the possibility of an earlier actress turning her hand to writing a play except, of course, an inherent and strong resistance to such a notion.

I suggest that the true identity of the authoress of this remarkable play is none other than the actress who sponsored it, Elizabeth Barry. Barry's working knowledge of Behn's dramatic style and structure places her in a unique position to claim Behn's direct influence on her writing. Her upbringing in the Davenant household would have equipped her with a level of education even if, as 'Ariadne' insists, she was 'unlearn'd, ignorant of any, but her Mother-Tongue, and very far from being a perfect Mistress of that too'.[44] *She Ventures and He Wins* is a very contemporary comedy, employing dramatic skills that Barry's extensive knowledge and experience of the business of theatre would have enabled her to deploy better than any aristocratic 'young lady'. The fast-moving pace of the dramatic action and the comic set-pieces created for players she knows suggest the hand of an experienced theatre woman. Alongside this, the persistently teasing tone of the epilogue, attributed to Motteux, suggests that the female playwright is well known to the play going audience:

> Our Authoress now is in, at your Devotion,
> Tho' she, perhaps to please you, want the Notion,
> Be gen'rous once, she'll quickly mend her Motion.
> For, pray take notice, 'tis her Maidenhead,
> (that of her Brain I mean) and you that wed
> Feel seldom easy Joys, till that is fled.
> ...
> 'Tis true, you wait awhile in expectation
> (When up the Curtain flies) of Recreation;
> But you all go, when ere the Play is done;
> Then down the Curtain drops, and whip you're gone
> And thence to tell ungrateful Truths you run.
> Be kinder; let our unknown Fair appease ye,
> Though you mislike her Play, her Face[45] may please ye:
> She hides it now, yet she mislikes the task,
> But knows how much you love a Vizard mask.
> Yet sure she must be safe among You here; [46]

By announcing that the 'Authoress ... is in', the epilogue plays on the obvious expectation that she is to be found in the audience and yet the image here is that when the audience 'all go' she is not among them. She belongs to the playhouse and is 'safe among you here'. What better place to 'hide' her identity than on the stage itself, behind the 'Vizard mask' of the actress whose 'Face' had long 'please[d]' the playgoing audience?

Barry's authorship of the play would throw an interesting light on her decision to write or play the unlikely part of Urania, the honest and virtuous vintner's wife; a part which deliberately situates her among the respectable merchant class and directly opposes her whorish reputation. In this play every trick and disguise planned by the women, including the provocative breeches role, is designed to expose the duplicitous nature of men and affirm the honesty of women. As Urania plans Wouldbe's humiliation, she assures her husband that if she is not successful 'may the Curse of being thought dishonest, without knowing the pleasure of it, fall upon me'.[47] For an actress continually branded as a 'mercernary whore' in satires and lampoons it is tempting to suggest that, via Urania's outburst, Barry is commenting on her own reputation.

From this perspective the play itself can be read as a remonstration against constructions of female identity; both general and personal. In the face of fierce competition and, at times, outright antagonism from the Patent Company, if Barry had acknowledged her authorship, an audacious move for any woman let alone an actress, her public identity would make her particularly vulnerable to personal attack: reason enough to keep her identity secret whatever the play's fortune. Another link to the actress can be found in the use of the pseudonym, Ariadne. Although it is of classical provenance the name does not appear repeatedly in plays of the period. The most notable 'Ariadne' can be found in Behn's *The Rover II* (1681), a play in which Barry created the part of the courtesan 'La Nuce'. Here, Ariadne, a breeches role, was played by Elizabeth Currer, an actress who frequently appeared with Barry until her disappearance from theatre records around 1690. Currer and Barry also created the sisters, Marcella and Cornellia, in Behn's comedy *The Feign'd Curtezans* (1679) which was probably revived in the same season in which *She Ventures and He Wins* was first performed. Barry's public position as the play's sponsor serves as the perfect vizard mask, a disguise which has worked to deflect attention from her identity as the play's author.

If considered in isolation, none of the suggestions above points conclusively to Barry as the anonymous playwright but, when put together, they constitute a strong case for arguing her authorship. Although documentary records fail to provide the hard evidence required to justify this argument absolutely, traditions of theatre practice can, in themselves, offer other forms of evidence. As the play's sponsor and a senior company member, Barry would have been in a position to read the play to the full company prior to production and, in the absence of the playwright, take the rehearsals. From this perspective *She Ventures and He Wins* can be seen not as a 'one-off' incursion into the world of the playhouse by a 'young lady' but an expression of a growing confidence and participation in the whole business of theatre by theatre women. The real 'failure' of this bold move lies not so much in a short run for her play but in a historiographical need to forget. The fusion of text and performance suggested by the creative engagement of an actress/playwright goes directly against the grain of a theatre history that continues to struggle with the implications of women as a central force in the public sphere of the playhouse. The tension between text and performance – between nascent constructs of high and low art – can be seen at work in the other group of women working on the Late Stuart stage.

A triumvirate of female playwrights

In contrast to 'Ariadne's' isolated position as the first female playwright produced by the Players' Company, Trotter, Manley and Pix openly supported one another during a season in which all three had work produced by the Patent Company at Drury Lane. It is beyond the scope of this book to deal in detail with plays produced by the Patent Company but, in order to trace the events which led to the triumverate's defection to the Players' Company in the following season, it is worth considering some of the pertinent productions and events that contributed to this radical move; a move that was contentious in the competitive company atmosphere of 1695.

Karen Ray paints a powerful, if somewhat romantic, image of the three playwrights as they 'storm into the theatre and demand their birthright as the daughters of Aphra Behn'.[48] These women did identify themselves as rightful successors to Behn and her fellow female writers but there are some significant ways in which Behn's identity as a writing woman was beginning to be rewritten. The image of Behn as the bawdy Restoration playwright was being replaced by a more respectable image that connected her with the literary traditions of the poetess – an image to which Trotter, Manley and Pix appear to have been anxious to attach themselves. Following her death in 1689, Behn's papers fell into the hands of her friend Charles Gildon, described by Germaine Greer as a 'literary jobber ... unencumbered by scruples about the use he might make of Behn's literary estate'.[49] Gildon's appropriation of Behn's life and works and in particular his emphasis on that higher expression of art, her poetic genius, may well have made her writing more acceptable to the book-buying public but, ultimately, worked to take her plays into the literary sphere and out of the playhouse.[50] The Patent Company was evidently interested in staking its own claim to Behn's work and mounted three new productions, performed at Drury Lane within the first six months of the 1695/6 season. It is interesting to note that two of these were adaptations of Behn's prose writing.

In November 1695 the Patent Company produced Thomas Southerne's adaptation of Behn's novel *Oroonoko* (1688). In Southerne's dedicatory epistle Gildon was probably the 'friend' who reported that Behn 'always told [Oroonoko's] story more feelingly than she writ it'.[51] Southerne heaps praise upon Behn, reminding the reader that his earlier play *The Fatal Marriage* (1694) also owed a debt to Behn's novel *The History of the Nun* (1689).[52] Although he remarks on her 'great command of the stage' and his desire to acknowledge his debt to her, the play's 'uncommon success' is firmly credited to Southerne.[53] In the following month Behn's romantic novel *Agnes de Castro* (1688) was adapted for the Patent Company by a 'young lady', soon to be identified as sixteen-year-old Catherine Trotter. Two months later, Behn's unperformed *The Younger Brother* was also produced by the Patent Company. Charles Gildon, who probably had a hand in preparing the manuscript, uses the dedicatory epistle to complain that the play's unsuccessful run was due to 'some Faction that was made against it, which indeed was very Evident on the First day, and more on the endeavours employ'd, to render the Profits of the Third, as small as could be.'[54] Of these three new Behn productions, the two adaptations from her prose works were apparently more successful than the play. It is arguable that the new adaptations were tailored to favour the changing sensibility of the audience whereas the unperformed play retained rather too much of Behn's Restoration libertinism – although Gildon's contribution may well have had something to do with its failure.

Catherine Trotter dedicated her adaptation of Behn's *Agnes de Castro* (1696) to the Lord Chamberlain, Charles Sackville, Earl of Dorset, who had been instrumental in supporting the Players' Company bid for a separate performing licence. Following the conventional apologies for her age and inexperience, Trotter declares that she 'Conceals her Name, to shun that of Poetess'.[55] Nancy Cotton notes that, of the three new writing women, Trotter had 'family connections and patrons among the nobility' and that the 'familiar dedication to a nobleman, its elevated subject, and its formal, bookish style publicized the author as a learned lady'.[56] The published edition of 1696 includes a commendatory poem 'to the author' signed Dela[rivier] Manley. Whether this was the idea of the precocious young playwright, her friend Manley, or Trotter's publisher, Samuel Briscoe, who had published most of Behn's work,[57] the poem clearly links the subject (Trotter) and the author (Manley) to the respectable poetic tradition of Katherine Philips (Orinda) and Behn (Fair Astrea):

> Orinda, and the Fair Astrea gone,
> Not one was found to fill the Vacant Throne:
> Aspiring Man had quite regain'd the Sway,
> Again had Taught us humbly to Obey;
> Till you (Natures third start in favour of our Kind)   5
> With stronger Arms, their Empire have disjoyn'd
> And snatcht a Lawrel which they thought their Prize,
> Thus Conqu'ror, with your Wit, as with your Eyes.
> Fired by the bold Example, I would try
> To turn our Sexes weaker Destiny.   10
> O! How I long in the Poetic Race,
> To loose the Reins, and give their Glory Chase;
> For thus Encourag'd, and thus led by you,
> Methinks we might more Crowns than theirs Subdue.   14
>   Dela Manley[58]

Many literary critics have rightly noted the strong proto-feminist tone of this piece; it is clear that it is not women's sex that is rendered 'weaker' but their 'destiny' in a man's world (line 10). But the strength of the argument for the female playwright is undercut by the conspicuous absence of any reference to 'Ariadne', who certainly could claim to have filled Behn's 'vacant throne' in the playhouse, however briefly, and who also linked her work to the Philips/Behn writing tradition. Neither Manley nor Trotter can have been entirely unaware of a play produced less than three months earlier and yet there is no mention of either Ariadne or her play. This omission could be explained by the need to demonstrate their loyalty to the Patent Company but Manley's repeated references to terms and imagery connected with the classical, and thus more respectable, poetic tradition offer another suggestion: that Manley is making a deliberate move to situate her work in the literary sphere. Initially at least, it seems that Manley and Trotter were interested in distancing themselves from the business of theatre and the identity attached to theatre women – even though Manley did not eschew the much needed financial benefit of the third night.

Manley's comedy *The Lost Lover* was performed at Drury Lane in March 1696. It did not meet with the same adulation which greeted Trotter's tragedy, for either the playwright or the play. Of the three female playwrights, Manley is certainly the most outspoken about the resistance to writing women and the least willing to preface her work with conventional apologies for her sex. The prologue for *The Lost Lover* issues a rebuke to those in the audience 'Who, if our Play succeeds, will surely say, / Some Private Lover helpt her on her way'.[59] In spite of Manley's claim that she was the daughter of a gentleman her name was continually attached to scandal and she, perhaps more than Trotter or Pix, urgently needed the financial benefits a successful writing career could bring.[60] The preface to the published edition of *The Lost Lover* smarts with indignation at the treatment she has received. Echoing Behn, Manley concludes: 'I am satisfied the bare Name of being a Woman's Play damn'd it beyond its own want of Merit' but, perhaps in an attempt to align herself with the learned Trotter, she adds: 'I will conclude with *Dionysius*, "That Plato and Philosophy have taught me to bear so great a Loss (even of Fame) with Patience"'.[61] Manley places a deliberate distance between herself and the business of theatre and seems keenly aware of the public/private split between literary and theatrical writing:

> I am convinc'd Writing for the Stage is no way Proper for a woman, to whom all Advantages but meer Nature, are refused; If we happen to have

a Genius for Poetry, it presently shoots to a fond desire of Imitation. Tho' it be lamely ridiculous, mine was indulged by my Flatterers, who said, nothing cou'd come from me unentertaining: like a Hero not contented with Applause from lesser Conquests, I find myself not only disappointed of my hopes of greater, but even to have lost all the glory of the former; Had I confin'd my Sense, as before, to some short Song of *Phillis*, a Tender Billet, and the freedom of agreeable Conversation, I had still preserved the Character of a Witty Woman.[62]

Manley had a problem: she had already committed her tragedy *The Royal Mischief* into the hands of the Patent Company and was determined to do all that she could to rescue her reputation, her play and, more crucially, her hope of an income. The new play was already in rehearsal at Drury Lane when the pragmatic playwright removed it from the company and took it to their rivals at Lincoln's Inn Fields.

Quite how this dramatic exit was effected is unclear. Milhous refers to the 'uproar Mrs Manley caused'[63] and Fidelis Morgan suggests that 'there were quarrels within the Drury Lane company over the production of this play'.[64] The image of the frustrated playwright watching her play badly rehearsed, whisking the parts from the actresses' hands and storming off to place them at the feet of Barry and Bracegirdle is tempting but fanciful. A more plausible explanation might be that the cool reception given to Manley's first play and the passionate content of this tragedy combined to convince the Patent Company that the play would not do good business. If Rich had, for a moment, believed that the Players' Company would make such a success of it he would not have parted with it so easily, however forcefully Manley objected to the inferiority of his players. Rich may have rightly anticipated criticisms against the 'warmth' of the play, however, the audience at Lincoln's Inn Fields liked it well enough to allow a run of six nights, giving Manley *two* third night payments.

Writing for the body of the actress

In her preface to the published edition, Manley mounts a spirited defence against the charge that her play was offensive and again, echoing Behn, argues that if it had been written by a man it would not have attracted the same level of criticism. Manley appeals directly to the female reader, inviting her to judge the integrity of the play and, in complete contrast to the distance she placed between her work and the business of theatre in the preface to her first play, links her justification for the leading character

Homais, the sexually voracious femme fatale of the piece, with Elizabeth Barry's successful interpretation of the character:

> I do not doubt when the Ladies have given themselves the trouble of reading, and comparing it with others, they'll find the prejudice against our Sex, and not refuse me the satisfaction of entertaining them, nor themselves the pleasure of Mrs. Barry, who by all that saw her, is concluded to have exceeded that perfection which before she was justly thought to have arrived at; my Obligations to her were the greater, since against her own approbation, she excell'd and made the part of an ill Woman, not only entertaining, but admirable.[65]

Manley is experiencing for herself the difference between the literary text and the performed text – between reading and seeing. There is a clear distinction here between the cooler comparisons suggested by the process of reading her play and the pleasure experienced by seeing it performed. Perhaps Manley was beginning to appreciate the advantage her work met with when placed in the hands of an actress with the experience and reputation of Elizabeth Barry.

Barry and Bracegirdle return to their more conventional pairing in this play – which may explain Barry's initial reservations about the part – with the deliciously wicked character of Homais giving her ample opportunity to display her renowned talent for portraying the lustful villainess, complemented by Bracegirdle's equally popular portrayal of the innocent heroine, Bassima. Just as contemporary criticism was divided between those who dismissed the play and its playwright. (Ramble: Whose is that? / Sullen: This is Mrs. Manley's; it made shift to live half a dozen days, and then expired')[66] and those who praised her ('There is a Force and a Fire in her Tragedy, that is the Soul that gives it Life'),[67] some modern critics are doubtful about the way Manley develops the representation of female sexual desire in her central character. It is worth pausing to look in detail at a short section from the play in order to consider the extent to which Barry uses her off-stage sexual identity in her on-stage representation of female sexuality.

Married to an elderly and impotent Prince, Homais is consumed with desire for his nephew, Levan. When she is advised to disguise her passion she replies:

> What To conceal desire when every
> Attom of me trembles with it I'll strip
> My Passion naked of such Guile, lay it
> Undresst and panting at his feet, then try
> If all his Temper can resist it.[68]

When she has successfully seduced Levan, the scene is shut upon the bedchamber. The shutters open again later in the scene to find Homais in post-coital bliss and more than reluctant to leave her chamber:

> Impossible, for I've Embraced a God.
> No Mortal Sence can guess his Excellence,
> Where the Divine Impress has bin
> A pleasing trickling cools through all my Veins
> And tempers into Love, what else would be
> Distraction.[69]

The passion with which Homais pursues and *enjoys* sexual fulfilment is inexorably linked with her villainous deeds. She persuades a former lover to kill her husband and the virtuous princess Bassima, who both stand in the way of her passion for Levan, and so, of course, she must die. For Elizabeth Howe, Manley's bold representation of female sexuality is undermined by the conventional conclusion: 'Homais' lovemaking seems ultimately to bring her nothing but failure and death … If there is a 'feminist' message in this play it is one that can easily be ignored. Presumably male spectators just relished the erotic spectacle of Homais' promiscuity – she and her kind can easily be seen as no more than another variation on the actress as sex object.[70] Howe rightly draws attention to the inherent contradiction in Manley's representation of transgressive female behaviour but she assumes the sole perspective of the dominant male spectator for whom the body of the actress is inevitably rendered as object to his male gaze. But what if we move beyond the notion of the dominant male spectator and consider playmaking and playgoing as part of a wider social and cultural network of meanings than the isolated experience of one visit to the playhouse?

Jacky Bratton's notion of 'intertheatricality' is useful here as it goes beyond the restrictions imposed by considering the individual dramatic text and the specific event of performance of that text to 'include an awareness of the elements and interactions that make up the whole web of mutual understanding between potential audiences and their players, a sense of knowledge, or better the knowingness, about playing that spans a lifetime or more, and that is activated for all participants during the performance event'.[71] The key term here is 'knowingness': the audience at Lincoln's Inn Fields undoubtedly knew something of the fracas that had resulted in Manley's play appearing here with the Players' Company, not at Drury Lane. This is the first new play by a woman since 'Ariadne' had opened the season but, this time, Barry and Bracegirdle are playing into their public identity, in their own theatre. An intertheatrical reading must take account of the 'mesh of connections'[72] between audience and players. The known presence of female audience members, as well as male, cannot be excluded from the network of meanings created by the playwright's text, the on-stage body of the actress, the 'knowingness' of her off-stage identity and the identity of the character she embodies and her audience 'sees'. An intertheatrical reading disrupts the clarity of any one assumption about the dramatic text and in so doing reveals the crucially disruptive element of performance. Manley expresses something of this in her praise for Barry who made 'the part of an ill Woman, not only entertaining, but *admirable*' (my emphasis). Manley's dramatic narrative may have fulfilled the conventional construct that demands death for the female sexual transgressor but Barry's performance disrupts that construct by making her admirable. This is achieved not only by what the actress does 'on the day' but by the wider knowledge and understanding her audience may have of her and the context in which she is performing.

The published edition of *The Royal Mischief* carried commendatory verses by Trotter and Pix, reinforcing the public support the three female playwrights gave to one another. Mary Pix was the last of the three to have her first play, *Ibrahim*, produced at Drury Lane in May 1696. Manley certainly sought critical recognition for her work but, like Behn before her, her writing was primarily motivated by the need to earn money. Her decision to take her play to Lincoln's Inn Fields was vindicated by the box-office returns and this move was surely motivated by the same desire that had led Barry and Bracegirdle to defect from the patent house two years earlier: to have greater control of their own work and receive greater financial benefits from its commercial success. Whether her former patrons at the patent house liked it or not – and they clearly did not – by breaking away from the patronage of the Patent Company and moving to the Players' Company, Manley aligned herself with the most experienced and powerful theatre women of her time. Manley's decision to defend the integrity of *The Royal Mischief* by referring positively to the public performance rather than relying on the literary text alone is significant. By specifically acknowledging her 'obligation'[73] to Elizabeth Barry, Manley is not only openly acknowledging the actress as co-creator of the leading female character but also as co-creator of the play's commercial success. In an atmosphere of fierce theatrical rivalry, where box-office receipts were ultimately far more powerful than literary garlands, it is not so surprising to find the Patent

Company at Drury Lane reacting fiercely against this united female incursion into the male dominated world of theatrical commerce.

Notes

1 Edward A. Langhans, 'The Vere Street and Lincoln's Inn Fields Theatres in Pictures', *Educational Theatre Journal*, 20 (1968), p. 179.
2 *The London Stage*, vol. 1, p. 450. Judith Milhous, *Thomas Betterton*, Appendix C, p. 247, also uses this source in her list of personnel at Lincoln's Inn Fields although she fails to include Anne Bracegirdle.
3 Milhous, *Thomas Betterton*, Appendix D, pp. 249–251, reproduces the sharing agreement in full, citing the source as Public Records Office, LC 7/3 for the 'fair copy' of the agreement and LC 7/1 for the copy text (which Milhous dates as October 1696 and also reproduces in full). There are some irregularities in the list of names but no variance in the pre-eminent position given to Betterton, Barry and Bracegirdle. I have retained the original spelling when quoting from this document.
4 I have included Anne Bracegirdle as part of the original Duke's Company as, although her first appearance was after the companies had united, her relationship with the Bettertons places her in the Duke's Company tradition.
5 John Verbruggen was recruited by the United Company but his relationship with the Players' Company was a difficult one. Although both Susannah (Mountfort) Verbruggen and her husband had intended to join the rebel company, they withdrew when it was made clear that Susannah would be offered only a salary rather than a full share. Both were offered favourable inducements to return to the Patent Company but John Verbruggen appears to have argued with the Patent Company early in the first full season and returned to the Players' Company.
6 Milhous, *Thomas Betterton*, p. 69.
7 p. 74.
8 Anon., *A Comparison Between Two Stages, With an Examen of the Generous Conqueror* (London: 1702), p. 12. This satirical exchange between three male critics is set out in dialogue form and sometimes attributed to Charles Gildon.
9 Cibber, *Apology*, ed. Lowe, vol. 1, p. 194. It is interesting to note that the theatre of the late seventeenth century resorted to the same tactics as theatre today. Although there is no record of what the 'promises' were (I doubt that the naming of a brick or a seat would have the same appeal as it does to sponsors today), free entrance to the first performances would have been of benefit to both parties in this sponsorship 'deal'.
10 Milhous, *Thomas Betterton*, p. 74.
11 p. 83.
12 Traditional theatre histories tend to refer to the company at Lincoln's Inn Field's as 'Betterton's company' and the company occupying Drury Lane

and Dorset Gardens as 'Rich's company'. From here on I shall refer to the former as the 'Players' Company' and to the latter as the 'Patent Company'.
13 The theatres were closed for three months following the death of Queen Mary in December. The patent house re-opened to poor houses in March with a revival of Behn's *Abdelazar* (1676). The refit at Lincoln's Inn Fields evidently delayed the Players' Company but the success of the play carried them through the rest of the season.
14 *A Comparison Between Two Stages*, p. 10.
15 Gerard Langbain (the Younger), *Lives and Characters of the Dramatick Poets* (1691), revised by Charles Gildon (London: 1700), p. 22. Downes, *Roscius Anglicanus*, also notes that it was 'Superior in Success, than most of the precedent Plays' (p. 44).
16 *A Comparison Between Two Stages*, p. 10.
17 William Congreve, *Love for Love* (London: Jacob Tonson, 1695), Prologue 'spoken at the opening of the New House'.
18 Cibber, *Apology*, ed. Lowe, vol. 1, p. 197.
19 Congreve, *Love for Love*, Epilogue.
20 Congreve, *Love for Love*, 'A Prologue for The opening of the New Play-House, propos'd to be spoken by Mrs. Bracegirdle in Man's Cloaths'. This prologue is also included in the 1710 edition but, not surprisingly perhaps, it is omitted from Ewald's nineteenth-century edition of Congreve's plays (1887). The line numbering is my own.
21 Howe, *The First English Actresses*, p. 182, records only one previous breeches role for Bracegirdle, Semernia in Behn's *The Widow Ranter* (1689); however, Bracegirdle also appeared in breeches in D'Urfey's *The Marriage-Hater Match'd* (1692) and was in breeches as the reluctant prologue speaker for the same play (see Chapter 3). Around the same time Bracegirdle took over the part of Hellena in Behn's *The Rover* but her popularity in breeches roles was only fully exploited after 1695 when Howe records that Bracegirdle created at least nine other breeches roles.
22 I have not been able to trace any references to explain the existence of or meaning behind the author's use of 'the Woman's Charter' here. It is possible that this refers to the agreement between actresses and theatre management concerning pay scales which were adjusted according to their marital status. The reference to the agreement being 'cancelled' leads me to suggest this as a direct reference to Elizabeth Barry's benefit payments which the Patent Company sought to stop; a move which contributed to the Players' rebellion.
23 See Susan Bennett, 'Decomposing History', p. 82.
24 Ibid.
25 p. 73.
26 'Ariadne', *She Ventures and He Wins* (London: Rhodes, Harris and Briscoe, 1696). This play is also included in *Female Playwrights of the Restoration: Five Comedies*, eds Paddy Lyons and Fidelis Morgan (London: J. M. Dent,

27 'Ariadne', Act I, sc.i, p. 2.
28 'Ariadne', Prologue. Line numbers are my own.
29 According to *The London Stage*, part 1, p. 452, the Patent Company mounted Scott's *The Mock-Marriage* at the same time. This was also a new play by a writer new to the stage. Neither play is mentioned by Downes and both receive mixed reviews in contemporary reports.
30 Prologues and epilogues frequently carry the name of the author if it differs from that of the playwright. Anonymous authors are usually referred to as 'from an unknown hand', or 'from a friend'. I have, therefore, worked on the premise that the female playwright wrote her own prologue/epilogue unless it is attributed elsewhere.
31 'Ariadne', *She Ventures*, Act I, sc. i.
32 Act I, sc. i.
33 Act I, sc. ii.
34 Act II, sc. i.
35 Act V, sc. i.
36 See Maximillian E. Novak, 'The Closing of Lincoln's Inn Fields Theatre in 1695', *Restoration and Eighteenth Century Theatre Research*, 14:1 (1975), pp. 51–2, in which the author argues that the failure of the play resulted in the closure of the theatre. There is no extant record of the length of the run and no evidence to suggest that the theatre was closed for any significant period of time, other than that provided by Novak's interpretation of the handwritten note attached to *The Post Boy*, details of which are included in the following note.
37 Elizabeth's Barry's sponsorship of this play is referred to in handwritten notes appended to cuttings from *The Post Boy*, 17–19 September 1695. I am indebted to the librarian at the William Andrews Clark Memorial Library, University of California, Los Angeles, for supplying me with a photocopy of the cutting and the handwritten addendum, dated 19 September in which the author also makes reference to the theatre being closed on the evening he or she had visited it.
38 'Ariadne', *She Ventures*, Act I, sc. i.
39 See Kathryn McQueen Kendall, 'Theatre, Society, and Women Playwrights in London from 1695 Through the Queen Anne Era', unpublished PhD dissertation, University of Texas at Austin, 1986, p. 17.
40 Constance Clark, *Three Augustan Women Playwrights* (New York: Peter Lang, 1986), p. 21.
41 p. 23.
42 Kendall, 'Theatre, Society and Woman Playwrights', p. 19.
43 Baker, *Biographia Dramatica*, vol. 1, p. 66.
44 'Ariadne', *She Ventures*, Preface.

45 In Lyons and Morgan, *Female Playwrights of the Restoration*, p. 107, 'mislike' has been transcribed as 'mistake' and the word 'face' has been replaced by '****'. Although the former may simply be a scribal error, the overt sexual inference attached to the latter is curiously misleading as it does not appear in the 1696 published edition.
46 'Ariadne', *She Ventures*, Epilogue.
47 Act I, sc. ii.
48 Karen J. Ray, '"The Yielding Moment": A Woman's View of Amorous Females and Fallen Women', *Restoration and Eighteenth Century Theatre Research*, 2 (winter 1996), pp. 39–48, p. 41.
49 Germaine Greer, *Slip-Shod Sibyls* (1995), reprinted London: Penguin Books, 1996, p. 196.
50 Gildon first published Behn's works under the title of *All the Histories and Novels written by the Late Ingenious Mrs Behn, entire in one volume … Together with the History of the Life and Memoirs of Mrs. Behn* (London: Samuel Briscoe, 1696). Editions of Behn's works were continually reprinted through the eighteenth century with additional material credited to Charles Gildon.
51 Thomas Southerne, *Oroonoko* (London: H. Playford 1696). The play is reprinted with additional notes by the editors, Maximillian E. Novak and David Stuart Rodes (London: Edward Arnold, 1977).
52 Behn's *The History of the Nun* was licensed in October 1688 but not published until 1689.
53 *A Comparison Between Two Stages*, p. 19, is fulsome in its praise for this 'uncommonly successful' play, although the production is not included in Downes, *Roscius Anglicanus*.
54 Aphra Behn, *The Younger Brother: or, The Amorous Jilt*, ed. Charles Gildon (London: 1696), Dedicatory Epistle.
55 Catherine Trotter, *Agnes de Castro* (London: H. Rhodes, R. Parker and S. Briscoe, 1696), Dedicatory Epistle.
56 Nancy Cotton, *Women Playwrights in England c. 1363–1750* (Toronto and London: Associated University Press, 1980), pp. 83–84.
57 On the back page of the 1696 edition of *Agnes de Castro* held by the British Library, there is an advertisement for five other plays printed for Rhodes, Parker and Briscoe, including '*She Ventures and He Wins*. By a Lady'.
58 Trotter, *Agnes de Castro*, Commendatory Poem.
59 Delarivier Manley, *The Lost Lover: or, The Jealous Husband* (London: R. Bently, F. Saunders, J. Knapton and R. Wellington, 1696), Prologue.
60 The stories surrounding Manley's reputation are explained (and excused) in her later sensational autobiographical works, *The New Atalantis* (1709) and *The Adventures of Rivella etc.* (1714). However, many modern scholars have questioned the extent to which she fictionalised her past.
61 Manley, *The Lost Lover*, Preface.
62 Preface.

63 Milhous, *Thomas Betterton*, p. 90.
64 Fidelis Morgan, *The Female Wits: Women Playwrights of the Restoration* (London: Virago, 1981), p. 39.
65 Delarivier Manley, *The Royal Mischief* (London: R. Bentley, F. Saunders, and J. Knapton, 1696), Preface: 'Epistle to the Reader'.
66 *A Comparison Between Two Stages*, p. 31.
67 Langbain, *Lives and Characters*, amended by Charles Gildon, pp. 90–91. If Gildon is also the author of *A Comparison Between the Two Stages* as has been suggested, it is evident that he was quite prepared to present both sides of the argument when it suited him to do so.
68 Manley, *The Royal Mischief*, Act III, sc. i, p. 20.
69 Act III, sc. i, p. 26.
70 Howe, *The First English Actresses*, p. 51.
71 Bratton, *New Readings*, p. 37.
72 p. 37.
73 Manley, *The Royal Mischief*, Preface.

5
COMPETITION AND CRITICISM

The Patent Company was in trouble. The big names of the Late Stuart stage were now to be found at Lincoln's Inn Fields rather than at Drury Lane or Dorset Gardens and the London playgoing audience seemed more inclined to put their hands in their pockets for the rebels. Christopher Rich had managed to retain some senior players, notably comedian Joe Haynes. Several players had initially shown interest in joining the rebels but were persuaded to remain, including Susannah Verbruggen (formerly Mrs Mountfort) who used her popularity in breeches roles to deliver a blatantly crowd-pleasing prologue to Southerne's *Oroonoko* in November 1695: 'You see, we try all shape, and shifts, and Arts / To tempt your favours, and regain your Hearts',[1] to which one might add – and your money. It seems more than likely, if not inevitable, that a level of ill-feeling existed among some of the players who were not invited to join the company at Lincoln's Inn Fields or, like the Verbruggens, found themselves offered less than advantageous conditions. On the other hand, the thirteen-year monopoly of the United Company was now over and the split provided new opportunities for players remaining at Drury Lane to play parts previously reserved by the rebel senior players. But none could escape the possibility that without their leading players, the Patent Company might fail.

The patent house employed a number of strategies to recover its share of the audience, including the repeated use of personal burlesque which, as Judith Milhous observes, 'gave Drury Lane actors a chance to show off in their own persons, as well as a chance to distort and exaggerate their rivals' habits'.[2] Here then was an opportunity for the Patent Company players to develop their own public identity and win their own audiences. One of the more intriguing aspects of this approach is that it implicitly demonstrates the strength of the Players' Company position and the extent to which the Patent Company players participated in the battle with the rival company. According to Colley Cibber the strategy emerged from the Patent Company's hurried decision to mount a competing production of Congreve's *The Old Batchelor* at the opening of the 1695/6 season:

upon Enquiry, it was found that there were not two Persons among them who had ever acted in that Play: But that Objection, it seems, (though all the parts were to be study'd in six hours) was soon got over; *Powel* had an Equivalent, *in petto*, that would balance any Deficiency on that Score, which was, that he would play the *Old Batchelor* himself, and mimick *Betterton* throughout the whole Part. This happy Thought was approv'd with Delight and Applause ... Accordingly the Bills were chang'd, and the bottom inserted,

The Part of the Old Batchelor *to be perform'd In Imitation of the Original.*

... To conclude, the Curiosity to see *Betterton* mimick'd drew us a pretty good Audience, and *Powel* (as far as Applause is a Proof of it) was allow'd to have burlesq'd him very well.[3]

George Powell's career is represented in theatre histories as having been blighted by vanity, jealousy and repeated overindulgence in drink and gambling[4] but Rich evidently thought well enough of him and may well have found his personal ambition useful in his battle against the rival house. Rich kept a tight rein on the management of the Patent Company but delegated some of the day-to-day managerial decisions to Powell, who clearly saw himself as a worthy successor and rival to Thomas Betterton.[5] Cibber does not provide a full cast list for the revival of *The Old Batchelor* or make specific reference to Barry and Bracegirdle, who had originally created the leading female characters, but they were certainly implicated in another Patent Company strategy which pleaded the energy and attraction of youth, only to be found at Drury Lane.

George Powell exploited this approach fully in the prologue to his adaptation of Beaumont and Fletcher's *Bonduca*, produced in September 1695:

> And therefore, if the Truth you would declare;
> Say Gallants, to your Smiles, who bids most fair;
> Our Growing Spring, or Fading Autumn there?
> Besides, though our weak Merit shines less Bright,
> ...
> To us, young Players, then let some smiles fall:
> Let not their dear Antiquities sweep all.
> Antiquity on a stage? Oh fye! 'tis Idle:
> Age in Good Wine is well, or in a Fiddle.
> Ay then it has a little musick there;
> But in an old, Decrepid, Wither'd Player;
> It looks like a stake[d] Maid at her last Prayer.[6]

Powell's counterattack rests on the argument that his company is younger and more vigorous. The thrust of his attack aims simply to brand the Players' Company as well past their sell-by date, with a particularly vicious dig at the women in the imagery of the 'Decrepid, Wither'd' witch-like 'Maid'. This campaign evidently proved a success at the box-office. The use of such satirical barbs reached new heights in a piece written for the opening weeks of the new season at Drury Lane in 1696 – a topical satire aimed directly at the female playwrights.

The female wits

Manley's open derogation of the standard of acting in the preface to the published edition of her first play, *The Lost Lover* (1696), implicitly includes Powell's performance as Sir Amorous Courtall. Powell was also at the head of the cast rehearsing *The Royal Mischief* when Manley withdrew the play and took it to the rival house. In an atmosphere of open warfare with the Players' Company, Manley's box-office success with *The Royal Mischief* must have been the final insult. What is certain is that Powell was responsible, at least in part, for the scathing satirical comedy directed not only against Manley and her fellow writing women but also against the actresses in the Players' Company.

The Female Wits was performed at Drury Lane early in the 1696 season. It is a satirical comedy set around the rehearsal for a new tragedy written by a woman. The central character, the female playwright 'Marsilia', is an overt caricature of Manley, and the play she prepares to rehearse a parody of *The Royal Mischief*. The comedy opens in Marsilia/Manley's house where she is quickly joined by two other playwrights who are to attend the day's rehearsal: 'Mrs. Wellfed', described in the cast list as 'One that represents a fat, Female Author' is clearly intended to be Mary Pix, while 'Calista', 'A Lady that pretends to the learned Languages, and assumes to herself the Name of Critick' caricatures Catherine Trotter.[7] The intention of the anonymous author(s) is clear from the opening lines of the play, which reveal Marsilia/Manley to be a vain duplicitous woman who, as the description in the cast list confirms, 'admires her own Works, and [is] a great Lover of Flattery'. Beneath the layers of comedy – and this is a very funny play – there is a more serious agenda. The mutual support these three writing woman publicly demonstrated for one another is undercut by revelations of their 'true' feminine nature: jealousy, competitiveness and disdain for one another's work. Although there are several exchanges in which Pix and Trotter are presented in a far from favourable light they are not treated as harshly as Manley, who is the main target for the author's contempt.

Marsilia/Manley is presented as an arrogant woman who admires her own appearance almost as much her poetry, which she insists on quoting at length to any who will listen. She refers to Mrs Wellfed/Pix as 'That ill-bred, ill-shap'd Creature' and then greets her affectionately, repeating the performance with Calista/Trotter who she pronounces to be: 'the vainest, proudest, senseless Thing. She pretends to Grammer, writes in Mood and Figure, does everything methodically – Poor Creature! She shews me her Works first. I always commend 'em, with a Design she should expose 'em, and the Town be so kind to laugh her out of her Follies.'[8] Ultimately, all three women are presented as proud and foolish creatures who are blinded by their pretensions to poetry. None, however, has such overweening ambition and vanity as Marsilia/Manley. Her maidservant, the aptly named Patience, soon remarks that 'Nothing but Flattery brings my Lady into a good Humour'[9] and, in order to feed her insatiable appetite for admiration, Marsilia has also invited three gentlemen to attend the rehearsal. The voice of reason is represented by Mr Awdwell, who is in love with Marsilia and continually tries to restrain her excesses; even though his love for her is undercut by the implication that he is her keeper and will soon tire of her. Mr Praiseall fulfils the promise of his name, while Lord Whiffle, whom Marsilia is evidently keen to impress, represents an empty-headed aristocrat. With her entourage about her Marsilia and the main action of the play move to the playhouse.

Lucyle Hook notes that the *The Female Wits* is broken up into sections which are linked with popular songs from earlier productions and suggests that, among other things, this structure indicates that the play was 'put together by group effort, and the evidence points to the actors at Drury Lane ... Joseph Haynes, Colley Cibber, Hildebrand Horden, and George Powell.'[10] Obviously, this group of authors had a thorough knowledge of the playhouse and, in particular, the rehearsal process around which the main action of the play is set. Marsilia/Manley continues to be presented in a wholly ridiculous light as she attempts to direct the cast of players. She repeatedly interrupts the rehearsal, either to bid the players to reach for increasingly absurd heights of emotion in their performance or to invite favourable comments from her coterie of foolish admirers. It is soon obvious that the plot makes no sense at all and, the more Marsilia attempts to explain it, the more ridiculous it becomes. The calamitous rehearsal reaches a climax when Marsilia finds herself facing a rebellious cast and threatens to play the leading lady herself. Ignored by their fellow playwright, Calista/Trotter and Wellfed/Pix, who have already concluded that Marsilia is 'very tedious', leave the players to try and make sense of this absurd tragedy. It is apparent that none can, or will, follow Marsilia's instructions as to how the play should be performed and finally the preposterous Marsilia storms off in a tantrum, demanding to 'go directly into Lincoln's Inn Fields' and thus to the rival company.

Lucyle Hook rightly draws attention to the significance of this play as an important piece of documentary evidence for theatre historians:

> The play illuminates at least four areas about which we know very little: the personalities of the three women playwrights at the beginning of their careers, the excellent portraits of some of the little known players, the acting techniques that are parodied so broadly that it is possible to recognize the original practice, and the rehearsal customs and stage directions employed which give new light or confirm what is already known.[11]

The importance of Hook's final point should not be underestimated. Some critics have argued that *The Female Wits* is primarily concerned with mirroring its more famous predecessor, Buckingham's *The Rehearsal* (1672)[12] but there is a wealth of information here, including quite specific details to be gleaned concerning the rehearsal process on the Late Stuart stage. At the very least this play provides irrefutable evidence that the female playwright, quite as much as her male contemporaries, attended rehearsals and directed the players. There are also some rare glimpses into the work of actresses and the way in which they negotiated their on- and off-stage identity. This last point, however, also suggested by Hook, must be treated with caution. There is evidently a far more subtle political agenda at the heart of this satire which, inevitably, calls into question the extent to which the play 'illuminates' the 'personalities' of the playwrights or the players represented here. As a direct counter attack to the success of *The Royal Mischief* at Lincoln's Inn Fields, *The Female Wits* actively works to rewrite the story of Manley's defection to the rival company; a move revealed in the Patent Company's representation of themselves via the 'excellent portraits' of the players.

From the moment the action of the play moves to the playhouse, it is clear that the authors are seeking the audience's sympathy for the indignities the patent house players suffered at Manley's hands and that they are relieved when she removes to the other house – in Lincoln's Inn

Fields. *The Female Wits* identifies the Drury Lane players by their real names and exploits aspects of their public identity in a move which works to reinforce the notion of verisimilitude: for example jokes are made at the expense of George Powell's reputation for hard drinking and, later, Mrs Cross's popularity as a singer and dancer are included in the plot. Crucially, the anonymous authors establish their disdain for not only the female playwright and her play but also the acting styles of their rivals in the Players' Company. Mrs Cross and Frances Knight capitalise on the Patent Company's successful burlesque of their rivals at the other house, especially when Marsilia/Manley demands that Knight should play her part in the style of Anne Bracegirdle's portrayal of Statira in Lee's *The Rival Queens*, first performed in 1677 and frequently revived by the Barry/Bracegirdle partnership. 'Dear Mrs. Knight, in this speech stamp as queen Statira does, that always get a clap. And when you have ended, run off, thus, as fast as you can drive.'[13] This not only offers ample opportunity for the younger actress to parody the tragic acting styles of her rivals but also implies that Marsilia/Manley's heroic tragedy, and her notions of how it should be played, were as outdated as the Players' Company who performed it.

In this cleverly constructed piece of theatre politics, the Patent Company author/players simultaneously promote themselves while annihilating Manley and undermining the success of the production at Lincoln's Inn Fields. The sense of personal triumph is demonstrated by Powell in the closing moments of the play when 'Mr Powell, Mrs. Knight, Mrs. Cross *etc.*, [enter] Laughing' to give a final account of Marsilia's undignified departure for the other house:

> Oh, my Sides! my Sides! the wrathful Lady has run over a Chair, shatter'd the Glasses to pieces: The Chair-Men, to save it, fell pell-mell in with her. she has lost part of her Tail, broke her Fan, tore her Ruffles, and pull'd off half my Lord Whiffle's Wig, with trying to rise by it. So they are, with a Shagreen Air, and tatter'd Dress, gone into the Coach: Mr Praiseall thrust in after 'em, with the bundle of Fragments [of the play] his Care had pick'd up from under the Fellow's Feet.[14]

Although the extent of Powell's role as co-author of this play is unknown, his prominence within the play as 'himself' suggests that he had no qualms about participating in this overt attack against the female playwrights and the rival company that housed their plays.

Powell was almost certainly behind the eventual publication of the play in 1704[15] and was most likely to have been the author of the preface, which openly confirms that Manley, Pix and Trotter were the subjects of the satire. He begins by praising his own performance and those of Mrs Powell as Mrs Wellfed/Pix and the late Susannah Verbruggen[16] as Marsilia/Manley. He then goes on to remind the reader of the play's success having been 'Acted six Days running without intermission' and indicates that it was only prevented from running longer 'to oblige the Taste ... of some particular Persons'.[17] The inference is clearly that the company at Lincoln's Inn Fields used their influence to have the play suppressed. It is perfectly possible, however, that the play had its full run and that Powell merely uses the suppression argument as a commercial ploy. In his concluding remarks about the female playwrights he reverts to the more obvious sexual slurs aimed at the writing woman: Pix and Trotter are 'in such a state of wedlock to Pen and Ink, that it will be very difficult for 'em to get out of it'; as for Manley, she is 'Known for a Correspondence with the Muses some time since, though she has of late discontinu'd it, (I presume for some more profitable Employ)'.[18] Following the production of *The Female Wits*, Manley left London for the country and she is not known to have written another play for ten years. When she did return to the stage her new tragedy, *Almyna*, was written anonymously and produced at Vanbrugh's Queen's theatre in December 1706, with Barry and Bracegirdle creating the leading female roles.

Innovation in the face of adversity

The Players' Company appears, publicly at least, not to have engaged with the personal slanging match launched by the Patent house, using instead prologues and epilogues to insist on the superiority of their productions and management style. According to Colley Cibber the full houses which the Players' Company had enjoyed in their opening season were soon in decline and, more importantly, the co-operative basis on which the company was formed was beginning to disintegrate: 'short was the Duration of the Theatrical power! For tho' Succes pour'd upon them at their first Opening that every thing seem'd to support it self, yet Experience in a year or two shew'd them that they had never been worse govern'd than when they govern'd themselves!'[19] This is clearly wishful thinking on Cibber's part; a view partially adopted by Milhous who concludes that 'Overall, Cibber's picture is fairly accurate ... But [the Players' Company] did not stumble as early as he implies.'[20] Box-office success was as essential and unpredictable then as it is in today's commercial theatre but it is evident, not least from the Patent Company's repeated attempts to undermine their rivals, that the Players' Company continued to maintain their supremacy for some considerable time. This is not to suggest that the co-operative management at Lincoln's Inn Fields escaped the inevitable difficulties brought about by internal company wrangles. Supporting players, especially singers and dancers, seem to have regularly moved between the two companies in the first few seasons[21] but the senior players, particularly the sharers, were expected to remain loyal to the company they had joined. Milhous and Hume note that the Lord Chamberlain issued an order to both companies forbidding them to offer enticements to 'any Actor, Actress, or Servant, belonging to the other company' on penalty of having their theatre closed.[22] Within a year of this edict Thomas Doggett had signed an agreement with the Patent Company who agreed to pay the comic actor £4 for every six acting days, plus a benefit during Lent. The second of the two documents relating to this agreement clearly reveals that Thomas Skipwith offered Doggett a series of enticements which appear to be designed to cause as much disruption to the Players' Company as possible: £100 signing bonus to be paid in two parts, a further £10 if Doggett leaves Lincoln's Inn Fields by 20 July and learns five new parts, or £20 if he quits the company within three weeks.[23]

Cibber does not spare Doggett in his account of the actor's many shortcomings but he concludes that Doggett's main reason for deserting the Players' Company was:

> that he look'd upon it as a sinking Ship; not only from the melancholy Abatement of their Profits, but likewise from the Neglect and disorder in their Government: He plainly saw that their extraordinary success at first had made them too confident of its duration, and from thence had slacken'd their Industry – by which he observ'd, at the same time, the old house, where there was scarce any other Merit then Industry, began to flourish.[24]

It is arguable that the Players' Company was relieved to let the troublesome Doggett go. Within the year he was raising a petition against Skipwith for non-payment of salaries and by November 1697 he had walked out of Drury Lane altogether.[25] There is moreover, no evidence to suggest that Cibber is correct in his accusation that the Players' Company lacked organisation and artistic industry; in many respects the available evidence suggests quite the opposite.

Under its own management, the Players' Company introduced a number of theatrical innovations. In anticipation of the growing demand for concerts and musical entertainments, the Players' Company increasingly sought to extend the theatrical repertoire. Pierre Motteux,[26] who worked almost exclusively at Lincoln's Inn Fields, first brought *Love's a Jest* to Lincoln's Inn Fields in June 1696, described by Milhous as 'experimental', being a 'new-style play, but with a great deal of interpolated music'.[27] Another innovation, sometimes attributed to Motteux, was the introduction of the double bill: an important development in the theatrical repertoire that would be of growing significance in the following decades. The most damaging accusation hurled at the Players' Company was that they did little to advance younger players. Milhous seems to agree with the decidedly ageist argument adopted by the Patent Company, suggesting that the 'elder actors were hanging on to their jobs with grim tenacity' and that the 'lack of opportunity was to create a morale and discipline problem: young actors had no lack of opportunity at Drury Lane'.[28]

Theatre histories have failed to engage with two vital ingredients here in sustaining successful commercial production. Firstly, the success and survival of the Players' Company depended entirely upon the senior players' appearance in both revivals and new plays: in a theatrical climate that was struggling to attract failing audiences it was the presence of Barry, Bracegirdle and Betterton, at the head of the great players of the age, that gave Lincoln's Inn Fields the commercial edge over the less established players at Drury Lane. Secondly, the Players' Company appears to have encouraged new performers to work alongside the experienced players, rather than replacing them – suggesting a hitherto unrecognised level of actor-training at work in the co-operative structure. The double bill of *The Anatomist: or The Sham Doctor* performed with Motteux's *The Loves of Mars and Venus* in November 1696 supports this notion and further suggests that it proved commercially profitable. This production had an uninterrupted run of five days and the cast list reveals that a number of junior members in the Players' Company appeared *alongside* senior players: Elinor Leigh and Elizabeth Bowman play the leads in *The Anatomist* alongside Bracegirdle, who is clearly the main attraction in *The Loves of Mars and Venus*.[29] This is hardly indicative of a company in a state of 'stasis and complacency'[30] as Milhous asserts. A letter from Robert Jennens to Thomas Coke, dated 19 November 1696 reveals quite how urgently the Patent Company needed to match the Players' Company mode of operating by, at the very least, producing a new and successful production.

> There has been for four or five days together at the play house in Lincoln's Inn Fields acted a new farce translated out of the French by Mr Monteux [sic] called the Shame [Sham] Doctor or the Anatomist, with a great concert of music, representing the loves of Venus and Mars, well enough done and pleases the Town extremely. The other house has no company at all, and unless a new play comes out on Saturday revives their reputation, they must break.[31]

The premiere of John Vanbrugh's first play, *The Relapse*, was performed on 21 November 1696 and appears to have saved the Patent house from the brink of disaster. Not only did the Patent Company now have a successful comedy; it also had a new playwright. But the two-company system offered wider opportunities for new playwrights too, and Vanbrugh's next comedy, *The Provok'd Wife*, was performed five months later in mid-April 1697 at Lincoln's Inn Fields. Cibber goes to some lengths to suggest that Vanbrugh was persuaded by one of the Players' Company's more powerful patrons, Lord Halifax, to take his new play to Lincoln's Inn Fields.[32] Cibber further argues that the patentees agreed to the arrangement and insists on Vanbrugh's true loyalty to Drury Lane, where all his subsequent plays were performed until, that is, Vanbrugh formed his own company to perform in a purpose-built theatre in 1705.[33]

Vanbrugh might have found it convenient to be seen to be bowing to the wishes of a man as powerful as Lord Halifax *and* retain his friendship with Skipwith. It is also possible that the Players' Company asked Halifax to intervene in an attempt to seduce the new playwright to their company. William Congreve, Vanbrugh's friend and effectively a writer in residence at Lincoln's Inn Fields, may also have encouraged Vanbrugh to give his play to the Players' Company. Congreve's only tragedy, *The Mourning Bride*, had just been performed at Lincoln's Inn Fields in February 1697. Barry and Bracegirdle created the central leading roles and it too proved to be hugely popular, running for an 'Uninterrupted 13 Days together'.[34] With Barry and Bracegirdle interested in creating the leading roles in *The Provok'd Wife*, it would be curious if Vanbrugh would fail to see the value of promoting his play through such a powerful working partnership.

Cibber is the main source of the received histories of this period but, as noted at various points above, his *Apology* comprises recollections made some considerable time after the events he records. The events that Cibber chooses *not* to include in his memoirs reveal something of the selective history he has inevitably chosen to record.[35] One such example may be found in the summer of 1696 when Cibber himself appears to have explored the possibilities open to him at Lincoln's Inn Fields. From the preface to his *Woman's Wit* (1697) it is apparent that he began writing the play for the Players' Company but he appears to have been dissatisfied by his treatment and returned, or was recalled, to the Patent Company in time to appear in the new season. Milhous suggests that Rich had heard about Cibber's new play and was anxious to ensure that this promising player/playwright returned to the Patent Company:

> On 29 October 1696, just three days after Verbruggen had concluded an agreement with the New Theatre, Cibber signed a contract that bound him to write exclusively for the Patent Company as long as he remained a member of it ... The terms, while surprisingly generous in monetary matters, did prevent Cibber from having anything to do with the other company if he wanted to keep his job at Drury Lane. He agreed to give *Woman's Wit* to Drury Lane; not to publish it until at least a month after the production opened; to reserve first refusal on all plays he might write in the future to Rich; and finally, he agreed not to write anything for any rival company.[36]

My purpose in considering the details of events that concern these male playwrights is in to establish the lengths to which both companies went to strengthen their position in a highly competitive market-place.

Predictably, documentary evidence for similar agreements that might have been made with the female playwrights is conspicuously absent. It is arguable that the generally low esteem in which the writing woman was held and, of course, her good fortune in getting her play accepted at all, made any agreement that tied her to one company unnecessary. If the Patent Company expected to retain any loyalty from the female playwrights they would have done well to attend to the central theme in Pix's *The Spanish Wives*: that despotism and cruelty can only lead women to acts of infidelity whereas freedom and generosity ensure their loyalty. This was Pix's second play, which, curiously, the Patent Company had decided to produce at Dorset Gardens, usually the venue for spectacular opera, and in the off-season month of August 1696 when virtually none of the main company, or its audience, were in London. Whether Pix approached the company at Lincoln's Inn Fields before or soon after *The Female Wits* was produced, or whether they actively recruited her, is not known. What is certain is that the Players' Company enjoyed a four-year monopoly on women's playwriting. There were perhaps stronger loyalties at work here than a written contract could provide, but certainly new creative opportunities provided by the

Barry/ Bracegirdle managerial and acting partnership. If at the beginning of the 1696/7 season Rich had been aware of the potential commercial success of the collaboration between the actress/managers and the female playwrights, he might not have let them slip from his hands so easily.

New plays, new partnerships

The first of Pix's plays to be produced by the Players' Company was a lively contemporary comedy, *The Innocent Mistress*, performed at the end of the season in June 1697. Aside from the dismissive reference to the Patent Company's attempt to boost audience figures by introducing animals as entr'acte items, new stage machinery and elaborate scenic designs, the prologue, written by Motteux, reveals an awareness of the need to heed the growing call for reform plays while still catering for the broader entertainment tastes of the Town:

> For there's in Plays, you know, a Reformation
> (A thing to which y'have no great inclination)
> I fear you'll seek some lo[o]ser Occupation[37]

Motteux appears to be negotiating with the fact that Pix is anticipating the need for contemporary comedy to deal with contemporary concerns – as well as provide contemporary high-energy entertainment. Before closing with the traditional plea for the female playwright, the prologue virtually apologises for and, therefore, asserts the play's overt moral intentions:

> Spare it, you who for harmless sports declare,
> Show that this age a modest Play can bear.
> Twice has our Poetess kind usage found;
> Change not her Fortune, tho' she chang'd her Ground.[38]

Pix's change of ground to the Players' Company coincides with several interesting changes in her playwriting. These changes anticipate a shift in emphasis that marks a period of prolific playwriting by women which is inseparable from the position of the actresses they were writing for. In other words, Pix is writing for performance in the context of a theatre in which the actress/managers occupy an unusually powerful position – on stage and off. On one level the play explores the subject familiar in Behn's earlier works: women's desire to control their own social and sexual destiny in a world operating by man-made rules. But

Pix extends this theme further than Behn ever did by employing fashionably recognisable settings, informal dialogue and a relaxed representation of the contemporary household – which includes the representation of the overworked and underpaid servant. In modern terms we might describe this as sit-com writing: an approach to the contemporary world that assumes a level of audience familiarity with the players, scenes and situations. This is intertheatricality at work, a tradition in which, as Jacky Bratton has argued, female writers 'could be said to be leaders … making plays within, instead of at odds with, the context in which the theatre artist works'.[39] Interestingly, Bratton's argument against the assumptions of a literary hegemony at work in theatrical writing concerns the 'disappearance' of Susanna Centlivre, who closely followed Pix in writing new plays for the theatre. My interest here is not to pre-empt that argument, or claim Pix as the 'first', but to identify other disappearances – or forgettings – and to suggest a broader application of intertheatricality that takes into account the importance of collaboration between the female playwright and the leading theatre women of the day – at this moment, Barry and Bracegirdle.

The Innocent Mistress is the first of Pix's four comedies to explore the familiar theme of love and marriage within a contemporary London setting: St James's Park, Locketts Coffee House and the Temple are all represented in this play. More importantly, through the two central love stories Pix demonstrates her ability to negotiate the shifting social interests of the Late Stuart stage. Mrs Beauclair and Sir Francis Wildlove evoke the witty 'gay couple' of the Restoration stage while the move toward the sentimental is revealed in the principled, platonic relationship between Bellinda and Sir Charles. Whereas Pix's previous works clearly presented female characters in a sympathetic light, the action in these plays, particularly in *The Spanish Wives*, was driven by male protagonists. Here, her central protagonists are the two women, created for and by the acting partnership of Elizabeth Barry and Anne Bracegirdle.

In previous chapters the range of parts and female 'types' played out in the Barry/Bracegirdle partnership has already been explored in some detail. But it is worth considering further the complexity of the interweaving of their off-stage identities, playing into and against the expectation of their on stage identities. The collaboration between writer and performer *with* their audience is exactly what intertheatricality is all about. Here, in the face of personal criticism, generated by the patent house and aimed at both the playwright and the actresses, Pix, Barry and

Bracegirdle create a contemporary comedy in which to play out and disrupt the performance of self in society. This is a play that depends upon intertheatricality to draw attention to social expectations and social posturing, to undercut pomposity – and, crucially, to dare to represent women as agents of their own actions. The collaborative creation of the play openly acknowledges its place as part of a larger theatrical code that, as Bratton puts it, 'consists not only of language, but of genres, conventions and memories – shared by the audience – of previous plays and scenes, previous performances, the actors' previous roles and their known personae on and off stage'.[40]

Elizabeth Barry plays Bellinda, a wealthy heiress who has fled from home to avoid a loveless marriage and now lives in London under an assumed name. She has fallen in love with Sir Charles Beauclair/Betterton but, on discovering him to be married, albeit a marriage of convenience to a rich social-climbing widow, is determined to remain the innocent mistress of the title. Anne Bracegirdle plays her friend, Mrs. Beauclair (Sir Charles' niece), a lively and intelligent woman who loves the rakish Wildlove/Verbruggen and uses various disguises – including breeches – to reveal his true character. The success of Pix's central female characters relies largely on the range of performance possibilities offered by the two central actresses: Barry is given ample scope to express heightened emotion in Bellinda's anguished speeches, while Mrs Beauclair provides Bracegirdle with numerous opportunities for quick-witted comedy. But Pix goes beyond the relatively straightforward narrative of 'good' women finding their men. Her complex, multilayered plot circulates largely around the sophisticated world of the aristocracy but she is unusually adept at exploring a more complex web of social interaction by presenting the perspective of those who dissent from the restrictions of the dominant social hegemony and, further still, by exposing the follies of those who aspire to it. Through the odious Lady Beauclair/Elinor Liegh, the rich widow now married to Sir Charles, and her coarse daughter, Peggy/Mrs Howard – a remarkably modern tragi/comic figure who attempts to hide her rapacious appetite for cake and wine from her mother – Pix reveals her thorough knowledge and evident dislike for the aspirant merchant class, contriving to have both women paired with equally odious men by the end of the play. Lady Beauclair's first husband, the aptly named Flywife, returns to London from the Indies, thus freeing Sir Charles to marry Bellinda, and Peggy finds her match in Spendall who – as his name suggests – marries her for her money.

In a play which sees every character coupled with the partner they deserve, a further marriage plot concerns the innocent Arabella who is determined to escape a plan hatched by her guardian, Cheatall – 'a very foolish Fellow, Brother to the ill-bred Lady Beauclair'[41] – to marry her and have her fortune. Although Arabella has a champion in the honest country gentleman, Beaumont, the complicated plan to help her escape, and the rather farcical plot that leads Cheatall to believe he is accused of Arabella's murder, is formed and executed by Lady Beauclair's disaffected maid, Eugenia. She involves Gentil, Cheatall's manservant, in an escapade designed from honest compassion but clearly with financial reward in mind:

Gentil	Whither so fast, Mrs. Eugenia?
Eugenia	Stop me not. I am upon an Act of Charity, trying to free the Immur'd Lady [Arabella]. I have been picking up all the Rusty Keys in the house in hopes to accomplish it.
Gentil	Why, you'll loose your place.
Eugenia	Hang my place – There's not one in the family understands a Grain of Civility except Sir Charles. And if he speaks to me my Lady pulls my Head-cloaths off – Come, I know you don't love that Lubberly Coxcomb, your Master – E'en joyn with me, assist in Arabella's Liberty, and recover her Fortune, and I dare engage she'll make ours.[42]

With a cast of nineteen, this comedy careers at almost breakneck speed from one situation to another and is only slowed by the impassioned and deliberately self-conscious scenes between the platonic lovers, Bellinda and Sir Charles. Pix was obviously interested in appealing to every element of the audience and, in the process, offers some sharp observations on a society caught between libertinism and the moves toward reform. In an early exchange between the two central heroines Pix exposes the inherent contradiction of a society which relishes Restoration wit and yet seeks to advocate virtue and honesty, especially in women. This dialogue must have delighted an audience familiar with the virtuous and whorish reputations of the two leading actresses and, in turn, allowed both playwright and actress to play on their public identity:

Mrs Beauclair/Bracegirdle	I must confess, though I am wild to the very verge that Innocence allows, yet when my Uncle, that dear good man, told me if e'er I meant to oblige him I must be a Companion, Friend, and Lover of his Mistress. The proposition startled me, but then I did not think there had been such a Mistress as my Bellinda, nor Platonick Love in real practice.

Bellinda/Barry   True, my dear Friend, our Love is to the Modern Age
                  unpractic'd and unknown.[43]

The Innocent Mistress reveals the extent of the underlying patriarchal anxiety about female behaviour, not least in the growth of a discourse that offers women a different vision of their future from the life of obedience prescribed for them in a patriarchal society. Barry and Bracegirdle play out that vision on stage and as sharer/managers the off-stage implications can hardly be missed.

Pix boldly links Bellinda's decision to flee from an undesirable marriage with attitudes and ideas gained through reading 'Plays and Romances, from thence she form'd herself a Hero, a Cavalier, that could Love and talk like them'.[44] To reinforce the point, Bellinda makes her first entrance 'with a book' and begins to describe her first meeting with Sir Charles in a tone which closely resembles an adventure romance and in which – of course – a visit to the playhouse plays a central role:

Bellinda   In short, 'twas thus: Coming from the play, masked, with a young lady, a fluttering fellow seized me, and, in spite of my entreaties, grew rudely troublesome. I was never used to such behaviour, and it thoroughly frighted me. Sir Charles, being near, saw my unfeign'd concern, and generously made the brute desist, then led me safely to a coach. Observing where I bid the coachman drive, he came to wait upon me. My fair friend again was with me, and 'twas by her persuasions that I saw him. We found his conversation nicely civil and full of innocent delight. I blushed and fondly thought this man my amorous stars, in kindness, destined for my happiness, but oh! …
Mrs. Beauclair   But oh, he was married, and that spoiled all.[45]

The comic timing of Mrs Beauclair's line undercuts the romanticism but simultaneously reinforces the notion of female desire for an idealised man, revealing the inevitable disappointment of reality. Bellinda's appetite for plays and romances – those fictional 'Seducers of women' – is seen to form her romantic desires but it also informs her determination to dissent from repressive social constructs: she will be neither a submissive daughter to her father's will nor a kept mistress in a libertine society.

It is interesting to find Barry creating the role of the bookish and virtuous Bellinda, while Bracegirdle plays the more knowing and dry-witted Mrs Beauclair. The layers of intertheatrical meaning being generated here extend to the female playwright as well as the actresses as their voices conjoin in the disruption of expected performances of self. The doubled voice of the female playwright/actress rails against the ignorance of the male playgoer/critic, personified by Spendall, as he launches an attack against the writing woman:

Spendall   I said, a she Wit was as great a Wonder as a Blazing star and as certainly foretold the World's turning upside down; yet, spight of that the Lady will write.
Mrs. Beauclair Brute! what did I ever write, unless it was thy character, and that was so adroit, you had like to hang'd your self?[46]

The heterogeneous nature of the audience that fails to see and engage with the theatrically represented self is linked to notions of ignorance – and this not reserved only for the foolish male spectator. The derided Lady Beauclair, an aristocrat by marriage rather than birth, is seen to resent bitterly Sir Charles's efforts to educate and thus improve her 'unquiet mind' by taking her to the playhouse: 'The first thing I saw was an ugly, black Divil kill his Wife, for nothing; then your Metridate, King o' the Potecaries, your Timon the Atheist, the Man in the Moon, and all the rest – Nonsense, Stuff, I hate 'em.'[47] The argument here clearly attempts to refute accusations that novels and plays exert an immoral influence on the female reader/spectator and Pix is obviously interested in demonstrating the benefits of education to the honourable woman. Mrs Beauclair and Bellinda are seen to be encouraged to be *more* virtuous by what they read/see, while the crude Lady Beauclair fails to appreciate or be moved by *any* of the dramatic tragedy or spectacle she has experienced in the playhouse. Crucially, her ignorance is used to feed the comedy and Pix uses this to tread the precarious path between offending her merchant-class audience and appealing to their interests in virtuous and honourable constructs of femininity.

The difficult task of appealing to every section of society represented in the audience is quite clearly expressed in the epilogue to *The Innocent Mistress* – also written by Motteux and spoken by the actor Barnabus Scudamore:

> We've sworn t'invite the grave part of the Nation;
> Rich Sparks with broad-brim-hats and little Bands,
> Who'll clap dry Morals till they hurt their Hands;
> Nice Dames? Who'll have their Box as they've their Pew,
> And come each Day, but not to ogle you:
> No, each side Box shall shine with sweeter Faces;
> None but Chains, Gowns and Coifs shall have their places,

> Their chit-chat News, Stockjobbing, and Law-causes.
> The Middle-Fry shall in the Gall'ry sit,
> And humh whatever against Cuckold's Writ.
> And City Wives from Lectures throng the Pit;
> Their Daughters Fair with Prentice trudge it hither,
> And throng as they do Lambeth-Wells this weather.
> Then all this stor'd, tho'Money's scarce this Age,
> We need not fear t' have a Beau-crowded Stage.
> So, for new guests we'll change, just as our Beaux
> Wear Doyly-Stuff, for want of better Cloths.[48]

Although many of the prefaces, prologues and epilogues discussed in earlier chapters attempted to embrace the growing diversity of their audience, Pix's *The Innocent Mistress* goes further by directly addressing the social tensions created in the audience's awareness and performance of its social diversity. The friendship between Bellinda's essentially sentimental heroine and Mrs Beauclair's witty, cross-dressed heroine presents seemingly different models of female behaviour while, at the same time, reinforcing notions of honour and virtue. Bellinda's high-mindedness is rewarded by her marriage to Sir Charles but then Mrs. Beauclair's wit and daring is also rewarded by her success in reforming the rakish Wildlove. The implicit repudiation of Restoration morals is matched by a sharp critique of the rising middle-class hegemony delivered via an entertaining mixture of wit and sentiment, farce and dramatic tension; amply fulfilling the prologue's claim to have 'something every taste to hit'.

Pix's play was well received and at least one critic publicly recognised that the female playwright was worthy of better treatment than she, or her fellow female playwrights, might expect: 'The play has its peculiar Merit; and as a Lady carried the Prize of Poetry in France this year, so in Justice, they are like to do in England; tho' indeed we use them more barbarously, and defraud them both of their Fame and Profit.'[49] The success of Pix's collaboration with Barry and Bracegirdle at Lincoln's Inn Fields was evidently sufficient to encourage Pix to create two new plays for the actress/managers in the following season. Traditional theatre histories are quick to attribute the success of the female playwrights at Lincoln's Inn Fields to the influence of male theatre practitioners, notably Congreve, who is generally considered to have influenced Pix – an assumption that will be challenged in a later chapter – and yet none has seriously considered the influence of the two actress/managers who brought their work to the stage. In the season following Pix's debut at

Lincoln's Inn Fields, four new plays by three female playwrights were produced at Lincoln's Inn Fields – with Barry and Bracegirdle in the leading roles. Since the theatres had re-opened in 1660 no single season had contained so much work by female theatre practitioners and no two actresses had occupied such an influential position in a London playhouse.

Notes

1 Southerne, *Oroonoko* (1696), Prologue. Susannah Verbruggen had returned to the Patent house having been refused a share in the Players' Company. The patentees, Skipwith and Rich, were evidently determined to keep her in the company by offering an unusually generous financial incentive in an agreement made between Skipwith and Susannah's husband, John Verbruggen. Susannah received a bonus of £75 on signing with the company and an assurance of 20 per cent of the profits or a minimum payment of £105 per annum. (See Milhous and Hume *A Register of English Theatrical Documents 1660–1737* (Carbondale: Southern Illinois University Press, 1991), 2 vols, vol. 1, p. 312. The editors cite their source as LC 7/3, fols 64–65.) Rich's reputation for non-payment suggests that Susannah may not have received the full amount agreed but, like her husband, been given a weekly payment on account.
2 Milhous, *Thomas Betterton*, p. 90.
3 Cibber, *Apology*, ed. Lowe, vol. 1, pp. 205–207.
4 Colley Cibber is the main source for the less than generous appraisal of Powell's acting career, a view that has largely been adopted in subsequent biographical references.
5 See Cibber, *Apology*, ed. Lowe, vol. 1, p. 189, concerning Rich's offer to give George Powell Betterton's parts – an offer which Powell accepted and which resulted in Betterton's decision to move to Lincoln's Inn Fields.
6 George Powell, *Bonduca: or The British Worthy* (London: Richard Bentley, 1696), Prologue. It seems most likely that this is a reference to the practice of burning women found guilty of witchcraft; the last execution of this kind took place in 1712. The gruesome image evoked here is the sight and sound of the (usually older) woman prior to or during her execution.
7 *The Female Wits: or, The Triumverate of Poets at Rehearsal* (London: William Turner, William Davis, Bernard Lintott & Thomas Brown, 1704). The play has been reprinted in facsimile of the original by the Augustan Reprint Society, Los Angeles: University of California, 1967, with an introduction by Lucyle Hook, and is also included in Fidelis Morgan, *The Female Wits*, pp. 392–433. Morgan's edition differs in some small but important details and so I have used the first 1704 edition held by the British Library for all quotations. It is worth noting that following Morgan's adoption of the phrase 'Female Wits' as the title for her collection of plays by seventeenth-century

female playwrights the term has been attached to this group of women in a positive way. The intention of its original application, however, is clearly pejorative.
8 *The Female Wits*, Act I, p. 5. There are no scene numbers given in the 1704 published edition and so I have provided pages numbers where possible.
9 Act I, p. 2.
10 Hook (ed.), *The Female Wits*, p. xii. Hook argues that the comedian Joe Haynes was probably the principal author. Haynes played Bayes in *The Rehearsal* (1672), a popular satire against Dryden (traditionally attributed to Buckingham) which was regularly revived as part of the theatrical season. Haynes was also a popular speaker of satirical prologues and epilogues. Hook argues that in the published edition of *The Female Wits* (1704), the preface states that the author died before publication (Haynes died in 1701) but this might well have been a strategy to deflect attention from the still living author(s).
11 p. xiv.
12 For example see Tiffany Stern, *Rehearsal from Shakespeare to Sheridan* (Oxford: Clarendon Press, 2000), pp. 124–194.
13 *The Female Wits*, Act II, p. 32.
14 Act III, p. 66.
15 The Players' Company was in a state of disarray by this point and subject to numerous published attacks aimed at 'the three Bs' (as Betterton, Barry and Bracegirdle were known). Publication at this point may well have worked to cash in on a general feeling of antipathy towards the management at Lincoln's Inn Fields.
16 Susannah Verbruggen died in 1703, the year before this play was published.
17 *The Female Wits*, Preface.
18 Ibid.
19 Cibber, *Apology*, ed. Lowe, vol. 1, pp. 227–228. Lowe corrects Cibber's given date of 1693 for the creation of the Players' Company but passes no further comment. Although it is possible that this was a scribal or printing error, it does seem to be another indication that Cibber's account of specific events must be treated with caution.
20 Milhous, *Thomas Betterton*, p. 81.
21 *The London Stage* roster of players for the 1695/6 season notes that Richard Leveridge and Miss Ayliff (both singers) appear for both companies.
22 Milhous and Hume, *A Register of English Theatrical Documents*, vol. 1, p. 315. The editors cite their source as the Lord Chamberlain's papers 7/3, folio 21 and note that the order of 16 April 1695 was confirmed and expanded on 25 July 1695 in 7/3, folio 70. It is worth noting the specific reference to the 'Actress' at this point, some five years earlier than noted in the *OED*, which suggests that the term did not come into use until 1700.
23 The details of this agreement are also recorded by Milhous and Hume, *A Register of English Theatrical Documents*, vol. 1, p. 318 who cite the Lord

Chamberlain's papers 7/3, folios 71–74. The difficulties caused first by Doggett then Verbruggen, who defected to the Players' Company, resulted in more activity from the Lord Chamberlain, who sanctioned this reciprocal exchange of leading players but issued orders against any further transfers in October 1696 and again in May 1697.

24 Cibber, *Apology*, ed. Lowe, vol. 1, pp. 230–231.
25 See Milhous and Hume, *A Register of English Theatrical Documents*, vol. 1, pp. 322–333. The editors comment on a series of documents relating to Doggett. Between 1697 and 1700 he did not play for either company but received a licence to perform in Norwich under the protection of the Duke of Norfolk. The only notable event in Doggett's three years as manager of a strolling company concerns a report in *Dawks Newsletter* dated September 1698 which gives an account of a performance at the Angel Inn in Norwich. Playing to a full house, the performance was stopped when the gallery broke, killing a young woman outright and injuring others. However unfortunate this particular incident was, it demonstrates that then, as now, there was money to be made on the road by touring companies, especially if they could boast a player from the London companies.
26 Motteux was born and educated in Rohan in Normandy. See David Erskine Baker, *Biographia Dramatica or A Companion to the Playhouse* (Dublin: T. Henshall, 1782), 2 vols, vol. 1, pp. 327–328, who notes that Motteux was fluent in several languages and 'acquired so perfect a mastery of the English language … [he] became a very eminent dramatic writer in a language to which he was not native'. Motteux evidently lived very comfortably on the proceeds of his plays and his interests as a merchant trader. Baker reveals something of the inherent suspicion toward foreigners (and their sexual morality) in the intriguing account of the circumstances surrounding Motteux's death in 1718: 'he was found dead in a disorderly house in the Parish of St Clement Danes, not without suspicion of having been murdered; though other accounts say, that he met with his fate in trying a very odd experiment'.
27 Milhous, *Thomas Betterton*, p. 102.
28 p. 88.
29 Of the younger actresses who appeared in this play Mrs Howard appears in *The London Stage* calendar of performances as having played substantial roles in at least two new plays in the first two seasons. Mrs Perrin is in the cast lists for at least five new plays in the same period. Other young actresses also appear frequently: Abigail Lawson made six appearances in new plays, Mrs Prince four, and there are several new names that appear alongside named roles more than once.
30 Milhous, *Thomas Betterton*, p. 88.
31 *The London Stage*, Part 1, p. 470, cites the source as HMC, 12th Report, Appendix, Part 2, Cowper MSS., 2, 367.
32 See Cibber, *Apology*, ed. Lowe, vol. 1, pp. 217–218.

33 Vanbrugh and Congreve gained a licence to perform at the new theatre in December 1704. At it's opening on 9 April 1705, the Queen's theatre was found to have acoustic problems and later in the season the company returned to Lincoln's Inn Fields while alterations were made at Queen's.
34 Downes, *Roscius*, p. 44.
35 See Maggie B. Gale and Viv Gardner (eds), *Auto/biography and Identity: Women, Theatre and Performance* (Manchester: Manchester University Press, 2004), for further discussion on autobiographical writing and performance.
36 Milhous, *Thomas Betterton*, pp. 86–87.
37 Mary Pix, *The Innocent Mistress* (London: J. Orme for R. Basset and F. Cogan, 1697), Prologue, attributed to Pierre Motteux.
38 Prologue.
39 Jacky Bratton, 'Reading the Intertheatrical, or, the Mysterious Disappearance of Susannah Centlivre', in *Women, Theatre and Performance: New Histories*, pp. 7–24, p. 16.
40 p. 15.
41 Cast list, identified in the published text as 'Names Represented'. The importance of identifying the particular actors and actresses involved in the creation of the play is highlighted here by an unusual layout for the period in which the player's name precedes that of the character and character description.
42 Pix, *Innocent* Mistress, Act III, p. 19.
43 Act I, pp. 4–5.
44 Act I, p. 4.
45 Act I, p. 5.
46 Act I, p. 7.
47 Act III, p. 24. These malapropisms, written some eighty-seven years before that term was coined after Sheridan's Mrs Malaprop in *The Rivals* (1775), evidently refer to recent productions. *The London Stage* listings for this season and the previous one lead me to suggest that the first reference concerns Southerne's adaptation of Behn's *Oroonoko* (1695), which was revived in early June 1697, the second refers to another recent revival of Lee's *Mithridates, King of Pontus* (1678). Shadwell's adaptation of Shakespeare's *Timon of Athens*, also known as *The Man-Hater* (1678), is thought to have been revived in the 1696 season and Settle's *The World in the Moon* (1697) was premiered at the same time as Pix's *Innocent Mistress*. Interestingly all the plays mentioned here appear to have been performed by the rival Patent Company.
48 Pix, *The Innocent Mistress*, Epilogue.
49 Langbain, *Lives and Characters*, p. 112.

6
Re-forming the stage

The season of 1697/8 marks a crucial period in theatre history and an extraordinary chapter in the history of theatre women. In no other season on the Late Stuart stage were so many new plays by female playwrights performed by the same company in the same playhouse. Competition between the two houses was still fierce and an act of overt plagiarism by the Patent Company fuelled the ongoing animosity. The Players' Company maintained its commercially successful edge over its rivals and this season can be seen to represent the peak of Barry and Bracegirdle's joint career as actress/managers at Lincoln's Inn Fields. But this was also the season in which the entire theatrical community was beleaguered by determined moves to curb the activities of the playhouse. Objections to the immorality of the stage were supported and refuted in a flurry of publications that marked out the battle lines. The place of women in the theatre – on and off stage – was part of that moral debate. The diversity of the work co-produced by female playwrights and actresses in this season is all the more remarkable when considered in the context of the upheavals caused by the anti-theatrical lobby.

Jeremy Collier's *Short View*

Moves to bring the two theatre companies under tighter control had begun to be enforced toward the end of the previous season in response to growing objections about the immorality of new plays. In June 1697 the Lord Chamberlain issued an order stating that 'new Plays Acted by both Company's of His Majesty's Comaedians are scandalously lew'd and prophane … I do hereby strictly Order that you do not presume hereafter to Act any new Play till you shall have first brought it to my Secretary, and receive my directions from him therein as you shall answer the contrary att your Perill.'[1] It is not possible to ascertain the level of seriousness with which the two companies responded to the renewed vigour of this already established edict but if they thought it a momentary flexing of moral/political muscle they underestimated the force of the opposition ranged against them. In the spring of 1698 the rumbling of Puritan discontent exploded into print with the publication of Jeremy Collier's *A Short View of the Immorality and Profaneness of the English Stage*.[2] Collier became something of a figurehead for the section of society that saw the 'Glorious Revolution' of 1688/9 – the Protestant victory over Popery – as an opportunity to reinstate the social ethics and instruments of control identified with the Puritan values of the Commonwealth and, therefore, suppressed following the Restoration in 1660. As Milhous observes: 'Scholars ... have known better than to suppose that Jeremy Collier came out of nowhere to smite the theatres. His *Short View* ... was only the high point in a rising clamor of protests. But the number of individuals who responded to his book in prefaces and pamphlets shows just how threatened the writers and actors felt. They had reason to panic.'[3] Collier's publication prompted and actively encouraged the judiciary to add their weight to the argument, resulting in the issue of a series of complaints against the profanity of the playhouse. Luttrell records that on 10 May 'the justices of Middlesex have presented the playhouses to be nurseries of debauchery and blasphemy' and two days later extended their censure to include playwrights and booksellers for writing, printing and selling plays, concluding 'that women frequenting the playhouses in masks tended much to debauchery and immorality'.[4]

Surprisingly perhaps, Collier does not attack female playwrights and his objections to the actresses mainly revolve around the immorality of the characters written for them and the lewdness of the dialogue they are given to speak. As Jean Marsden points out in her convincing discussion of the anti-theatrical debate: 'Collier suggests that the erotic behavior of a lower class woman, the actress, *in her own character*, is of little moment. It has no natural or political implications and does not threaten the structure of society. It is the fictional representation which constitutes the danger because, Collier fears, ladies in the audience will identify with the character on stage, not with the actual actress.'[5] Although Marsden's article is primarily concerned with the connection between female spectatorship and female sexuality her argument reveals a subtle but crucial move in Collier's writing which, ultimately, works to undermine the powerful presence and creative activity of theatre women.

The process of occlusion

In a season containing at least four new plays by writing women and performed in a playhouse with a strong female leadership, why does Collier's attack on the immorality of the playhouse fail to include any mention of their work?[6] Sister Rose Anthony poses the same question and attempts to provide an explanation.

> For some reason known best to himself he does not attack women dramatists; he does not even mention Mrs. Behn who was certainly entitled to his ire. Neither does he refer to the plays of Mrs. Manley, Mrs. Pix, and Mrs. Trotter ... His leniency with the women dramatists may be attributed to a certain gallantry and to consideration of them, both of which qualities are evident throughout his anti-stage works.[7]

If this is the explanation, the problem here is that the notion of Collier's gentlemanly 'gallantry' works to reinforce patriarchal attitudes in the construct of the female 'other' and what constitutes feminine behaviour. The provenance of Collier's thinking has some bearing here, as it would surely be unthinkable for an essentially high-church clergyman like Collier even to countenance the notion of 'woman' as a proactive creator of meanings – whether in the playhouse, which he admits he never visits, or in the realm from which his attack is launched: the literary text.

The woman's 'natural' place in the private domestic sphere is essentially seen as being a passive receptacle, a receiving/spectating woman; hence the concern with how female characters, not actresses, might influence the female spectator. The woman in the public sphere is 'unnatural' and Collier's concern is with the way that this unnatural woman is being *created* by the male playwright. Collier implicitly acknowledges the power of the intertheatrical but simultaneously strips women of their agency in that theatrical exchange. He is concerned that the female spectator might be polluted by the representation of a female *character* behaving dishonourably but assumes that, by definition, all actresses are dishonourable: the actress/whore trope. So, the individual identity of the actress, on or off stage, is of no concern. Similarly, the female playwright can be ignored because, as a woman first, it is against her 'nature' to participate in public discourse. The occlusion of theatre woman has begun. Collier's tract can be seen as a benchmark in a hegemonic process that refuses to consider plays as belonging to the theatre, insisting instead on their appropriation as text alone and so belonging within a literary heritage and discourse.[8]

It is not my intention to dwell on Collier's work but I cannot help but note the irony that John Payne Collier – who claimed descent from Jeremy Collier – was a major figure in the construction of the nineteenth-century theatre history we have inherited which is, as Jacky Bratton puts it, 'a history that is, at its very basis, hostile to its own subject: the traffic of the stage'.[9] Jeremy Collier and the anti-theatrical lobby played some part in establishing the ongoing debate and fascination with the stage, generated it seems by a deep hostility to its subject. My interest here is to draw attention to particular responses in the flurry of published exchanges between Jeremy Collier, his supporters and his detractors in order to consider the extent to which the controversy affected the Players' Company and the traffic of the stage at Lincoln's Inn Fields: notably their writer in residence, William Congreve.

Collier attacked most of the leading male playwrights of the day and many went into print in their own defence. Congreve was not the first to pick up the gauntlet but his *Amendments of Mr Collier's False and Imperfect Citations, etc.*, published in July 1698, makes it clear that he is prepared to meet Collier on the *literary* ground from which the attack was launched and in which Congreve also had a stake. Congreve is interested in defending the stage but far more in justifying his own dramatic works as they appeared in print. Congreve begins by turning the accusations of immorality back on his traducer declaring that he will 'restore those Passages to their primitive station, which have suffer'd so much in being transplanted by him [Collier]: I will remove 'em from his Dunghil, and replant 'em in the Field of Nature; and when I have wash'd 'em of that Filth which they have contracted in passing thro' his very dirty hands, let their own innocence protect them'.[10] Congreve answers Collier's specific attacks against the immorality of his comedies by arguing that 'Men are to be laugh'd out of their Vices in Comedy' going on to demonstrate his own literary credentials and familiarity with the classical arguments for Poetry and, inevitably, blurring the lines between the reception of performance and reading the text. He argues that 'the Business of Comedy is to delight as well as instruct',[11] and attempts to defend each play in detail against Collier's four central charges of 'Immodesty, Profaneness, Abuse of the Clergy, and Encouragement of Immorality'.[12] Congreve then delivers the most passionate and personal counter attack that takes the argument back into the playhouse and invokes the sexualised male gaze: '*Sometimes to report a fault is to repeat it.* The spectator in the Pit shall plainly perceive, that he [Collier] loves to look on naked Obscenity; and that he only flogs it, as a sinful Paedagogue sometimes lashes a pretty Boy, that looks lovely in his Eyes, for Reasons best known to himself.'[13] Congreve is keenly aware that Collier's attack on the theatre is only the tip of a much larger moralistic iceberg, increasing in size as it moves inexorably to control and contain the liberal inclinations of the Town: 'I am not the only one who looks on this Pamphlet of his to be a Gun levell'd at the whole Laity, while the shot only glances on the Theatre; what he means by the Attack, or what may be its Consequences, I know not, and I suppose he cares not ... He has assaulted the Town in the seat of their principal, and most reasonable Pleasure. Down with the Theatre right or wrong.'[14] Although Collier ignored specific theatre women in his sometimes vitriolic attack, another critic, apparently supporting Collier's position, used the publication of Congreve's defence as an opportunity to take a public swipe at both the playwright and the players, while delivering some vicious sexual slurs against the female playwrights along the way.

Set in a dialogue between 'Mr Smith' and 'Mr Johnson', the preface to *Animadversions on Mr. Congreve's Late Answer to Mr. Collier*, published in 1698, leaves the reader in no doubt as to which side the anonymous author supports: 'Mr Congreve has set out a Book in Vindication of his Plays from Mr Collier's. Most of the other Scribling sparks o'th Town, have discharg'd their little Artillery and their Spleen as well as he, but not one Breach have they made yet in Mr Collier's Bastions; they are too well Lin'd against the disorderly Fire of such Poppers.'[15] The author's dedicatory epistle 'To the Ingenious Mr ......' attacks many of the popular male playwrights of the day but his references to the female playwrights bears out Congreve's accusation that Collier and his supporters may argue for morality but are most often to be found employing the very obscenities they complain about.

> Or could I write like the two Female things
> With *Muse Pen-feather'd*, guiltless yet of Wings
> And yet, it strives to Fly, and thinks it Sings.
> Just like the Dames themselves, who slant in Town,
> And flutter loosely, but to tumble down.
> The last that writ, of these presuming two,
> (For that *Queen Ca——ne* is no Play 'tis true)[16]
> And yet to Spell is more than she can do,
> Told a High Princess, she from Men had torn
> Those *Bays*, which they had long engross'd and worn.
> But when she offers at our Sex thus fair,
> With four fine Copies to her Play – O rare!
> If she feels Manhood shoot – 'tis I know where.
> Let them scrawl on, and Loll, and Wishat [*sic*] ease,
> (A Feather oft does Woman's Fancy please.)
> Till by their Muse (more jilt than they) accurst,
> We know (if possible) which writes the worst.
> Beneath these Pictures, sure there needs no name,
> Nor will I give what they ne'er got in Fame.[17]

Following this vituperative attack, 'Mr Johnson' delivers a 'short essay on the stage' which reveals such a deep-seated dislike of the players that it seems that the author was more interested in using the opportunity of this public debate to vent his personal antipathy toward the players rather than support the more general case against the theatre. 'I would by no means have a Player made a sharer, for then he grows so Sawcy immediately, that the Poet and the Actor tread the Stage with equal Foot; nay, and the Actor in a little while, shall Ten to One, pretend to turn Poet too. Actors should indeed never have more Sense than generally they have; a Parrot-like sort of Cant, so they can but change their Tone is sufficient for them.'[18] The frustrated tone that complains about the player assuming the same social and intellectual level as the poet resembles the work of Robert Gould in *The Play-House, A Satyr* (c. 1685) – especially in his observations on the actress: 'I would have all the Actresses oblig'd by their Articles, to a considerable Forfeiture, upon proof of the abuse of their Vertue, or rather be Expell'd the Theatre; for I think no Woman, after she has play'd the Whore notoriously, can be fancifully receiv'd upon the Stage for a Heroine.'[19] It is more than likely that the reader is being directed toward the most famous whore/heroine of the time, Elizabeth Barry, the actress against whom Gould bore a particular grudge.[20] For their part, it might seem that having been excluded from the published debate, theatre women were silenced but that it is to exclude the importance of the business of theatre as an essential part of cultural discourse.

Getting on with the business of theatre

If Collier and others sought to ignore the individual identity of the actress and her creative influence in dramatic discourse, Barry and Bracegirdle were clearly aware of the importance of their position to both the playwright and the audience. The interplay between their on/off stage personae and the strength of their collaborative partnership at Lincoln's Inn Fields is demonstrated in their delightfully playful appearance as joint epilogue speakers for Vanbrugh's *The Provok'd Wife*, performed in April 1697. Written 'By another Hand', this overt piece of metatheatre is spoken by Lady Brute/Barry and Bellinda/Bracegirdle.

Lady B.   No Epilogue!
Bell.   I swear I know of none
Lady   Lord! How shall we excuse it to the Town?

Bell.	Why, we must e'en say something of our own	
Lady	Our Own! Ay, that must needs be precious stuff	5
Bell	I'll lay my Life they'll like it well enough.	
	Come Faith begin –	
Lady	Excuse me, after you.	
Bell	Nay, pardon me for that, I know my Cue.	
Lady	O for the World, I would not have precedence	10
Bell	O Lord!	
Lady	I Swear–	
Bell	O Fye!	
Lady	I'm all Obedience	
	First then, know all, before our Doom is fixt,	15
	The Third Day is for us –	
Bell	Nay and the Sixth	
Lady	We speak not from the Poet now, nor is it	
	His Cause – (I want a Rhime)	
Bell	That we sollicite.	20
Lady	Then sure you cannot have the Hearts to be severe	
	And Damn us –	
Bell	Damn us! Let 'em if they dare.	
Lady	Why, if they should, what Punishment remains?	
Bell	Eternal Exile from behind our Scenes	25
Lady	But if they're kind, that Sentence we'll recall	
	We can be grateful –	
Bell	And have wherewithall	
Lady	But at Grand Treaties hope not to be Trusted	
	Before Preliminaries are adjusted	30
Bell	You know the Time, and we appoint this place;	
	Where, if you please, we'll meet and sign the Peace.[21]	

Unlike the usual pleadings given to the female epilogue speaker, there is an assured, authoritative tone in this quick-fire exchange. The comic timing can only be implied on the page but, as with all published plays of the period, the reader is given the cast list in order to invoke, to remember, the performance they have first witnessed in the playhouse – a quite different approach to our modern use of play-texts. Here, Barry and Bracegirdle play into the construct of the actress as merely a mouthpiece for the playwright's words (lines 1–3) but, in the absence of his words, provide their own (lines 4 onwards) and speak on their own behalf (lines 18–20). It is hard to avoid the sense that these two women are in command of the space they occupy, the playwright whose work they perform and whose financial reward they will apparently enjoy.[22] Crucially, the self-conscious representation of their authority acknowledges their power to punish their audience (lines 24 and 25) but also their reliance upon their 'kind[ness]' (line 25). At this point, the actress/managers were evidently confident that they had both.

The play chosen to open the 1697/8 season was an extravagant tragedy written, once more, by an anonymous 'Young Lady' who provided a perfect vehicle for both leading actresses. *The Unnatural Mother*, performed in September 1697, was the first of four plays by female playwrights to be performed at Lincoln's Inn Fields in a turbulent theatrical season. The published edition is unusual in that it is does not include a cast list but the 'unnatural mother' of the title, the wicked step mother Callipia, has all the marks of the vengeful, sexually voracious mistress that Barry excelled in. Her innocent step daughter, Bebbemeah, epitomises the virtuous victim role which Bracegirdle had equally made her own. The tragic plot is set in the exotic 'Kingdom of Siam' and is typically complex and convoluted, revolving directly around Callipia's desire for sexual fulfilment and power. Poisonings, stabbings and incest are interwoven with scenes of pagan funeral rituals, romantic songs and pastoral dances eventually concluding with the suicide of the now demented villainess, Callipia, whose crimes are made known through the timely appearance of spirits and ghosts. Modern literary criticism has tended to largely ignore the play or, like Margarete Rubik, cite it as an example of the 'low ebb' tragedy had reached by the turn of the century, concluding that it 'must range at the very bottom of the scale' and noting that the 'title figure lacks the passionate vitality of Manley's Homais [in *The Royal Mischief*] and is a mere monster'.[23] Rubik's description of the plot as an 'incongruous mixture of horror tragedy, love romance, pastoral, farce and ghost story',[24] if read from the perspective of performance rather than literature, reveals a play that has something for everyone; a winning and necessary device in the competitive atmosphere of the Late Stuart stage.

The Unnatural Mother is dramatic spectacle, built on a bold and skilful use of stagecraft which, when combined with the heightened emotional dialogue, is prescient of much later melodramatic writing. Allardyce Nicoll attributed the play to 'Ariadne', a suggestion which has been dismissed on the basis that 'there is no resemblance between the frothy intrigue comedy, *She Ventures,* and the villainess tragedy'.[25] The publication of the play suggests that it was popular enough to be considered commercially viable although, interestingly, there are none of the usual dedications, commendatory verses or prefaces that accompany the majority of published texts. If this was the work of one of the female wits, or perhaps Barry or another actress trying her hand at playwriting, the prologue makes clear the reasons she chose anonymity:

> A Woman now comes to reform the Stage,
> Who once has stood the Brunt of this unthinking Age;
> Yet shou'd her Pen, her Beauty cannot fail;
> But, oh! She vows she'l not her Charms unvail,
> Nor shall you know, harsh Men, at whom you rail.
> Then how you censure this her Play beware,
> Lest thro' the Poetess you wound the Fair:

The suggestion that the playwright has already withstood the brunt of public censure leads me to consider Manley as the possible author.

Playing in the face of plagiarism

If the female playwrights were becoming hardened to their plays being publicly attacked, they evidently did not expect to be overtly plagiarised. In the same month that *The Unnatural Mother* received its first production, the Patent Company also premiered a new play written by its actor/manager, George Powell. *Imposture Defeated: or, A Trick to Cheat the Devil* was a double-plot comedy which, for the greater part, replicates Pix's plot for her new comedy *The Deceiver Deceived*. Powell initially denied having seen Pix's manuscript but, as he had not even bothered to change the name Pix had given to the central character, he had to produce another argument in his preface to the published edition. "'Tis true, such a one she brought into the house, and made me a solicitor to the company to get it acted, which when I had obtained, she very mannerly carried the play to the other house; and if I had really taken the character from her, I had done no more than a piece of justice."[26] In other words, she got what she deserved. Powell's disdain for the female playwright evidently led him to underestimate seriously the support she now had from the company at Lincoln's Inn Fields. According to one contemporary report, a large group from the Players' Company arrived at Drury Lane to cry the play down.

> The mighty Man of Wit [Congreve] at the representation of this Play was seen very gravely with his Hat over his Eyes among his *chief Actors and Actresses, together with the two She-Things called Poetesses*, which write for his House, as 'tis noble called, thus seated in state among those and some other of his ingenious critical Friends, *they fell altogether upon a full cry of damnation,* but when they found the malicious Hiss would

not take, this very generous, obliging Mr. Congreve was heard to say we'll find a new way for this spark, take my word there is a way of clapping a Play down.[27] (my emphasis)

While this account places Congreve at the centre of the group, I would suggest that the formidable sight of Pix, Barry, Bracegirdle and other leading figures from Lincoln's Inn Fields must have proved a disturbing sight to their rivals.

The Players' Company responded to this latest attack from the Patent Company more substantively by producing Pix's *The Deceiver Deceived* some eight weeks later. Pix's prologue makes no attempt to hide the playwright's sense of outrage and her intention is clearly to expose the plagiarist, Powell, by publicly laying the case before her audience:

> Deceiv'd Deceiver, and Imposter cheated!
> An Audience and the Devil too defeated!
> All trick and cheat! Pshaw, 'tis the Devil and all,
> I'll warrant ye we shall now have Cups and Ball;
> No, Gallants, we those tricks don't understand;
> 'Tis t'other House best shows the slight of hand:
> Hey Jingo, Sirs, what's this! Their Comedy?
> *Presto* be gone, 'tis now our Farce you see.
> By neat conveyance you have seen and know it
> They can transform an Actor to a poet.
> With empty Dishes they'll set out a Treat,
> Whole seas of Broth, but a small Isle o Meat:
> With Powder-le-Pimp of Dance, Machine and Song,
> They'll Spin ye out short Nonsense four hours long:
> With Fountains, Groves, Bombast and airey Fancies
> Larded with Cynthias, little Loves and Dances:
> Which put together, makes it hard to say,
> If poet, Painter, or Fidler made the Play.
> But hold, my business lies another way.
> Not to bespeak your praise by kind perswasions,
> But to desire the favour of your patience.
>   Our Case is thus:
> Our Authoress, like true women, shew'd her Play
> To some who, like true Wits, stole't half away.
> We've Fee'd no Councel yet, tho some advise us
> T'indite the Plagaries at *Apollo's* Sizes?
> But ah, how they'd out face a Damsel civil:
> Who've impudence enough to out face the Devil:
> Besides, shou'd they be cast by prosecution,

> 'Tis now too late to think of restitution;
> And faith, I hear, that some do shrewdly opine
> They trade with other Muses than the nine.
>   I name no names, but you may easily guess,
> They that can cheat the Devil can cheat the Flesh.
> Therefore to you kind Sirs, as to the Laws
> Of Justice she submits her self and Cause,
> For to whom else shou'd a wrong'd Poet sue,
> There's no appeal to any Court but you.[28]

Powell's disregard for the female playwrights was evidently not shared by the male writers at Lincoln's Inn Fields. The published edition of *The Deceiver Deceived* also contains 'A dialogue in the fourth Act, between Mr. Bowman and Mrs Bracegirdle: The words by Mr. Durfey and set by Mr Eccles' and another in the fifth act 'Written by Mr. Motteux; set to Musick by Mr Eccles'. The sixteen-strong cast includes all the leading actors in the Players' Company, with Barry and Bracegirdle once again playing the leading female protagonists.

Set in Venice, this rather predictable love and marriage comedy is not one of Pix's best plays and was not particularly successful, although it was retitled and produced again in 1699 as *The French Beau*.[29] Pix takes the familiar plot of the young wife, Olivia, married to the old and miserly husband, Bondi, but provides what must have been a visually entertaining twist to the inevitable adultery plot. Bondi has feigned blindness in order to avoid the expenses of an election campaign for public office. Believing her husband to be blind, Olivia allows a former lover to openly court her and of course her husband, who actually sees everything, is caught in the trap of his own deceit. Powell's version of the plot takes the wife and her lover into the bedchamber where they are inevitably caught by the husband. Pix's lovers come tantalisingly close to committing the final act of adultery but Olivia eventually chooses the path of virtue and fidelity. Powell bragged that his play pleased the audience more, having a longer run of five days, and attempted to dismiss the whole affair as female jealousy, but Pix continued to defend her position by launching a further attack against Powell in the published edition dedicated to Sir Robert Marsham:

> I look upon those that endeavour'd to discountenance this Play as Enemys to me, not that, and had the Play been never so good they wou'd have shew'd their Teeth: Yet sure, if you be so Noble to protect it, their good manners (that is, if they understand any) tho their spite remains will make em cease to Cavil at the Work, when such a worthy name

Adorns the Frontpiece. I must not trouble you with the little Malice of my Foe, nor is his Name fit to be mentioned in a Paper addrest to Sir *Robert Marsham*, he has Printed so great a falsehood, it deserves no Answer; yet give me leave without being thought Impertinent or Prolox, to say I now am pleased and treated by those who please every Spectator with a Candour and Sweetness not to be exprest.[30]

Pix is explicitly issuing a warning to her traducers here. Not only does she have powerful and influential patrons but she has also the creative support of those 'who please every spectator'; the actress/managers at Lincoln's Inn Fields.

Public identity and publicity

Barry and Bracegirdle were enjoying particular popularity in this season, reflected in an unusual decision to include their likeness in a royal painting.[31] Early in 1698 the court painter, Sir Godfrey Kneller, began work on a portrait of King William which depicts the triumphant sovereign astride his horse.[32] In the right-hand foreground of the portrait are two emblematic figures of Britannia and Flora. Lucyle Hook was the first to suggest that the models for these two figures are none other than the two leading actresses of the day, Barry and Bracegirdle.[33] Working from a footnote in Horace Walpole's *Aedes Walpolianae* (1743) which reads: 'Mrs Barry and another Actress sat for the two Emblematic Figures, on the foreground, in the great Picture',[34] she quickly identifies the unnamed actress as Bracegirdle.[35] Elizabeth Howe is among several theatre historians to accept Hook's evidence and the potential importance of 'a painting from life of the two greatest actresses of the period at the height of their careers by the greatest artist of the time'.[36] What is more important, however, is that these two actresses should be recognisably present in a piece of overt royal propaganda at all.

Hook's account suggests that Kneller deliberately draws attention to the theatrical provenance of his models.

> In the Hampton Court picture, Mrs Barry is playing the theatrical role of Britannia. Kneller makes special use of her as the greatest actress of the time, placing her in a kneeling position reminiscent of many of her great tragic roles. He shows the intense expression of her eyes as she gazes in awe at the king; he has not defined her mouth clearly because he wishes the lips to give the impression of movement.[37]

Standing in front of the portrait, recently rehung in William's throne room at Hampton Court, there is a theatrical energy in the painting, created largely by the spatial relationship between the three figures. William sits astride his horse looking directly at the viewer, Barry is, as Hook notes, looking directly at the King but her kneeling position and the expression in her eyes suggest a beseeching, pleading look, reinforced by the fact that her half outstretched right hand is holding a sprig of herbs – possibly myrtle as a sign of peace. In some ways Bracegirdle seems separate from this scene; her gaze is directed between and beyond the other two figures, although she has a white rose in her right hand as if to strew the King's path with blooms. It is a very 'staged' scene with Bracegirdle as Flora representing the more ethereal figure as her hair and shoulder wrap are caught in the movement of air. Barry is downstage of her and, in contrast, clearly connected with the ground. Kneller has used earthier colours for her dress and the horn filled with fruit and grain follows the left-hand line of her body. It is certainly surprising to find the image of an actress being used to personify the passion of a country for her King. Even more so when she is flanked by another actress representing the personification of the nation's poetic flowering. The general feeling of the painting and the position of the female figures is clearly intended to invoke admiration rather then possession in the eye of the viewer who was, at the time, intended to be a male member of William's court.

The question remains as to why Kneller chose to include the actresses in this royal commission. Was he influenced by those who had a particular interest in the prosperity of the theatres or was it his intention to remind the Late Stuart monarchy of the importance of the links between court and playhouse? Dramatic discourse could play a part in winning the hearts and minds of the audience, much as television does today, or maybe Kneller was as enamoured of the Barry/Bracegirdle partnership as the rest of the theatre-going audience. As Hook notes: 'the fact that the models for the emblematic figures were the leading actresses of the day must have been common knowledge and of some interest to the limited Court circle that was admitted to the audience chamber at Hampton Court.'[38] Barry and Bracegirdle's recognisable presence in this portrait works to reinforce the complex socio-political relationship between the aristocratic court and their royal servants in the playhouse; a relationship that has always excluded the middle ranks. The theatrical reforms of the eighteenth and nineteenth centuries begin to take shape in the closing years of the seventeenth century as the growing political voices of the middle ranks sought to influence cultural discourse via moves to reform, or even silence, the activities of the playhouse. From this perspective, Collier's opening attack might be seen as establishing some of the ground for an ongoing and heated moral debate.

Negotiating with reform

The publication of Collier's *Short View* triggered a stream of published responses that, fuelled by the growing influence of the Societies for the Reformation of Manners, would continue uninterrupted for nearly seven years. Eleven new anti-theatrical attacks and, in response, some eight vindications of the stage were published between 1698 and 1705.[39] Just two months after the publication of Collier's *Short View*, Catherine Trotter joined in with the debate. Her tragedy *The Fatal Friendship* was premiered at Lincoln's Inn Fields in May 1698 and, as Kendall observes, 'it would seem that Catherine Trotter wrote the dedication of *The Fatal Friendship* with a copy of the *Short View* at her side'.[40] Trotter was evidently keenly aware of the dangers of being caught in the cross-fire of the debate and skilfully negotiates the contesting discourses by including references to both sides in the published edition of her play.

Trotter begins by openly acknowledging that as a writing woman she will be criticised but there is something of a triumphant tone in this dedication as she claims the influential protection of another woman, the heir to the throne, Princess Anne:

> when a Woman appears in the World under any distinguishing Character, she must expect to be the mark of ill Nature, but most one who seems desirous to recommend her self by what the other Sex think their peculiar Prerogative. This, Madam, makes me fly to the Protection of so great a Princess, though I am sensible so high an Honour must raise me many more Enemies. Making me indeed worthy of Envy, which I am but too well secur'd from in my self (though an undertaking so few of my Sex, have ventur'd at, may draw some Malice on me) but 'tis my happiness that the thing which will most reasonably make me the object of their Enmity, will be my safety against the effects of it. What insolence dare injure one they find in your Royal Presence, and under your illustrious Patronage?[41]

There is a feeling that Trotter was not wholly convinced that Anne's patronage *was* enough to protect her from her enemies, for her dedication is immediately followed by no fewer than four commendatory poems. One set of verses clearly places her alongside her male contemporaries in the forefront of the bid to save the stage.

> Tis thus you may support the sinking Stage,
> Thus learn the Scriblers that infect this Age;
> To Mourn how Nature stinted their poor lot
> And leave for humbler arts their Plays and Plot:
> Let Congreve, Granvile, and the few who yet,
> Support the credit of our Poets Wit;
> With you the Empire of the Stage maintain,
> Nor suffer Fools so oft t'usurp your reign;
> Then perfect Plays would perfect joys inspire,
> Touch to the Soul, and waken dead desire:
> Deny each chatt'ring Ape his fancy'd part,
> And teach us to revere your Sacred Art.[42]

Although the writer supports the activity of the playhouse, she leans more heavily on the arm of literary genius by reinforcing the female playwright's literary credentials and identifying Trotter as the inheritor of the female poetic tradition established by Katherine Phillips and Aphra Behn:

> The fam'd Orinda's, and Astrea's Lays
> With never dying Wit, bles'd Charles's Days,
> And we suppos'd Wit cou'd no higher rise,
> Till you succeeding, Tear from them the Prize,
> More Just Applause is yours who check the Rage,
> Of Reigning Vice, that has debauch'd the Stage,
> And dare shew Vertue in a vicious Age:[43]

Trotter and her publisher evidently considered the mood of the time precarious enough to warrant the inclusion of these heavily defensive verses in the published edition of her play.

Fidelis Morgan considers *The Fatal Friendship* to be 'a tragedy of situation rather than character' and suggests that, in contrast to the many ranting tragedies of the same period, 'like the language of her play, Catherine Trotter's characters are notable for their restraint'.[44] Thomas Betterton played the hero, Gramont, and Kynaston was brought in to play his rich and overbearing father, Count Roquelaure. Both father and son are in love with the same woman, Felicia, played by Anne Bracegirdle. The fact that Felicia and Gramont have secretly married and had a son, who has conveniently been kidnapped by pirates, provides one of the central plot devices in the play. While Felicia's brother encourages her to marry the Count, the Count insists that Gramont should marry Lamira, a wealthy and passionate widow, played by Elizabeth Barry. Gramont is also bound to his friend Castalio who has been wrongfully imprisoned and nurses a secret passion for Lamira. The play splits the dramatic focus between the beleagured hero, Gramont, and his fatal friendship with Castalio (Gramont accidentally kills Castalio and then finally kills himself) and the relationship between Lamira and Felicia who are forced into enmity by the actions and desires of the men around them. The scenes between the two women – once friends and now rivals – are among the best in the play. Once again they are tailor-made for the Barry/Bracegirdle partnership.

Trotter explores the corrupting influence of money, the conflict between duty/obedience and love, and forgiveness and revenge. The central theme concerns the way that circumstance and the actions of others can provoke both men and women to act against their true nature. Even the vengeful Lamira is seen to be fundamentally 'good' by the end of the play, leading some modern critics to question the effectiveness of a tragedy in which 'all the dramatis personae have to be basically good at heart, which leaves no possibility for dramatic conflict, unless it be based on chance, fate or character inconsistency – all of which are employed to excess'.[45] What this and other critics miss is the strong moral message running throughout the play and which Trotter spells out in the final speech:

> ... [Gramont] was by *nature* honest, just, and brave,
> In many trials showed a steady virtue,
> Yet by one sharp assault at last was vanquished.
> None know their strength; *let the most resolute*
> *Learn from this story to distrust themselves,*
> Nor think by fear the victory is less sure,
> *Our greatest danger's when we're most secure.*[46]
>
> (my emphasis)

This strongly Reformist message, embodied in a play with plenty of dramatic tension, was a box-office success. Even those in the audience who were sympathetic to Collier must have found plenty of material that fulfilled his prescription that 'The Business of *Plays* is to recommend Vertue and discountenance Vice; to Shew the Uncertainty of human Greatness, the suddain Turns of Fate, and the Unhappy conclusions of Violence and Injustice.'[47] The themes certainly anticipate the preference for domestic drama which dominated the next century and which, to some extent, the female playwrights established. via their representation of a female perspective. It would be quite incorrect, however, to assume that female playwrights limited their work to representations of the micro-political sphere of the domestic family household.[48]

The personal is political

In the following month Elizabeth Barry played the title role in another tragedy, *Queen Catherine: or, The Ruines of Love,* written by Mary Pix. This was a bold attempt at a tragedy for several reasons, not least that, as Clark points out,[49] the play is set in the historical gap between Shakespeare's *Henry VI* (part III) and *Richard III*. The Shakespeare connection was exploited in the prologue, spoken by Thomas Betterton, himself a keen 'borrower' and adapter of Shakespeare's plays. This move obviously seems very risky to a twentieth-century critic, swayed by Shakespeare's iconic status, in a way that the late-seventeenth-century writer clearly was not, but this is not to say that the move was any less bold.

> Shakespear did oft his Countries worthies chuse
> Nor did they by his Pen their Lustre lose.
> Hero's revive thro' him, and Hotspur's rage,
> Doubly adorns and animates the Stage:
> But how shall Woman after him succeed,
> And what excuse can her presumption plead.
> Who with enervate voice dares wake the mighty dead;
> To please your martial men she must despair,
> And therefore Courts the favour of the fair:
> From huffing Hero's she hopes no relief,
> But trusts in Catherine's Love and Isabella's grief.[50]

The historical specificity of the subject and the Shakespeare connection reinforce Lincoln's Inn Field's claim to the higher moral ground of legitimate theatre. Who else could play the Queen of that dramatic realm but Barry, with Bracegirdle as her loving friend and ward, Isabella? The prologue reinforces the collaborative strength of theatre women who not only lay claim to the theatrical legacy of earlier playwrights but also shift the focus of the dramatic action to centre on women. Although the central theme is concerned with domestic love, it is woven into the macro-politics of great historical events in English history. The plot turns on Edward IV's love for Henry V's widow, Catherine. As she is in love with Owen Tudor, Edward's passion soon turns to revenge but Catherine is a strong and noble Queen whose first entrance is set up by Edward's description of her as a 'Warlike Queen, / Who wields her self the sword'. Edward tricks the innocent Isabella and gains entry to the castle in order to dispose of his rival Owen Tudor. In a secondary plot, Isabella is torn between loyalty to her Queen and the desires of her heart. To avoid consummating a forced marriage to a man she does not love,

Isabella eventually runs on to his sword and dies. Racked by sorrow for both Owen Tudor and Isabella, Catherine gives in to the madness of grief but soon recovers herself in order to fulfil her duty: to protect her family and work toward peace in her country.

The play was moderately successful, running for four nights. Pix and the Barry/Bracegirdle partnership present the image of strong female leadership and, as Kendall puts it, 'it is women, the play suggests, who keep the world on its axis. Without the calm, sensitive, guiding hand of women, the kingdom would fall into chaos.'[51] Pix dedicated the published edition of the play to 'The honourable Mrs Cook of Norfolk'. Perhaps she, like everyone else, was keenly aware that the next monarch on the English throne would be a woman, and a play about the nobility and virtue of an earlier queen was a fairly astute commercial move. Catherine Trotter added her weight to the play by writing the verse epilogue: a playful piece delivered by a very young protégée of Elizabeth Barry's, 'Miss Porter'.[52]

> What Epilogues are made, for who can tell,
> 'Twere worth the pains to write and speak 'em well.
> If they cou'd gain your favour for bad Plays,
> But by their merit you'll condemn or praise:
> 'Tis but a form, no matter then by whom,
> Or what is said, and therefore I am come
> ...
> Methinks I'm now grown tender of its fate
> Who knows but I may come to act Queen Kate.[53]

Although the young speaker claims to have no interest in the task of pleading for the play, it is clear by the closing lines that her interest is sharpened by the prospect of, one day, playing the leading role and, by implication, following in the footsteps of Elizabeth Barry. The strong sense of celebrating an established female tradition, in both the country and the playhouse, is hard to avoid.

Notes

1. Milhous and Hume, *A Register of English Theatrical Documents*, vol. 1, p. 324, cite the source for this document as LC 5/152, p. 19, noting that the order was reported in *The Post Man* 3–5 June 1697.
2. Jeremy Collier, *A Short View of the Immorality and Profaneness of the English Stage* (1698), reproduced from a copy in Cambridge University Library (Menston: Scolar Press, 1971).
3. Milhous, *Thomas Betterton*, p. 112.

4 Narcius Luttrell, 'The N. Lutterell Collection', 5 vols. of collected printed matter dating between 1659 and 1730. A facsimile held by the British Library from the original held by the Newberry Library, Chicago, vol. 4, p. 378.
5 Jean I. Marsden, 'Female Spectatorship, Jeremy Collier and the Anti-theatrical Debate', p. 884.
6 The London Stage list of new plays is, of course, partial as much of the evidence relies upon the publication date of the play and not all new plays were published. In the first full season of competition, running from September 1695 to July 1696, eleven new plays are recorded at Lincoln's Inn Fields, thirteen at Drury Lane and two at Dorset Gardens (then under Patent Company control). The figure drops in the following season, September 1696 to July 1697, with seven new plays at Lincoln's Inn Fields, eight at Drury Lane and two at Dorset Gardens. Lincoln's Inn Fields produces eight new plays between September 1697 and July 1698, four of which are by female playwrights. The Patent Company produces seven new works at Drury Lane and appears to produce only a few revivals at Dorset Gardens.
7 Sister Rose Anthony, *The Jeremy Collier Stage Controversy 1698–1726* (New York: Benjamin Blom, 1937), p. 28. This relatively early work remains one of the most thorough examinations of the anti-theatrical debates at the turn of the eighteenth century, prompting the publisher to reissue the book in 1966.
8 See Bratton, 'Reading the Intertheatrical' and *New Readings*, for more on the appropriation of the dramatic text and the implications of this move on the history of theatre women.
9 Bratton, *New Readings*, p. 88.
10 William Congreve, *Amendments of Mr Collier's False and Imperfect Citations etc.* (London: J. Tonson, 1698), p. 4.
11 p. 8.
12 p. 13.
13 p. 81.
14 pp. 102–103.
15 *Animadversions on Mr. Congreve's Late Answer to Mr. Collier* (London: John Nutt, 1698), Preface.
16 Mary Pix's *Queen Catherine* was performed in June 1698, one month before this attack was published.
17 *Animadversions*, Dedicatory Epistle.
18 pp. 78–79.
19 pp. 80–81. This is yet another example of a primary source in which 'Actresses' are identified prior to the date of 1700, usually accepted as the moment at which the term was in full use. The context of this usage reinforces the strength with which the actress/whore trope was recognised and the blurring between the on- and off-stage identity of the woman who was an actress.
20 See Chapter 2 for more on Gould's manuscript *The Play-House, A Satyr* (c. 1685). This satire was printed with new additions in *The Works of Mr Robert*

Gould (London: W. Lewis, 170), vol. II, 'Advertisement', in which Gould records his surprise when Elizabeth Barry refuses to produce his new play at Lincoln's Inn Fields: 'All that this could obtain from the Mighty Actress was plainly to tell me, She was not so good a Christian as to forgive; and indeed, I really and readily believ'd Her: For as I had not myself, so I never heard of any other Person that Accus'd Her of Vertue.'

21 John Vanbrugh, *The Provok'd Wife* (London: Richard Wellington & Bernard Lintott, 1698), Epilogue.

22 Vanbrugh's decision to give his benefit to the Players' Company appears unusual at a time when many playwrights wrote to earn a living. It reveals, however, the emerging conflict between the aristocratic writer (writing for the love of his art) and the professional writer (writing to earn a living). Toward the end of the century many professional writers, including Congreve and, to some extent, Trotter, appear to have struggled with the growing gulf between the identity attached to the professional writer and the literary poetic genius. Vanbrugh may have preferred to be associated with the former rather than the literary hacks and 'scribblers' (like Robert Gould) competing to have their plays performed.

23 Margarete Rubik, *Early Women Dramatists*, p. 87.

24 Ibid.

25 Constance Clark, *Three Augustan Women Playwrights*, pp. 20–21. Clark cites Allardyce Nicoll, *A History of Restoration Drama, 1660–1700* (Cambridge: Cambridge University Press, 1923), p. 161.

26 George Powell, *Imposture Defeated: or, A Trick to Cheat the Devil*, London: R. Wellington, 1698, Preface.

27 *Animadversions on Mr Congreve's Late Answer to Mr Collier*, p. 34. Clark, *Three Augustan Women Playwrights*, pp. 204–206, also gives a full account of this event and is content to agree with the traditional assumption that Congreve was Pix's mentor and chief defender in this case, going on to suggest that the detail included in the account points to George Powell as its anonymous author. In the light of the author's vehement dislike for theatre personnel I would rather suggest that the case for Robert Gould as the author is more convincing.

28 Mary Pix, *The Deceiver Deceived* (London: R. Basset, 1698), Prologue.

29 The *London Stage*, Part 1, p. 503 includes this entry and cites G. Thorn-Drury, 'An Unrecorded Play-title', *Review of English Studies*, 6 (1930), p. 316, as the source.

30 Pix, *The Deceiver Deceived*, Dedicatory Epistle.

31 Nell Gwynn was probably the most painted actress of the period but many of her portraits were clearly intended for the private chambers of Charles II. Paintings of Barry are rare and those of Bracegirdle usually portray her in dramatic roles.

32 The large portrait (18 x 15 ft) which celebrates William's victorious return to England after the Peace of Ryswick (November 1697) was commissioned to

hang in William's presence room in the King's apartment at Hampton Court on the large end wall facing the throne is where it is hung today.

33 Lucyle Hook, 'Portraits of Elizabeth Barry and Anne Bracegirdle', *Theatre Notebook*, 15 (1960), pp. 129–137. Hook makes an interesting discovery of the original single portrait of Elizabeth Barry made by Kneller in preparation for his larger work, which was then copied by Harding in 1792 (long after Barry's death) and handed over to an engraver (Knight). This rather crude third generation of the original inevitably distorts the image, almost to caricature, and yet continues to be used as a representation of her likeness. Hook's findings successfully explain the contradiction between the coarse image represented in the much-used Harding/Knight engraving and the descriptions of Barry as one of the most beautiful and fascinating women of her day.

34 p. 130. The actresses may well have 'sat' for the painting in the way Walpole suggests but it is equally possible that Kneller worked from other pictorial sources depicting the actresses in character. The painting is generally regarded as an idealised image of the King, who was not the six-foot Adonis that this portrait suggests, and it may be that the two women were represented in similar vein.

35 Following her retirement from the stage in 1707 Bracegirdle appears to have avoided any public mention of her name in print until after her death in 1748. Using other portraits, both visual and textual, Hook, 'Portraits of Elizabeth Barry and Anne Bracegirdle' pp. 131–132, demonstrates that Flora is indeed a likeness of Bracegirdle and makes a convincing argument for the fact that it is highly unlikely that any other actress would be paired with Barry at this point in theatre history.

36 p. 132. Howe includes this portrait in her discussion of the Barry/Bracegirdle partnership in *The First English Actresses*, pp. 156–162, fig.12. The portrait is also cited in the entries for Barry and Bracegirdle in the *Oxford Dictionary of National Biography* (2004).

37 p. 136. It is possible that Kneller saw Barry as Boadicea in Charles Hopkins's *Boadicea Queen of Britain* which was performed at Lincoln's Inn Fields in November 1697 and that the pose represented in the portrait reflects something of this specific performance. John Downes, *Roscius*, notes that ''twas a well Writ Play ... it was lik'd and got the Company Money' p. 44.

38 Hook, 'Portraits of Elizabeth Barry', p. 135.

39 See Anthony, *The Jeremy Collier Stage Controversy*, pp. 296–297, for a chart of all the published exchanges around the anti-theatrical debate between 1698 and 1726.

40 Kendall, 'Theatre, Society, and Women Playwrights', p. 83.

41 Catherine Trotter, *The Fatal Friendship* (London: Francis Saunders, 1698), Dedicatory Epistle.

42 Commendatory Verse, signed P. Harmon.

43 According to Clark, *Three Augustan Women Playwrights*, p. 78, these anonymous verses are now attributed to Lady Sarah Piers, Trotter's friend and

patroness who, with Manley, Pix, Trotter, Centlivre and others, also contributed verses to *The Nine Muses; or Poems Written by Nine Severall Ladies upon the Death of the late famous John Dryden, Esq.* (London: Richard Basset, 1700).

44 Morgan, *The Female Wits*, p. 145.
45 Rubik, *Early Women Dramatists*, p. 68.
46 Trotter, *The Fatal Friendship*, Act V, p. 56.
47 Collier, *A Short View*, Introduction, p. 1.
48 The representation of a female perspective has led to the general assumption that women can write only 'small' domestic plays – an assumption that continues in modern criticism. While female playwrights undoubtedly offer insights into the 'nuclear' domestic unit, it is evidently incorrect to suggest that their writing fails to address larger political issues, as Pix's next play demonstrates.
49 Clark, *Three Augustan Women*, p. 264.
50 Mary Pix, *Queen Catherine: or, The Ruines of Love* (London: Wiliam Turner and Richard Basset, 1698), Prologue.
51 Kendall, 'Theatre, Society, and Women Playwrights', p. 276.
52 Highfill, ed., *A Biographical Dictionary*, vol. 12, pp. 91–96, includes a detailed and lengthy biography for Mary Porter based largely upon information included in Betterton's *The History of the English Stage* (1741). What is clear is that Elizabeth Barry was Porter's mentor, taking a particularly active part in the development of her craft. On the older actress's retirement Mary Porter took over many of her leading tragic roles.
53 Pix, *Queen Catherine*, Epilogue.

7
Old stories, new histories

The personal and professional confidence which marks the work of the actress/managers and female playwrights in the closing years of the seventeenth century becomes increasingly strained as the company moves into the eighteenth century. Competition between the two houses led to the importation of expensive theatrical attractions from abroad, which drained the financial resources of Lincoln's Inn Fields, and once again the formation of a new united company was under serious discussion. Both houses faced growing pressure from the anti-theatrical lobby, which was attracting increasing support from the judiciary and, on her succession in 1702, the approval of the last Stuart monarch, Queen Anne. Censorship of plays was applied with renewed vigour, and on the threshold of a new century the leading players found themselves faced with lawsuits for the use of profane and immoral language on the public stage. In a time which Judith Milhous identifies as 'the darkest period for the English theatre since the Commonwealth',[1] the entire theatrical community was fighting for survival.

Inevitably, the female theatre practitioners at Lincoln's Inn Fields faced an escalation of hostility toward them from forces both outside and inside the theatrical community. 'Petticoat Authors' were the object of derision and abuse in satires which reinforced the writer/actress/whore trope with new vigour.[2] Barry was, once again, reviled as a proud, mercenary whore while Bracegirdle's virtuous reputation was openly mocked in sexually graphic lampoons. More seriously, the actresses' managerial position within the company was undermined when moves were made to place Betterton in overall charge of the Players' Company. Shortly after, all three were accused of skimming company profits for themselves and failing to pay the rest of the company. In spite of the opposition ranged against them, the actress/managers resisted moves to curb their authority and, alongside the female playwrights, continued to negotiate their way through the treacherous waters of the anti-theatrical lobby. Ten new plays by female playwrights were produced between 1699 and 1705, including three by one of the most successful female playwrights of the eighteenth century, Susanna Centlivre, who will be discussed later in this chapter.

Pix and Congreve: history and hype

In May 1699 the Players' Company produced Mary Pix's tragedy *The False Friend: or, The Fate of Disobedience*. The villainess of this morally didactic melodrama was played by Elizabeth Bowman, with Barry and Bracegirdle paired as the two tragic heroines. The prologue, spoken by Mr Hudson, leaves the audience in little doubt that Pix was intent on allying herself with the cause of moral reform or, as Constance Clark puts it, 'Pix had obviously made the professional choice to join rather than to fight'.[3]

> Amongst Reformers of this Vitious Age,
> Who think it Duty to refine the Stage:
> A Woman, to Contribute, does Intend,
> In Hopes a Moral Play your Lives will Mend.[4]

The play itself is considered 'rather dull' by some critics even though it keeps up a frantic pace with murders, poisonings and grief-stricken madness.[5] In many ways Pix appears to follow the rather frenetic plot pattern found in *The Unnatural Mother* (1697) but fails to execute it with the same level of theatrical verve. One of the more intriguing aspects of this production is Barry's choice of the part of the tragic victim, Adellaida, rather than the outrageous villainess, Appamia, which is certainly the meatiest of the female roles. The chill winds of reform may have suggested the political expedience of playing the headstrong but essentially innocent victim rather than the flamboyant vengeful mistress role she was usually associated with.

In the following season the Players' Company ventured to produce two new contemporary comedies. The first was Congreve's *The Way of the World* which, although by no means a disaster, was received with less enthusiasm than was expected. In a letter to a friend, an evidently disappointed theatre goer, Lady Marow, entirely dismisses it: 'Congreve's new play doth not answer expectation, there being no plot in it but many witty things to ridicule the Chocolate House, and the fantastical part of the world.'[6] Downes's comments are barely more enthusiastic but much more intriguing: '*The Way of the World*, a Comedy wrote by Mr. Congreve, twas curiously Acted; Madam *Bracegirdle* performing her part so exactly and just, gain'd the Applause of Court and City; but being too Keen a Satyr, had not the success the Company Expected.'[7] In what way Downes considered it to have been 'curiously acted' is unclear, especially as he has nothing but praise for Bracegirdle's performance. What is clear is that this new play failed to meet the expectations of both the audience and the company who had enjoyed the profits from revivals of Congreve's earlier comedy, Love for Love, and his equally successful tragedy The Mourning Bride.

It seems fairly evident that The Way of The World suffered from what we would now refer to as being 'over-hyped'. Three months before the play was produced Vanbrugh had written to the Earl of Manchester bemoaning the poor state the Players' Company was in: 'Matters running very low with 'em this Winter; if Congreve's Play don't help 'em they are undone. 'tis a Comedy and will be play'd about Six weeks hence, nobody has seen it yet.'[8] For a play that 'nobody' had seen, the expectations were already remarkably high. Congreve's very public dispute with Collier and his ardent defence of both the theatre and his own work must also have contributed to the sense of anticipation surrounding his new play in both supporters and critics alike. Added to this was the gossip surrounding his relationship with Anne Bracegirdle, who, once again, created the leading female role in the witty heroine, Millament, and spoke the epilogue in which Congreve's own expectations for the play's reception are clearly expressed: 'After our Epilogue this crowd dismisses / I'm thinking how this Play'll be pulled to pieces.'[9] Congreve was right to anticipate the comparative failure of the play's first production but its subsequent meteoric rise in the dramatic and literary canon have served to overshadow another new comedy produced in the same month by the Players' Company.

Pix's The Beau Defeated: or, The Lucky Younger Brother is the third of her four comedies to be performed at Lincoln's Inn Fields between 1697 and 1703 and, once again, provides a vehicle for the company's two leading actresses. This is a well-crafted comedy with a keen satirical edge which appears to have attracted no attention from contemporary writers although it has been noted by some twentieth-century critics.[10] It is worth pausing to consider this play in some detail as the London setting and the concern with the preoccupations of contemporary society are presented from a wholly female perspective. This approach is not in itself new but Pix's representation of the *kinds* of women that populate London society has a biting edge that is more usually associated with her male contemporaries – especially Congreve. Pix cleverly constructs and exposes the socially aspirant city widow Mrs Rich, the fraudulent gamester Lady La Basset, her sycophantic gambling companion Mrs Trickwell and the dipsomaniac landlady Mrs Fidget in sharply observed and carefully constructed comic scenes. Her representation of positive female characters, of all classes, is equally effective and avoids the cloying virtue attached to her heroines in *The Innocent Mistress* (1697).

The main plot concerns the marital ambitions of two wealthy widows. The contrasts between the socially ambitious Mrs Rich, played by Elizabeth Barry, and the romantically ambitious Lady Landsworth, played by Anne Bracegirdle, could not be more marked. The play opens with a comic plot-setting scene which plunges the audience into the world of the absurd city widow, Mrs Rich, who is determined to marry a title and sever her ties with her late husband's family. Pix exposes the social chasm between the impoverished aristocracy of the town and the nouveaux riches of the city; the financial needs of the former and the social aspirations of the latter being the catalyst for the play's comic and dramatic action.

Mrs Rich: An Affront ... Ah! I die: An affront! ... I faint: I cannot speak. A Chair quickly.
Betty: (*Giving a Chair*) An affront! To you, Madam, an affront! Is it possible?
Mrs Rich: But too true, my poor Betty. Oh! I shall dye. To disrespect me in the open street! What Insolence!
Betty: How, Madam! Not to show respect to such a person as you? Madam Rich: the Widow of an honest Banker, who got Two Hundred Thousand Pounds in the King's service? Pray madam, who has been thus insolent?
Mrs Rich: A Dutchess; who had the confidence to thrust my Coach from the Wall, and make it run back above twenty yards.
Betty: A very impertinent Dutchess ...[11]

The actress playing the supporting, but pivotal, role of the servant Betty is not identified in the published edition. From the company rosters for this season it is reasonable to suggest that Mary Porter, Barry and Bracegirdle's protégée, had the skills to work as both comic feed to Barry's Mrs Rich and sympathetic ally to the virtuous Lady Landsworth/Bracegirdle. It is the astute Betty who questions the wisdom of Mrs Rich's determination to marry the penniless beau, Sir John Roverhead, and warns her mistress against the wiles of Lady La Basset and her sidekick, Mrs Trickwell – two inveterate gamblers who fleece Mrs Rich at every opportunity.

As Mrs Rich sweeps out, the second wealthy widow, Lady Landsworth, takes the stage – and also confides in the long-suffering servant, Betty. Having patiently endured a marriage to an aged husband, Lady Landsworth now enjoys the financial reward of his inheritance and is determined to create her own destiny by choosing a husband she loves.

She is a spirited woman who is quite prepared to 'invert the Order of nature, and pursue, tho' he flies', 'I have the freedom to make my own choice, and the whole World the Mart'.[12] Of course, Lady Landsworth does find such a man and, like Charlotte in 'Ariadne's' *She Ventures and He Wins*, uses disguise to test his true nature.

The issue of disguise is at the heart of this play. Pix explores the social anxieties surrounding who people *appear to be*, by their dress and manner, and who *they really are*. Using a series of clever plot turns and highly comic set-pieces, the play exposes the gullibility of Mrs Rich and her friends. Lady La Basset and Sir John Roverhead are exposed as imposters – he a servant and she a cast-off mistress – who have used their disguise to make money from gullible city widows. Mrs Rich's humiliation is further compounded by her discovery that she has been tricked into secretly marrying the country squire, the Elder Clerimont, having been persuaded by his cousin, Mrs Clerimont, that the appearance of his uncouth manners and broad country dialect are merely to disguise his true identity as a beau. But it is in the final moments of the play that the marked differences between the earlier comedies of the Restoration and this fine example of the Late Stuart stage are revealed. The Restoration playwrights, including Behn, would have not spared the object of their derision, Mrs Rich, in the way that Pix does here. The move toward the reform comedy is firmly established as the 'honourable' characters welcome the now chastened widow into their company. The closing speech, however, tips the scales toward the 'new' audience of the city in the final moralising message delivered by the widow's brother-in-law, the city gentleman, Mr Rich:

> you see how the near these pretenders to Quality had brought you to ruin: The truly Great are of a quite different character.
>
> > The Glory of the World our British Nobles are,
> > The Ladies too renowned, and Chaste and fair:
> > But to our Citizens, Augusta's Sons,
> > The conquering Wealth of both the India's runs;
> > Tho' less in Name, of greater Power by far,
> > Honours alone, but empty 'Scutcheons are;
> > Mixt with their Coin, the Title sweetly sounds,
> > No such Allay as Twenty Thousand Pounds.[13]

Pix handles the social politics in such a way that both the city and town are presented in a favourable light. This overt admission of the economic relationship between the two groups celebrates the shift in social relations and virtually advertises the benefits to both social groups.

Pix did not put her name to the published edition of this or her subsequent comedy and the prologue makes several references to a male author.[14] Clark offers various speculative explanations for, as she puts it, 'an established author using such a screen at this point', including the possibility that Pix was responding to 'pressure from the management or players for fear of losing business on account of a play advertised as by a woman'.[15] But Pix appears to have no problem with attaching her name to the tragedies performed by the Players' Company in the following season. Most of Jeremy Collier's examples of immorality in the playhouse come from comedy; a point that Pix is unlikely to have overlooked, particularly as her play followed Congreve's, who was already deeply entrenched in a running battle with the reformers. The players were also increasingly vulnerable as moral objections extended beyond the writing to the *playing* of comedy which, by its realistic performance style, reinforces the sense of verisimilitude and contains a greater potential for socio-political disruption. In this kind of political atmosphere the male playwright could rely, to some extent, on his place in the patriarchal hegemony as a basic line of defence, whereas the female playwright could only resort to the screen of anonymity and the presumed 'natural' identity of the male author. The work of occlusion was gaining ground and that returns the argument to the question of why Congreve's plays are canonised, while Pix is all but forgotten.

The problem of 'remembering'

Breaking through the layers of theatre history that have privileged, in this case, Congreve over Pix brings us back to the importance of intertheatricality and the ways in which it has been used to reinforce the dominant stories of success in theatre history. The almost constant revival of Congreve's plays, especially in the twentieth century, depends upon intertheatricality for its success. The accretion of past performances, places of performance and audience reception generates a raft of meanings that give weight to each new revival of the play. The fact that *The Way of the World* did not do very well at the box-office in 1700 has no bearing on the potential success of a revival in modern theatre. The decision to produce the play now depends more on its familiarity as part of the current theatrical repertoire; a familiarity increasingly driven by the playwright's inclusion in the school curriculum and national examination system. The measure against which Pix's play would be judged has been laid down in the canonisation of Congreve against whom Pix and her work would be judged. It is this act of comparison that Susan Bennett identifies as most damaging in the composition of traditional theatre history and from which she argues for a 'decomposing' strategy that goes beyond 'elasticizing our existing histories' and demands that we pay more attention to 'how we forget' and 'what composition of theatre history will have us, fully and appropriately, remember'.[16]

The power of occlusion, then, goes beyond the immediate exclusion of Pix's play from the literary dramatic canon; after all, feminist revision recovered the text some time ago. But that work, albeit of great importance, cannot bridge the chasm of historical exclusion and see such work returned to the place it was created for – the repertoire of the playhouse. Even if *The Beau Defeated* were to be revived at the Royal National Theatre today, its absence from performance history would inevitably invite unfavourable comparison with Congreve's very present works. We cannot undo the history we have. We cannot create a history of performance and reception for Pix's play in the nineteenth and twentieth centuries – they did not exist. But we can, as Bennett puts it, 'look to [theatre history's] very architecture in order to effect change'.[17] Pix and Congreve were contemporaries, both writing for the same company and both creating notable female characters in collaboration with London's two leading actresses, Barry and Bracegirdle. In order to understand more fully the ways in which the work of these theatre women has been forgotten and the concomitant pursuit of a history posited on notions of male genius established, the foundations blocks of that architecture need to be exposed. The occlusion of theatre women is part of an ongoing agenda in the eighteenth century that sought to bring the playhouse and its personnel under the control of political hegemonic interests. The Licensing Act of 1737, the ultimate tool of appropriation and control of theatre, was some way off but the process which brought that into being had been under way for some time.

Control and controversy

At the turn of the new century the activities of the playhouse were under renewed scrutiny by external authorities. In November 1700 a newly appointed Lord Chamberlain, Lord Jersey, ordered that Betterton was to be given 'sole management' of the Players' Company, 'with power to reward those who are diligent, and to punish such as he finds negligent in their business'.[18] Even Milhous acknowledges that the move was 'most unusual' but her desire to demonstrate that Betterton cannot be blamed for the eventual demise of the Players' Company, as his powers were limited to 'insist[ing] on discipline, not overall direction and control of the sort he had once exercised over the Duke's and United companies',[19] leads her to ignore the wider implications of this attempt to influence the day-to-day management structure of the company – and its audience. Female spectators were also subjected to new edicts as, in the same month, the Lord Chamberlain issued an order forbidding women to wear masks in the playhouse.[20] Following a fight at Drury Lane in December, a presentment from the Grand Jury of Middlesex accused both houses of 'debauching and ruining of the Youth', causing frequent breaches of the peace and being 'full of prophane, irreverant, Lewd, indecent and immoral expressions, and tend to the great displeasure of Almighty God'.[21] More seriously, for the players at least, John Verbruggen was the first of several actors and actresses to be tried for 'using prophanely and jestingly the name of God upon the stage'.[22]

Joseph Krutch gives a detailed account of a number of cases brought against players from December 1700 onwards.[23] Initially at least, these appear largely to involve players from the Lincoln's Inn Fields company. All the leading players are mentioned in the indictments, including Barry and Bracegirdle. According to Krutch, the players avoided action against them only by securing a series of delays, finally launching a successful appeal on the grounds that if a play was passed by the Master of Revels, however many years earlier, the players assumed it fit to be acted. Of more immediate concern to the entire theatrical community was that spies for the reform lobby were evidently reporting on specific players and playwrights, creating an atmosphere of suspicion parodied in *A Comparison Between Two Stages*. Written anonymously and published in 1702, this satirical piece was set out in the form of a dialogue between 'Ramble' and 'Sullen', two gentlemen, and 'Chagrin', a cynical critic of the day.

Sull: But did you hear the News
Ramb: What News?
Sull: The Trial between the Play-Houses and Informers, for Prophane, Immoral, Lewd, Scandalous, and I don't know how many sad things utter'd and spoken on the Stage.
Chag: Who were the Persons that spoke 'em, and what were the words?
Sull: Batterton, Bracegirdle, Ben. Johnson, and others; but the words may not be repeated: Are you so cunning? For ought I know, Critick, you're a Spy; they are fly Rogues, they say, and lurk in all Companies for matter of Accusation, that a Man is not safe, tho' he be with the Minister of the Parish

Ramb: Why, thou scandalous Rascal! Dost thou take us for Reformers and Trepans?
Sull: Nay, I don't accuse you of being any way reform'd; but they say, they have made it criminal to repeat the words; is not that strange?
Chag: Ay by my Faith is't; in time they'l make it dangerous to ask What's a clock, lest it be interpreted, that at such an Hour a Man has an Appointment with a Mistress.[24]

The humour barely conceals the anxiety about censorship and its implications on private, as well as public morals. With this level of tension and suspicion about and leading players facing prosecution, it is little wonder that the Players' Company was demoralised.

Pix's new tragedy *The Double Distress* was performed in March 1701 and, as the prologue suggests, the company was seriously beginning to question its own future.

> Well, we've shew'n all we can to make you easie,
> Tumblers and Monkeys, on the stage to please you:
> If all won't do we must to Treat incline
> And women, rather then be starv'd, will join.
> 'Tis quickly done, the Racket Walls remain,
> Give us but only time to shift the Scene,
> And Presto, we're in a Tennis Court again.[25]

This prologue suggests that some theatre women, however reluctantly, were pragmatic about the choices before them. At some point over that winter Betterton entered into discussions with the patent house concerning the possibility of creating a new united company. Trotter's prologue to *The Unhappy Penitent*, performed at Drury Lane in February 1701, demonstrates that a new theatrical union was a subject under public discussion and indicates that theatre women were even advocating such a move:

> But now the peaceful Tattle of the Town,
> Is how to join both Houses into one,
> And whilst the blustering hot-brain'd Heroes fight,
> Our softer Sex pleads gently to unite.[26]

It may have suited Trotter to see the two companies unite but there were few reasons for Barry and Bracegirdle to advocate a return to the patent house. It would be speculative to suggest that the actress/managers actively obstructed negotiations with the patent house but, as Milhous puts it, 'for whatever reason, the possibility of a new union came to naught'.[27]

New playwrights, new plays and old gossip

In the season of 1701/2 the Players' Company appears to have produced only four new plays, the lowest number since their formation in 1695. Milhous notes that 'Lincoln's Inn Fields rather oddly concentrated on tragedy in its new productions',[28] a strategy which may well have been intended to minimise the censure of the anti-theatrical lobby by avoiding the obvious 'low' associations of comedy. The first tragedy of the season was *Antiochus the Great: or, The Fatal Relapse*, by Jane Wiseman, in which Elizabeth Barry played the leading female role. This is Wiseman's only play to be performed and, therefore, assumed to be the only play she wrote. Little is known about this new female playwright who is said to have been a servant to a Mr Wright of Oxon and, according to Baker, 'having much leisure time, she employed it in reading plays and novels'.[29] Following an evidently profitable third night, Wiseman married a vintner, bought an inn and retired to Westminster. Although Wiseman's play did well enough for the playwright, the company was still struggling. The death of King William in March 1702 created more difficulties as both houses were ordered to close until after the coronation of Queen Anne on 23 April. *The London Stage* includes an extract from a letter written by Sir John Perceval, dated 11 March 1702, in which he acknowledges the financial hardship endured by the players following the cessation of business at the height of the season: 'none will suffer by the King's death but the poor players, who are ready to starve ... none will trust them for a pot of ale'.[30]

The presence of a female monarch seems to have done little to relieve the opposition faced by the female theatre practitioners in the closing years of the Lincoln's Inn Fields' company. Kendall argues that 'during the time of Anne outright misogyny was tantamount to treason'[31] but the rise in direct personal attacks against theatre women proves that this was far from the case. In the same year that Anne succeeded to the throne, Thomas Brown published *Letters From the Living to the Dead* which includes a fictional exchange between the deceased female playwright, Aphra Behn, and Anne Bracegirdle, mischievously entitled "From Worthy Mrs Behn the Poetess, to the famous Virgin Actress":

> I am sensible 'tis as hard a matter for a pretty Woman to keep her self Honest in a Theatre, as 'tis for an Apothecary to keep his Treacle from the Flies in hot Weather; for every Libertine in the Audience will be buzzing about her Honey-pot, and her Vertue must defend it self by Abundance of Fly-flaps, or those Flesh-loving Insects will soon blow

upon her Honour, and when once she had a Maggot in her Tail, all the Pepper and Salt in the Kingdom will scarce keep her Reputation from stinking.[32]

Although the opening lines of this extract have been included in several histories of seventeenth-century theatre, there has been no consideration of the shift in attitudes toward Bracegirdle. Anne Bracegirdle's 'virtuous' public identity at the beginning of her career appears to have lost its appeal and here, in a move that is still popular with modern tabloids and fanzines, Bracegirdle's personal reputation is being publicly and explicitly derided via a fictional kiss-and-tell confession in which the actress admits to the financial deals she strikes with her lovers or keepers: 'Then he begins to mix his fine Words with fine Presents; he gives, I receive, returning a side Glance for a Diamond Ring; two Smiles for a Gold Watch; a Kiss for a Pearl Necklace; and at last, for a round Sum, the ultimate of my Favours; of which, in one Month's time, he is as much tir'd, as a Child is of a Barthlomew Nick-Nack, and so we separate again, both fully satisfied.'[33] The actress/whore trope is pressed home as the manipulative dissembler reveals herself to be a heartless mercenary, admitting that she is also a plaything, a knick-knack bought at a fair and discarded when the novelty has gone – but not without recompense.

A similar attack against Bracegirdle's public identity appears in *A Comparison Between Two Stages* where the cynical Sullen and Chagrin express their objection to the way the actress/managers at Lincoln's Inn Fields have 'grown so damn proud of late'.

Sull: But does that Romantick Virgin still keep up her great Reputation?
Chag: D'ye mean her Reputation for Acting?
Sull: I mean her reputation for not acting; you understand me.[34]

Curiously, Elizabeth Barry is actually praised by the third speaker, Ramble, but this merely gives Chagrin the opportunity to press home his attack on Bracegirdle, concluding that she is 'a haughty conceited Woman, that has got more Money by dissembling her Lewdness, than others by possessing it'.[35] These objections continue to reveal the underlying anxiety about the financial independence these women achieved – an anxiety which most obviously appears in the vehement opposition expressed toward the very existence of female playwrights:

Chag: I wonder in my Heart we are so lost to all Sense and reason: What a pox have the Women to do with the Muses? I grant you the Poets call the Nine Muses by the Names of Women, but why so? Not because

	the Sex had any thing to do with Poetry, but because in that Sex they're much fitter for Prostitution
Ram:	Abusive, now you're abusive Mr Critick
Chag:	I tell you we are abus'd: I hate these Petticoat Authors; 'tis false Grammer, there's no feminine for the Latin word, 'tis entirely of the Masculine Gender, and the Language won't bear such a thing as a She-Author.[36]

The appearance of Susanna Centlivre

The most prolific and commercially successful playwright of the eighteenth century had her first play, *The Perjur'd Husband* produced at Drury Lane in October 1700. Susanna Centlivre (formerly Mrs Carroll) took her next play, a comedy entitled *The Beau's Duel: or, A Soldier for the Ladies* to the Player's Company where it was performed at the end of the season in June 1702. Barry and Bracegirdle are notably absent in the leading female roles, which are played by Mrs Prince and Mary Porter. A conventional account would doubtless suggest that the two actress/managers were now rather too old to create young heroines but I suspect that the court cases in which both Barry and Bracegirdle were named were still close enough to make the two actresses wary of exposing themselves to further censure. Centlivre's next play, *The Stolen Heiress*, was also produced by the Players' Company in December 1702. Interestingly, Centlivre also resorted to the kind of screen that Pix had employed for her comedies by not advertising her name in either piece. Although the published edition of the *Beau's Duel*, dedicated to Sir Samuel Brown, is signed by Susanna Carroll, she does not attach her name to the frontispiece or the dedication in the rather weaker tragicomedy, *The Stolen Heiress* and, significantly, the prologue refers to an anonymous male author.

Susanna Centlivre's inauspicious and sporadic early productions belie the impact of her work in commercial theatre in later years. This is far from the explosive entry of Trotter, Manley and Pix, or indeed Behn, and one might argue that the deep-seated opposition to theatre women prevented her from making the splash that greeted the work of her predecessors. But if we read against the grain of that history we might also see that Centlivre's early career reveals a different perspective. The arrival of a 'new' female playwright or actress tends to be heralded as a mark of progression, 'a "rise" from absence to presence, from mute to "motormouth"'[37] as Maggie Gale and Viv Gardner have put it. The identification of the 'new', the 'exceptional' theatre woman reinforces the notion that this is male territory in which female incursion is at best unusual or at worst anonymous – the supporting actress for example is rarely mentioned in the annals of theatre history. But Centlivre joins an already established body of theatre women: she is part of a continuum of theatre women living and working, writing and performing in the commercial theatre. Her rather slow rise to recognition may well be partly due to the particular atmosphere that led female playwrights to adopt anonymity but it is also an indication that she is learning her craft and, crucially, working her own way in a theatre system that has a thriving and established body of women in its midst. Centlivre does mark a rising generation of new theatre women but it is a generation building on an already established theatre practice. Her friendship with Pix and other writing women is as important as her collaboration with Barry and Bracegirdle, for whom she wrote the first of her popular plays on the fashionable obsession with gambling – a play which will be discussed later in this chapter.

Rumblings from within

Centlivre's arrival on the London theatre scene coincides with a shift in relations between the two main companies. From the outset of her career, Centlivre established a satisfactory working relationship with both houses: she took her next new comedy, *Love's Contrivance*, to Drury Lane, where it was performed in June 1703. This, with the movement between the two companies of various players, lends credence to Milhous's suggestion that the season of 1702/3 marks an end to the fierce competition between the two houses who had now 'arrived at a hitherto unrecognized *modus vivendi*'.[38] Milhous gives various examples of apparent co-operation between the two companies, arguing that 'each theatre was much more concerned with establishing a steady audience pool than with undermining the other's repertory'.[39] But then the Patent Company had no need to keep up its attack on its rivals, especially the actress/managers, as the job was being done for it by others.

The most damaging accusations against the actress/managers appear in John Verbruggen's petition to the Lord Chamberlain, presented in the spring of 1703.[40] Verbruggen complains that following his recruitment into the Players' Company in 1696, his share of the company profits has been unsatisfactory. His main grievance is that Barry, Bracegirdle and Betterton have refused to produce the accounts in order to verify the debts incurred and demonstrate the accuracy of the payment to the sharers. If these complaints merely represented the grievances of one leading actor it might be possible to dismiss them but Verbruggen includes a list of other player/sharers who make a far more damaging indictment. 'And as for Mr Bowman Bright Underhill & Mrs Leigh they are aggrieved in the same manner & observe that Mr Betterton Mrs Barry & Mrs Bracegirdle have made Gains to themselves by benefit plays and otherwise.'[41] The accusation that the three leading player/managers were skimming profits at the expense of other members in the company appears to have stuck, even though there is no evidence concerning the outcome of Verbruggen's case against them. Milhous argues that Verbruggen's petition demonstrates that the cooperative standing of the company had finally disintegrated and that 'this trio does seem in effect to have headed Lincoln's Inn Fields by this time'.[42] With some of the original founder members of the company suspecting them of foul play, the player/managers were vulnerable to attack from all quarters and the need for commercial success to meet their obligations all the more pressing.

Revivals were not pulling in the crowds, and Pix's new play, *The Different Widows*, performed in November 1703, seems to fared no better with the audience. Pix was not courageous enough or, perhaps, foolhardy enough to risk attaching her name to this comedy and it is the *only* Pix comedy for which Barry and Bracegirdle did not create the leading roles. It is not a strong play, although not as bad as might be suggested by Clark's summation: 'This bit of fluff is a potpourri of elements from previous Pix comedies.'[43] Pix is not alone in including ingredients from other plays, possibly with the intention of avoiding criticism by employing elements that were already tried and tested. The epilogue, spoken by Mary Porter, is rather too apologetic, admitting past faults, justifying each character in recommendation of the play and advocating, once more, the stage as a tool of reform rather than the cause of immorality:

> Long have we suffer'd, and the injur'd Stage
> Labour'd beneath the censure of the Age;
> We own our Faults, and pardon crave to day,
> When we present you with a modest Play.
> Here no Lewd Lines offend the chaster Ear,
> No jests obscene raise Blushes in the Fair;
> This we cou'd wish Collier himself wou'd hear.
> 'tis purely drawn after the City Fashion,
> Here's nothing taught, but thorough Reformation.
> Here vice is sham'd, and Lewdness is suppresst:

> Virtue's rewarded and her Friends carest.
> If some lewd characters at first appear'd,
> They're reclaim'd, or Punishment they shar'd.[44]

The reference to Collier, some five years after his first publication, demonstrates the extent to which the anti-theatrical lobby still threatened the activities of the playhouse and quite how much the move toward sentimental reform comedies had advanced.

The beginning of the end at Lincoln's Inn Fields

In 1703/4, the last full season at Lincoln's Inn Fields, there were certainly more revivals than new works and a significant rise in the appearances of singers and dancers in entr'acte entertainments to please the audiences' appetite for novelty. Afterpieces were becoming an established part of the evening programme, and the Players' Company enjoyed a considerable success with Farquhar's afterpiece, a farce entitled *The Stage Coach* which was performed in January 1704. Although Barry and Bracegirdle had fewer new plays in which to create new characters, they both had considerable personal successes in two new plays produced during the season. Bracegirdle was well received in the title role of *Abra Mule*, a sentimental tragedy by Joseph Trapp which ran for most of January 1704, and in the following month Barry and Bracegirdle's acting partnership proved equally successful for John Dennis's tragedy *Liberty Asserted*. Dennis's preface to the published edition singles Barry out for particular praise: 'But that of Sakia by Mrs Barry was acted so admirably and inimitably, as that no Stage in Europe can boast of any thing that comes near to her Performance.'[45]

Barry and Bracegirdle also appeared together in the anonymous tragedy *Zelmane*, which was the first new play to be produced by the Players' Company in the season of 1704/5. *The London Stage* notes that the dedicatory epistle suggests that the play was 'left unfinished by "M[ountfor]t", but the *Diverting Post*, 28 Oct., states that it was written by Mrs Mary Pix'.[46] This was Pix's last play to be produced by the Players' Company at Lincoln's Inn Fields and marks the end of the exclusive working relationship established with the company when *The Innocent Mistress* was performed there in 1697. Barry and Bracegirdle's ten-year occupancy of Lincoln's Inn Fields and their unique role as actress/managers was also coming to a close. In the spring of 1705 the Players' Company had effectively disbanded and entered into a new agreement under Vanbrugh's management.

There are various and somewhat conflicting accounts concerning the events that led to the 'Little Theatre' in Lincoln's Inn Fields being abandoned and the establishment of a theatre company in Vanbrugh's newly built Queen's theatre in the Haymarket. *The London Stage* suggests that 'taking the opportunity to perform in a new theatre ... Betterton and his fellow actors left Lincoln's Inn Fields'.[47] John Downes asserts that 'About the end of 1704, Mr Betterton Assign'd his License, and his whole Company over to Captain Vanbrugg to Act under his, at the Theatre in the Hay Market'.[48] Milhous and Hume's editorial footnote states that there 'is no other evidence of the nature of the deal struck between the Lincoln's Inn Fields actors and Vanbrugh' but adds a note that the performing licence, dated 14 December 1704, was issued to Vanbrugh and Congreve.[49] In her earlier work, Milhous devotes an entire chapter to the events following the opening of the Queen's theatre to the union of 1708 when Rich regained the monopoly of the London theatres and which Milhous marks as the end of 'the Lincoln's Inn Fields' experiment'.[50] Her argument is based upon the notion that 'only with the official abolition of competition between acting companies was the spirit of the venture wholly extinguished'[51] – but the formation of the Players' Company was about far more than creating 'competition' between acting companies.

From its inception the Players' Company created an alternative cooperative company in which actresses and female playwrights might enjoy the same status as their male counterparts – within the same company at least. I tend to agree with Cibber's account of events, even though his dating continues to be unreliable, in which he recognises that the ethos of the Players' Company ended when they left Lincoln's Inn Fields in 1705:

> 'tho we [the Patent Company] had then the better Audiences, and might have more of the young world on our Side, yet this was no sure Proof that the other Company were not, in the truth of action, greatly our Superiors. These elder Actors, then ... having only the fewer true Judges to admire them, naturally wanted the support of the Crowd whose taste was to be pleased at a cheaper Rate and with Coarser Fare ... In the Year 1706, when this house [Queens, Haymarket] was finish'd, *Betterton* and his Co-partners dissolved their own Agreement, and threw themselves under the direction of Sir *John Vanbrugh* and Mr. *Congreve*, imagining, perhaps, that the conduct of two such eminent Authors might give a more prosperous Turn to their Condition.[52]

Milhous dismisses Cibber's account of events, arguing that Betterton's creative influence was apparent in the early productions in the new theatre. As Milhous has chosen to completely ignore Barry and Bracegirdle's managerial position in the company it is not surprising that she chooses to finish her study in 1708, a year before Betterton's final retirement, and seeks to establish his part in the productions of operas and straight plays at the Queen's theatre. But the co-operative organisation of the Players' Company, led by the actress/managers, ended when Vanbrugh took over the licence and the company relinquished its managerial status to Vanbrugh. However skilled at their craft, Barry, Bracegirdle and Betterton were simply not as popular as they once had been and this made them increasingly vulnerable to the opposition ranged against them. What Cibber rightly recognises is that for Barry and Bracegirdle, Betterton's 'Co-partners', the decision to 'dissolve' their partnership and 'thr[ow] themselves under the direction' of Vanbrugh and Congreve was a mutual decision and one which seems to have been driven by pragmatism.

Playing for high stakes

In what can only be interpreted as a defiant final gesture, the last new play to be produced by the Players' Company at Lincoln's Inn Fields was Susanna Centlivre's *The Gamester*, performed in February 1705. This is the first of two Centlivre comedies to deal with the contemporary preoccupation with gambling – a theme first touched on by Pix in *The Beau Defeated*. The argument for Centlivre as part of a continuum in theatre practice by women is usefully demonstrated here. Her stagecraft reaches new levels in this play and the situations and characters created in *The Gamester* were built upon in her next and enduringly successful gambling play, *The Bassett Table*, performed at Drury Lane in November 1705. All the leading players at Lincoln's Inn Fields appear in the seventeen strong cast for *The Gamester*, with Barry creating the part of Lady Wealthy, 'a very vain coquettish Widow, very rich, sister to Angellica',[53] who was played by Bracegirdle. In *The Bassett Table*, Lady Wealthy becomes Lady Reveller, and is played by one of the stars of the eighteenth-century stage, Ann Oldfield. But here, in *The Gamester*, the final Players' Company production, Barry and Bracegirdle are paired once again in a new and topical contemporary comedy written by a female playwright.

The unusually straight forward plot was largely taken from a French play in which the hero is utterly ruined by his continued gambling. In Centlivre's play, Valere, the gamester of the title, is also unable to keep his vow to quit the gaming tables but is saved from ruin by the virtuous Angellica/Bracegirdle. It is surely not merely coincidental that in the last new play to be created by the female practitioners at Lincoln's Inn Fields the weak male hero is liberated and reformed by the courageous and inventive actions of a strong woman. Centlivre's skill as a theatre craftswoman is demonstrated in the way she delivers the kind of sentimental reform comedy the audience could approve of but also provides them with the kind of dramatic action and comic set-pieces they enjoyed – something for everyone. The play opens with a scene in which an exhausted servant complains about the all-night gambling activities of his master, a scene which doubtless held particular appeal to the audience in the upper gallery. The Barry/ Bracegirdle partnership makes full use of the contrasting female identities that had worked so well for them at the height of their careers. Bracegirdle's virtuous heroine is set in counterpoint to Barry's vain Lady Wealthy – who takes a malicious delight in finding ways to obstruct her sisters' happiness – but the move towards the sentimental is also inescapably present. Just as Angellica/Bracegirdle reforms her lover, so Wealthy/Barry is reformed by the love of a good man, Lovewell, played by Betterton.

The most effective and theatrically innovative scene takes place at the gaming table where all the excitement and anticipation of the moment is brilliantly conveyed as Valere risks everything on the roll of the dice. Into the middle of this scene Angellica arrives disguised as a young gentleman gambler and proceeds to win Valere's remaining money, his watch and his ring and, finally, accepts his wager of a small diamond encrusted portrait of herself. Valere inevitably loses this too but begs the 'young man' to let him keep Angellica's picture:

Val: … take the Diamonds, but I must have the Picture –
Angel: The Picture, Sir?
Val: Ay, the Picture, Sir
Angel: I won it, Sir, and I shan't restore it, I assure you.
Val: But you shall restore it, Sir, er'e you and I part.
Angel: If I shou'd draw a duel upon my hands here – I'm in a fine condition (aside) – Nay, Sir, if you are angry good by
Val: Nay, nay, nay (runs between him and the Door) you shan't carry off the Picture by Hercules – Looke'e, Sir, either take my Bond, or fight me for't – (Draws)
Angel: Sir – (trembling) what shall I do, I must be oblig'd to discover my self (aside)[54]

The comic tension builds as the anticipation of Angellica/Bracegirdle being forced to either a duel and/or the conventional discovery scene seems inevitable. Bracegirdle's popularity in breeches role, with all its traces of Restoration daring, gives way to the sentimentalisation of women as Angellica/Bracegirdle is saved by the arrival of two gentlemen who enable her to effect an escape with her disguise intact. Left alone, Valere 'comes forward' to deliver a highly sentimental but effective cliffhanger speech to close the act:

> Now I behold what a Monster this darling sin has made me, and loath myself for my long race of Folly –
>
> > Now I repent, but oh it comes to late,
> > And 'tis but Justice now that she shou'd hate;
> > He that flys Vertue still to follow Vice,
> > 'tis fit, like me, he loose his Paradise.
>
> End of the Fourth Act.[55]

Final bows

The Players' Company disbanded when the theatres closed for the Easter week in March 1705. The players signed new agreements with Vanbrugh and opened his newly designed Queen's theatre on 2 April 1705. Owing to bad acoustics at the new theatre they returned to the Lincoln's Inn Fields site at the end of the season and performed there again at the beginning of the 1705/6 season but there is no hint of a return to the autonomy they had formerly enjoyed. As members of Vanbrugh's[56] company, Barry and Bracegirdle relinquished their unique position as actress/managers and returned to the non-sharing status of salaried players. This is not to suggest that plays by female playwrights ceased to be produced or that Barry and Bracegirdle ceased to make a creative contribution to the plays they performed in.

In the ten years between the dissolution of the Players' Company and Queen Anne's death in 1714 – the point at which the Late Stuart stage ends – there were thirteen plays by female playwrights produced on the London stage, nine of which were written by Susanna Centlivre. Bracegirdle appeared in her comedy *The Platonick Lady* in 1706 and, in the same season, Barry created the honourable heroine in Trotter's unsuccessful tragedy *The Revolution of Sweden*. In the same year Barry and Bracegirdle also created the two leading roles in Pix's comedy *Adventures in Madrid*, a patriotic play which makes much of the repressive conditions married women endure in Spain and celebrates the freedom enjoyed by British wives. It is worth noting, however, that the two heroines are liberated by their English heroes, rather than their own devices, and that they marry on their liberators' terms rather than their own. It is tempting to consider the extent to which the fate of Pix's female characters parallels Barry's and Bracegirdle's situation in the closing years of their professional careers.

After a decade of independence, the female theatre practitioners were, once again, operating under the direction and protection of a male management, although Vanbrugh seems to have been a more sympathetic manager than Christopher Rich and clearly honoured his financial commitments. It may well have been that this less controversial theatrical environment encouraged Delarivier Manley to return to the theatre with a new tragedy, *Almyna*, performed in December 1706. Manley evidently did not feel confident enough to put her name to a play which so overtly championed women's rights to education and was disappointed with a short run of only three performances even though no expense was spared on the elaborate production. This was also the last play in which Barry and Bracegirdle appeared together in an acting partnership which had been first established in 1688.

Bracegirdle retired from the stage immediately after the production of *Almyna* in 1706 and was followed soon after by Barry in 1708. Their unique position as actress/managers and co-partners with Thomas Betterton is celebrated in the epilogue to his retirement benefit performance of Congreve's *Love for Love*, performed on 7 April 1709. It does not seem without significance that Betterton chose the play that had opened the Players' Company venture at Lincoln's Inn Fields for his farewell performance and that Barry and Bracegirdle both came out of retirement for the performance.[57] Bracegirdle repeated the prologue that she had used at the play's first performance and although only Barry is identified as the epilogue speaker, it is clear that she is joined on stage by Bracegirdle and that some of the lines are intended to be double-voiced.

> So We, to former Leagues of Friendship true,
> Have bid once more, our Peaceful Homes *Adieu*,
> To aid old THOMAS, and to Pleasure you –
> Like Errant Damsels boldly we Engage,
> Arm'd as you see for the Defenceless Stage;
> Time was, when this Good Man no help did lack,
> And scorn'd that any *She*, should hold his Back,
> But now – so Age and Frailty have ordain'd
> By two at once,* he's forc'd to be sustain'd;
>   *Mrs Barry and Mrs Bracegirdle*[58]

There is a teasing, tongue-in-cheek quality to these lines and the sense of an 'in-joke' around the fact that the two women had always 'sustain'd' Betterton, a notion reinforced by the asterisk which indicates the point at which Barry and Bracegirdle both clasp the actor round the waist.[59] The image created by the patriarch of the Restoration and Late Stuart stage being held up on either side by two of the leading actress/managers of the day is striking. The power of this image in performance can only be imagined but it conveys something of their ownership of the stage space as they address an audience from whom they can confidently anticipate a good reception. This final appearance of the Barry/Bracegirdle partnership demonstrates the extent to which these theatre women were truly shareholders in a vital part of theatre history – in spite of subsequent attempts to forget the full range of their work at Lincoln's Inn Fields between 1695 and 1705.

Notes

1 Milhous, *Thomas Betterton*, p. 113.
2 *A Comparison Between Two Stages*, p. 26 uses this disparaging term to describe the female playwrights.
3 Clark, *Three Augustan Women*, p. 264.
4 Mary Pix, *The False Friend: or, The Fate of Disobedience* (London: Richard Basset, 1699), Prologue.
5 Clark, *Three Augustan Women*, p. 266.
6 *The London Stage*, Part I, p. 526, an extract from a letter to Arthur Kay from Lady Marow, dated 12 March 1699/1700.
7 Downes, *Roscius*, p. 45.
8 *The London Stage*, Part 1, p. 521.
9 William Congreve, *The Way of the World* (London: Jacob Tonson, 1700), Epilogue.
10 Fidelis Morgan, *The Female Wits*, p. 47, acknowledges the play to be 'a very funny comedy' and illustrates the point by including three short extracts. She also reprints the play in its entirety in her collection of comedies (see Lyons and Morgan, *Female Playwrights of the Restoration*, pp. 161–234). Patsy S. Fowler's article 'Rejecting the Status Quo: The Attempts of Mary Pix & Susanna Centlivre to Reform Society's Patriarchal Attitudes', *Restoration and Eighteenth Century Theatre Research*, 9, 2 (winter 1996), pp. 49–59 offers a considered critique of the play but discusses Pix retrospectively through the lens of Centlivre's success. The play is not included in the most recent edition of women's plays from the period, *Eighteenth Century Women Playwrights*, ed. Derek Hughes, 6 vols, vol. 2, *Pix and Trotter*, which includes only Pix's *The Deceiver Deceived* and *Queen Catherine*.

11 Mary Pix, *The Beau Defeated: or, The Lucky Younger Brother* (London: Turner & Basset, [1700]), Act I, sc. i.
12 Act I, sc. i.
13 Act V, sc. ii.
14 Some early records attributed this play to a 'Mr Barker', a point noted by Baker, *Biographia Dramatica*, who clearly attributes the play to Pix in both volumes of his work: see vol. I, p. 358 and vol. II, p. 30.
15 Clark, *Three Augustan Women Playwrights*, p. 267.
16 Bennett, 'Decomposing History', in Worthen with Holland, *Theorizing Practice*, p. 84.
17 p. 84.
18 Milhous, *Thomas Betterton*, p. 115, cites the source as Lord Chamberlain's papers 5/153, folio 23.
19 pp. 115–6. This acknowledgment of Betterton's limited influence calls into question the general assumption that Betterton was always effectively the leader of the company, adding weight to the case for Barry's and Bracegirdle's extended managerial authority.
20 This was obviously an attempt to curb the activities of prostitutes and courtesans in the playhouse although, as I have discussed in earlier chapters, many fashionable women, including Pepys's respectable wife, Elizabeth, used masks in public. Evidently the order was ignored as it was reissued in 1704.
21 Alfred Jackson, 'The Stage and the Authorities, 1700–1714 (as Revealed in the Newspapers)', *Review of English Studies*, 14 (1938), pp. 53–62, p. 57, citing *The Post Man*, 17–19 December, and Luttrell, 'The N. Luttrell Collection', vol. 4, p. 720.
22 Jackson, 'The Stage and the Authorities', p. 56, citing *The Flying Post*, 28–30 November, and Luttrell, 'The N. Luttrell Collection', vol. 4, p. 712.
23 Joseph Wood Krutch, *Comedy and Conscience After the Restoration* (New York: Columbia University Press, 1924), revised 1949. See pp. 169–191 for detail of the events surrounding the court cases and reprints of related correspondence between the players and the authorities.
24 *A Comparison Between Two Stages*, pp. 142–143.
25 Mary Pix, *The Double Distress* (London: R.Wellington, 1701), Prologue.
26 Milhous, *Thomas Betterton*, p. 119.
27 p. 120.
28 p. 146.
29 Baker, *Biographica Dramitica*, vol 1, p. 473.
30 *The London Stage*, Part 2, p. 15.
31 Kathryn McQueen Kendall, *Love and Thunder – Plays by Women in the Age of Queen Anne* (London: Methuen Drama, 1988), Introduction, p. 9.
32 Thomas Brown, *Letters from the Dead to the Living* (1702), in *The Works of Mr Thomas Brown*, (London: Sam Briscoe, 1707), 3 vols, vol. 2, pp. 165–175, pp. 166–167.
33 p. 174.

34 *A Comparison Between Two Stages*, p. 17.
35 p. 199.
36 p. 26.
37 Gale and Gardner, *Women Theatre and Performance: New Histories, New Historiographies*, p. 5.
38 Milhous, *Thomas Betterton*, p. 152.
39 p. 165.
40 See Appendix E, pp. 252–254. Milhous reproduces the document in full as an appendix to her discussion, pp. 160–164. See also pp. 152–159 where Milhous links Verbruggen's claims to a series of lawsuits initiated by Sir Edward Smith who attempted to collect undistributed and undisclosed profits from both companies on behalf of a group of minor shareholders.
41 p. 253.
42 p. 161. It is, perhaps, not without significance that Milhous chooses this moment of particular difficulty within the company to acknowledge Barry's and Bracegirdle's full managerial status.
43 Clark, *Three Augustan Women Playwrights*, p. 275.
44 Pix, *The Different Widows: or, Intrigue All-A-Mode* (London: Henry Playford and Bernard Lintott, [1703]), Epilogue.
45 John Dennis, *Liberty Asserted* (London: Bernard Lintott, 1704), Preface.
46 *The London Stage*, Part II, p. 80.
47 p. 75.
48 Downes, *Roscius Anglicanus*, pp. 47–48 and Downes, *Roscius* eds Milhous and Hume, pp. 98–99.
49 p. 99, n.353. Milhous, *Thomas Betterton*, p. 191 reproduces the licence granted by Queen Anne and published in the *London Gazette*, 21–25 December 1704, in which Vanbrugh and Congreve are named as the sole licensees.
50 Milhous, *Thomas Betterton*, p. 219.
51 p. 220.
52 Cibber, *Apology*, ed. Lowe, vol. 1, pp. 319 and 320. Lowe's footnote corrects Cibber's '1706', citing Downes as the source for a date of 1704 for the agreement between the companies, further noting that the Queen's theatre opened on 9 April 1705.
53 Susanna Centlivre, *The Gamester* (London: William Turner and William Davis, 1705), Dramatis Personae.
54 Act IV, p. 56.
55 p. 56.
56 Congreve's position in the management of the Queen's Company appears to have been short lived, if ever fully realised. See Cibber, *Apology*, ed. Lowe, vol. 1, p. 326.
57 Barry returned to the stage, retiring for a second and final time in June 1710. She died in November 1713 at the age of fifty-five. According to *A Biographical Dictionary*, Barry died a comparatively wealthy woman: she left an estate of mills in Newbury to a Gabriel Ballam, and the remainder of her

estate to her executors John Custis and Abigail Stackhouse. She also made several individual bequests ranging from £20 to £200 which she left to Anne Bracegirdle 'to save Mrs. Bracegirdle harmless from any debt of the Play-House'. Perhaps the debts that the actress/managers claimed for Lincoln's Inn Fields were as large as they reported and Barry had not forgotten the difficulties of repaying them. Bracegirdle is also said to have been left £1000 by the Earl of Scarsdale about the time of her retirement. She died in 1748.

58 Pierre Danchin, *The Prologues and Epilogues of the Eighteenth Century, The First Part 1701–1720* (Nancy: Presses Universitaires de Nancy, 1986), 2 vols, vol. 2, pp. 427–430, p. 430.

59 p. 430. An editorial note indicates that when first published in 1709 (probably to be sold at the benefit performance) the physical action was not included in the text but was added in future editions published in 1714 and 1733.

8
CERTAINLY NOT A CONCLUSION

> Who would have thought that this past century was so immediately vulnerable to the erasure of women from its history?[1]

This book began by considering the way history works and challenging the working of historiographical method in the traditional representation of women's theatre histories. It has questioned the divide that happened after the event as it were, as the business of the theatrical past of women was asset-stripped and appropriated by the highest bidder: the playwright and her dramatic text to literature, the actress to biography or the byways of historical gossip. In pursuing an alternative history, one that tells the story of influence and collaboration between theatre women, the focus of this book has necessarily been tightened to look afresh at a specific period, a particular group of actresses and female playwrights and their work in the business of commercial theatre. An awareness of the traffic of the playhouse has been at the centre of this enquiry. The playhouse as the place of performance, in which the commercial exchange between performer and audience is transacted, created a cultural space in which the collaboration between early theatre women was established. In the closing chapter, the focus sharpened still further as Elizabeth Barry and Ann Bracegirdle brought their own collaborative partnership to a close in the early years of the eighteenth century. Their part in the story has reached its end – the story of theatre women that follow them, however, is far from over. But where do we go from here?

There are many other stories of collaboration to be unearthed, many other periods of theatre history to be revised. But there are perhaps broader questions relating to feminist histories and challenges for feminist historiography: how do we continue to recover women's work and make it present and, more importantly perhaps, do our historical revisions cut deeply enough? Susan Bennett has expressed some concern about the present and the future of feminist historiography: 'As I have looked at the emergence of interest in women's dramatic writing in the context of British theatre history, it has become patent that the primary impact of revisionist work has often been at what might be seen as a local level – a period study, a genre study, a consideration of a particular company or theatre site – rather than in any overarching narrative of British theatre.'[2] Bennett is troubled that the micro-narrative – an approach which has been unashamedly adopted in this book – not only works to reinforce women's exclusion from grand theatrical narratives in the historically distant past but also, as the quotation that opens this chapter suggests, threatens to perpetuate that exclusion as theatre historians begin to catalogue and interpret theatre and performance in the recent past of the twentieth century. Bennett is rightly suspicious of a historiography that works only in the margins but, as her own research interest in the twentieth-century female dramatist reveals, feminist theatre historiography could be said to collude with this marginalization by focusing on individual female achievement when we should, I suggest, be looking instead for networks of influence and collaboration – not only in the subjects we choose to revise but also in our own methods and academic practice.

The revision of women's theatre history, past and present, is, like the lives of its performers and the work of performance it seeks to recover, a collaborative act. Surely we collaborate with one another as we identify the lacunae, as we seek to fill the many gaps created by the grand narratives of the past and acknowledge each others' work in footnotes and bibliographies. Ours is an incremental history that deepens in complexity as the threads from past and present are woven together. Its strength lies in its resistance to the hegemonic notions of objectivity and national identity that are the marks of the overarching narratives we inherit. Its future depends upon its ongoing determination to defy linearity and go beyond geographical or disciplinary boundaries. Its methods and methodologies are continually developing as we seek new ways of seeing; new ways of reading text and performance; new meanings in our critical texts on performance; new collaborations. If we deny collaboration, then we deny the very basis upon which the theatre practices we examine are built.

Collaboration can be seen in the growth of interdisciplinary approaches that have emerged from the insistent rise of cultural history and its impact on all aspects of academic enquiry. Mira Rubin argues that 'crucial to the making of the "cultural turn" have been the wider effects of feminist interests and aspirations'.[3] The second book in this series of *Women, Theatre and Performance* demonstrates that wider effect and the potential of interdisciplinary collaborations by bringing together the voices of female playwright/performers with female academic scholars in gender studies, contemporary performance, theatre history, applied drama and video documentation to consider ways in which women from Britain, Europe, North America and American Latina have written about and performed themselves. The eleven case-studies in *Auto/Biography and Identity* bring feminist perspectives to bear in their exploration of the stories of women writing and/or performing themselves between the late nineteenth and the twenty-first century.[4] Part of the Foucauldian legacy to the doing and making of history is that it draws attention to an embodied history, one that can be most vividly seen in theatre history. Experiments in practice-based research have begun, albeit cautiously, to push the envelope of embodied memory and historical theatre practice, providing new opportunities for interdisciplinary collaborations and, in particular, fresh insights into women's theatre history.[5] Such experiments in new ways of seeing continually emerge as we push the boundaries of our theoretical and historical practice.

The personal is political

This book, then, is a monograph (the all important single-authored text which continues to be the main requisite for academic promotion in our universities) but as it works to builds new understandings of women's theatrical past it also self-consciously builds on the work of past story-tellers – it collaborates with their work, bringing new perspectives and making new connections. This is true in a personal as well as an academic sense. I have dedicated it to three theatre women: my grandmother, Evelyn Howard, my mother, Joan Berly and my daughter, Rebecca Everett. Together, we represent four generations of actresses working in the professional theatre between 1906 and 2006. My interest in the history of early theatre women arises from that family legacy and the network of connections spanning a century within the business of theatre. Our material remains include photographs, programmes and cuttings of reviews but the most treasured legacy, passed down from woman to woman, is a now-battered black make-up box, bearing the initials of each one and the date of our first professional performances.[6] But this represents a greater legacy, one that runs deeply through our sense of family history and the shared experience of theatre practice. This theatrical genealogy is, of course, hidden from view, as we have each used the name given to us by our fathers. The maternal lineage may be obscured but the presence of such genealogies (and there are many more unknown than known) defies the marginalisation of theatre women by demonstrating the ongoing work of successive generations of women at each level and in all aspects of theatre history.[7] These small stories, found in the network of connections between women, familial or otherwise, continually question the stability of the grand narratives of history that ignore them.

If feminist histories are to disturb the myopic perspective of the overarching narrative of theatre history, it is surely not by providing another version of the same thing but by demonstrating the implicit limitations of such a project and its concomitant claim for objectivity – not only in relation to its subject interests but also in its relation to its historiographical practice. Feminist histories might be seen as palimpsests, multilayered, multivisioned works, with each new writing building on the meanings created by the writing beneath. This incremental history is polyphonic. It is about women's presence in theatre and in its history: an ongoing project in which this book willingly collaborates.

Notes

1 Susan Bennett, 'Gender and Nation in British Theatre History: Rethinking the 1950s', position paper circulated to delegates in the Feminist Historiography Group at the American Society for Theatre Research, Annual Conference, Las Vegas, November 2004. Used here by kind permission of the author. No page numbers.
2 Ibid.
3 Miri Rubin, 'What Is Cultural History Now?', in *What Is History Now?*, ed. Cannadine, pp. 80–94, p. 84.
4 Gale and Gardner (eds), *Auto/biography and Identity: Women Theatre and Performance*.
5 See *Nineteenth Century Theatre & Film*, 29:2 winter 2002 (guest editors Jacky Bratton and Gilli Bush-Bailey) for an account of an AHRB-funded Innovations Research project in which historians in theatre, music, costume, dance and fight-arrangement worked on a practice-based project with a company of professional actors on the plays of nineteenth-century playwright/actress/manager Jane Scott.
6 My grandmother, Evelyn Howard, joined the Fred Terry company in 1906 and retired from the profession when she married my grandfather, a retired army officer, in 1919. My mother, Joan Berly, made her professional debut in pantomime in 1937. Her acting career was interrupted by the Second World War but after the war she returned to the theatre as a stage manager. Later, she ran her own business hiring out stage properties, worked as a theatrical

agent and as artist's 'booker' for the BBC. She gave up her professional career when I was born in 1955. In 1967 I performed at the Royal Festival Hall as part of the children's corps de ballet in Festival Ballet's *Sleeping Beauty*. My work as an actress in television, radio and theatre ended in 1992, when I embarked on an academic career. My daughter, Rebecca Everett, graduated from LAMDA in 2002. She has recently formed her own company, producing seasons of new and under-performed plays at London fringe venues. In August 2005 she played the female lead in the premiere of Joy Wilkinson's *Fair* at The Finborough.

7 See Bratton, 'Claiming Kin: An Experiment in Genealogical Research', in *New Readings*, pp. 171–199, for a detailed discussion on the ways in which the genealogies of theatre families can contribute new insights into women's theatre histories.

Bibliography

In all sections the place of publication is London, unless otherwise stated.

Primary sources

Dramatic texts

Anon., *The Unnatural Mother* (R. Bagget, 1698).
—— *The Fickle Shepherdess* (Turner, Davis and Nutt, 1703).
—— *The Female Wits: or, The Triumverate of Poets at Rehearsal* (William Turner, William Davies, Bernard Lintott, Thomas Brown, 1704).
—— *The Lunatick* (B. Bragg, 1705).
'Ariadne', *She Ventures and He Wins* (Rhodes, Harris and Briscoe, 1696).
Behn, Aphra, *The Feign'd Curtezans: or A Night's Intrigue* (Jacob Tonson, 1679).
—— *The Roundheads: or The Good Old Cause* (D. Brown, 1682).
—— *The Lucky Chance: or An Alderman's Bargain* (W. Canning, 1687).
—— *The Emperor of the Moon* (J. Knight and F. Saunders, 1687).
—— *The Widdow Ranter: or The History of Bacon in Virginia*, ed. Charles Gildon (James Knapton, 1690).
—— *The Younger Brother: or The Amorous Jilt* [with alterations and a memoir, by Charles Gildon] (J. Harris, 1696).
Centlivre, Susannah, *The Perjur'd Husband: or, The Adventures of Venice* (Bennet Banbury, 1700).
—— *The Beau's Duel: or, A Soldier for the Ladies* (D. Brown and N. Cox, 1702).
—— *The Stolen Heiress: or, The Salamanca Doctor Outplotted* (William Turner and John Nutt, [1702]).
—— *The Gamester* (William Turner and William Davis, 1705).
—— *The Basset-table* (1706).
Congreve, William, *The Old Batchelor* (Peter Buck, 1693).
—— *Love for Love* (Jacob Tonson, 1695).
—— *The Way of the World* (Jacob Tonson, 1700).
—— *Five Plays Written by Mr. Congreve* (H. Hills, 1710).
Craufurd, David, *Courtship A-la-mode* (J. Barnes, 1700).
Dennis, John, Dennis, *Liberty Asserted* (Bernard Lintott, 1704).

BIBLIOGRAPHY

Doggett, Thomas, *The Country-Wake* (Samual Briscoe, 1696).
Dryden, John, *Don Sebastian King of Portugal* (Jo Hindmarsh, 1690).
—— *Cleomenes the Spartan Heroe* (Jacob Tonson, 1692).
D'Urfey, Thomas, *The Marriage-Hater Match'd* (Samuel Briscoe, 1692).
—— *The Richmond Heiress: or A Woman Once in the Right* (Samuel Briscoe, 1693).
Manley, Delarivier, *The Lost Lover: or The Jealous Husband* (R. Bentley, F. Saunders, J. Knapton and R. Wellington, 1696).
—— *The Royal Mischief* (R. Bentley, F. Saunders and J. Knapton, 1696).
Mountfort, William, *The Successful Straingers* (James Blackwell, 1690).
Pix, Mary, *Ibrahim, The Thirteenth Emperour of the Turks* (John Harding and Richard Wilkin, 1696).
—— *The Spanish Wives* (R. Wellington, 1696).
—— *The Innocent Mistress* (J. Orme for R. Basset and F. Cogan, 1697).
—— *The Deceiver Deceiv'd* (R. Basset, 1698).
—— *Queen Catherine: or, The Ruines of Love* (William Turner and Richard Basset, 1698).
—— *The False Friend: or, The Fate of Disobedience* (Richard Basset, 1699).
—— *The Beau Defeated: or, The Lucky Younger Brother* (Turner and Basset, [1700]).
—— *The Czar of Muscovy* (B. Bernard Lintott, 1701).
—— *The Double Distress* (R. Wellington, 1701).
—— *The Different Widows: or, Intrigue All-A-Mode* (Henry Playford and Bernard Lintott, [1703]).
Powell, George, *Bonduca: or, The British Heroine* (Richard Bentley, 1696).
—— *The Cornish Comedy* (D. Brown, T. Bennet, K. Gately, 1696).
—— *Imposture Defeated: or, A Trick to Cheat the Devil* (R. Wellington, 1698).
Settle, Elkanah, *The Ambitious Slave: or A Generous Revenge* (1694).
Shadwell, Thomas, *The Scowrers* (James Knapton, 1691).
—— *The Volunteers* (James Knapton, 1693).
Southerne, Thomas, *The Wives Excuse: or Cuckolds Make Themselves* (Samuel Briscoe, 1692).
—— *The Maid's Last Prayer: or Any Rather than Fail* (Bentley and Tonson, 1693).
—— *Oroonoko* (H. Playford, 1696).
Trotter, Catherine, *Agnes De Castro* (H. Rhodes, R. Parker, S. Briscoe, 1696).
—— *The Fatal Friendship* (Francis Saunders, 1698).

Vanbrugh, John, *The Provok'd Wife* (Richard Wellington and Bernard Lintott, 1698).

Wiseman, Jane, *Antiochus the Great: or, The Fatal Relapse* (William Turner and Richard Basset, 1702).

Non-dramatic texts

Anon., *A Satyr on The Players* (c. 1682) in 'Satyrs and Lampoons', British Library, MS Harley 7317, pp. 96–100.

—— *Animadversions on Mr. Congreve's Late Answer to Mr. Collier* (John Nutt, 1698).

—— *Session of Ladyes* (1688) in 'Satyrs and Lampoons', British Library MS Harley 7317.

—— *The Player's Tragedy: or A Fatal Love* A New Novel (Randal Taylor, 1693).

—— *The Session of the Poets, Holden at the Foot of Parnassus Hill* (E. Whitlock, 1696).

—— *A Comparison between the two Stages, with an Examen of the Generous Conqueror* (1702), sometimes attributed to Charles Gildon.

—— *The Players turn'd Ackademicks: or, a description (in Merry Metre) of their translation from the theatre in Little Lincolns-Inn-Fields, to the tennis-court in Oxford* (1703).

Astell, Mary, *A Serious Proposal to the Ladies for the advancement of their true and greatest interest ... By A Lover of her Sex* (R. Wilkins, 1694).

Aston, Anthony, *A Brief Supplement to Colley Cibber, Esq; His Lives of the Late Famous Actors and Actresses* (c. 1769) in Cibber, *An Apology for His Life* (1748), ed. Robert W. Lowe (John C. Nimmo, 1889), vol. 2, pp. 297–318.

Betterton, Thomas, *The History of the English Stage from the Restauration to the Present Time, Including the Lives, Characters and Amours of the Most Eminent Actors and Actresses*, compiled by Edmund Curll and William Oldys from the notes of T. Betterton (E. Curll, 1741).

Brown, Thomas, *Amusements Serious and Comical* (John Nutt, 1700).

—— *Letters from the Dead to the Living* (1702), in *The Works of Mr. Thomas Brown* (Sam Briscoe, 1707), 3 vols, vol. 2.

Bulwer, John, *Manwatching: Chirologia, or the Naturall Language of the Hand* (Tho. Harper for Henry Twyford, 1644).

—— *Chironomia, or the Art of Manuall Rhetorique* (Tho. Harper for Henry Twyford, 1644).

—— *Pathomyotomia* (W. W. for Humphrey Moseley, 1649).

Cibber, Colley, *An Apology for the Life of Mr. Colley Cibber* (John Watts, 1740).

—— *An Apology for the Life of Mr Colley Cibber* (c. 1740), with notes and supplement by Robert W. Lowe (John C. Nimmo, 1889), 2 vols.

Collier, Jeremy, *A Short View of the Immorality, and Profaneness of the English Stage* (1698), reproduced from a copy in Cambridge University Library (Menston: Scolar Press, 1971).

Congreve, William, *Ammendments of Mr Collier's False and Imperfect Citations etc.* (J. Tonson, 1698).

Downes, John, *Roscius Anglicanus* (H. Playford, 1708).

—— *Roscius Anglicanus* (1708) ed. Montague Summers (Fortune Press, [1928]).

—— *Roscius Anglicanus* (1708) *A New Edition*, ed. Judith Milhous and Robert Hume (The Society for Theatre Research, 1987).

Drake, Judith, *An Essay in Defence of the Female Sex* (A. Roper and E. Wilkinson; R. Clavel, 1696).

Gildon, Charles, *The Life of Mr. Thomas Betterton* (Robert Gosling, 1710).

—— *All the Histories and Novels written by the Late Ingenious Mrs Behn, entire in one volume ... Together with the History of the Life and Memoirs of Mrs. Behn*, ed. Charles Gildon (Samuel Briscoe, 1696).

Gould, Robert, *The Play-House, A Satyr* (c. 1685), British Library MS, Add. 30492.

—— *The Works of Mr Robert Gould*, 2 vols (W. Lewis, 1709).

Langbain, Gerard (the Younger), *Lives and Characters of the Dramatick Poets* (1691), revised and amended edition (1698), attributed to Charles Gildon.

Luttrell, Narcisus, 'The N. Luttrell Collection', 5 vols of material printed between 1659–1730. The British Library holds a facsimile, the original being bought by American collector Louis H. Silver (1961), now held by Newberry Library, Chicago.

Manley, Delarivier, *The New Atalantis. With Secret Memoirs and Manners of Several Persons her Contemporaries* (John Morphew and John Woodward, 1709).

—— *The Adventures of Rivella: or, The History of the Author of the Atalantis. With Secret Memoirs and Characters of several considerable Persons her Contemporaries.* (1714).

Pepys, Samuel, *The Diary of Samuel Pepys*, ed. Robert Latham and William Matthews (G. Bell and Sons, 1970–83), 11 vols.

Wright, James, *Historia Histrionica: An Historical Account of the English Stage* (1699), in Cibber, *An Apology for His Life* (1748), ed. Robert W. Lowe (John C. Nimmo, 1889), vol. 1, xxi–li.

Secondary sources

Anthony, Sister Rose, *The Jeremy Collier Stage Controversy 1698–1726* (New York: Benjamin Blom, 1937), reissued 1966.

Aston, Elaine, *An Introduction to Feminism and Theatre* (Routledge, 1995).

Avery, Emmett L., 'Lincoln's Inn Fields, 1704–1705', *Theatre Notebook*, 5 (1950), pp. 13–15.

—— (ed.), *The London Stage 1660–1800: A Calender of Plays, Entertainments and Afterpieces Together with Casts, Box-receipts and Contemporary Comment Compiled from the Playbills, Newspapers and Theatrical Diaries of the Period*. Part II, *1700–1729* (Carbondale: Southern Illinois University Press, 1960).

Backsheider, Paula, *Spectacular Politics* (Baltimore: Johns Hopkins University Press, 1993).

Baker, David Erskine, *Biographia Dramatica or A Companion to the Playhouse* (Dublin: T. Henshall, 1782), 2 vols.

Bassnett, Susan, 'Struggling with the Past: Women's Theatre in Search of a History', *New Theatre Quarterly*, 5: 18 (1989) pp. 107–112.

Bate, Jonathan, *The Genius of Shakespeare* (New York and Oxford: Oxford University Press, 1998).

Bellchambers, Edmund, 'Memoirs of the Actors and Actresses Mentioned by Cibber', taken from his Edition of *Apology* (1822) reprinted in *Apology*, ed. Robert W. Lowe, 2 vols (John C. Nimmo, 1889), vol. 2, pp. 319–371.

Bennett, Susan, *Theatre Audiences* (1997), 2nd edition (Routledge, 2003).

—— 'Theatre History, Historiography and Women's Dramatic Writing' in *Women, Theatre and Performance: New Histories, New Historiographies*, ed. Maggie B. Gale and Viv Gardner (Manchester: Manchester University Press, 2000), pp. 46–59.

—— 'Decomposing History (Why Are There So Few Women in Theater History)', *Theorizing Practice: Redefining Theatre History*, ed. W. B. Worthen with Peter Holland (Basingstoke: Palgrave Macmillan, 2003), pp. 71–87.

Bratton, Jacky, 'Reading the intertheatrical, or, the Mysterious Disappearance of Susannah Centlivre', in *Women, Theatre and Performance: New Histories, New Historiographies*, ed. Maggie B. Gale and Viv Gardner (Manchester: Manchester University Press, 2000) pp. 7–24.

—— *New Readings in Theatre History* (Cambridge: Cambridge University Press, 2003).
Burling, William J., '"Their Empire Disjoyn'd": Serious Plays by Women on the London Stage, 1660–1737' in *Curtain Calls: British and American Women and the Theater, 1660–1820*, ed. Mary Anne Schofield and Cecilia Macheski (Athens: Ohio University Press, 1991), pp. 311–324.
Burton, Sarah, 'The Public Woman: An Investigation into the Actress-whore Connexion' unpublished PhD dissertation, University of London, 1998.
Canfield, Douglas, and Deborah C. Payne (eds), *Cultural Readings of Restoration and Eighteenth-century English Theater* (Athens, GA: University of Georgia Press, 1995).
Carter, Philip, 'Men About Town: Representations of Foppery and Masculinity in Early Eighteenth-century Urban Society' in *Gender in Eighteenth Century England*, ed. Hannah Barker and Elaine Challus (Longman, 1997), pp. 31–57.
Case, Sue Ellen, *Feminism and Theatre* (Macmillan, 1988).
Clark, Constance, *Three Augustan Women Playwrights* (New York: Peter Lang, 1986).
Clark, W. S., 'Corpses, Concealments, and Curtains on the Restoration Stage', *Review of English Studies*, 13 (1937), pp. 438–48.
Clifford, A. (ed.), *The Tixall Letters; or, The Correspondance of the Aston Family, and their Friends, during the Seventeenth Century* (Edinburgh: 1815).
Copeland, Nancy, 'Reviving Aphra Behn: *The Rover* in the "Restoration" Repertoire', *Restoration and 18th Century Theatre Research*, 14: 1 (summer 1999), pp. 1–18.
Cordner, Michael (ed.), *Sir John Vanbrugh: Four Comedies* (Penguin, 1989).
Cotton, Nancy, *Women Playwrights in England c. 1363–1750* (Toronto and London: Associated University Press, 1980).
Crouch, Kimberly, 'The Public Life of Actresses: Prostitutes or Ladies?' in *Gender in Eighteenth Century England*, ed. Hannah Barker and Elaine Challus (Longman, 1997).
Danchin, Pierre (ed.), *The Prologues and Epilogues of the Restoration, 1660–1700* (Nancy: Presses Universitaires de Nancy, 1981–1988), 7 vols.
—— (ed.), *The Prologues and Epilogues of the Eighteenth Century: The First Part 1701–1720* (Nancy: Presses Universitaires de Nancy, 1986), 2 vols.

Davis, Tracy, C., 'Questions for a Feminist Methodology in Theatre History', in *Interpreting the Theatrical Past*, ed. Thomas Postelwait and Bruce A. McConachie (Iowa: University of Iowa Press, 1989), pp. 59–79.
—— *Actresses as Working Women* (London and New York: Routledge, 1991).
—— 'The Contex Problem', *Theatre Survey*, 45: 2 (November 2004), pp. 203–209.
Diamond, Elin, *Unmaking Mimesis* (Routledge, 1997).
Donkin, Ellen, 'Mrs. Siddons Looks Back in Anger: Feminist Historiography for Eighteenth-century British Theater', in *Critical Theory and Performance*, ed. Janelle G. Reinelt and Joseph R. Roach (Ann Arbor: University of Michigan Press, 1992), pp. 276–291.
—— *Getting into the Act* (Routledge, 1995).
Drougge, Helga, 'Love, Death, and Mrs Barry in Thomas Southerne's Plays', *Comparative Drama*, 27: 4 (winter 1993), pp. 408–425.
Essex, John, *The Dancing-Master* (1728), a translation of Pierre Rameau, *Le Maitre a Danser* (Paris, 1725).
Evans, Richard J., 'Prologue: What Is History? – Now', in *What Is History Now?*, ed. David Cannadine (Palgrave Macmillan, 2002), pp. 1–18.
Ewald, Alexander C. (ed.), *Congreve: The Best Plays of the Old Dramatists* (Mermaid, 1887).
Ferris, Lesley, *Acting Women: Images of women in the Theatre* (Basingstoke: Macmillan, 1989).
Fishman, Jenn, 'Performing Identities: Female Cross-dressing in *She Ventures and He Wins*', *Restoration Studies in English Literary Culture 1660–1700* (spring 1996), 20: 1, pp. 36–51.
Fitzgerald, Percy, *A New History of the English Stage* (Tinsley Bros, 1882), 2 vols.
Fortier, Mark, *Theory/Theatre: An Introduction* (1997), 2nd edition (Routledge, 2002), p. 164.
Fowler, Patsy, S., 'Rejecting the Status Quo: The Attempts of Mary Pix and Susanna Centlivre to Reform Society's Patriarchal Attitudes', *Restoration and 18th Century Theatre Research* (winter 1996), 9: 2, pp. 49–59.
Franceschina, John, *Homosexualities in the English Theatre* (Westport: Greenwood Press, 1997).
Fraser, Antonia, *The Weaker Vessel* (1984), reprinted (Arrow Books, 1997).

Gagen, Jean, *The New Woman: Her Emergence in English Drama 1600–1730* (New York: Twayne, 1954).
Gale, Maggie B., and Viv Gardner (eds), *Women, Theatre and Performance: New Histories, New Historiographies* (Manchester: Manchester University Press, 2000).
——— *Auto/biography and Identity: Women, Theatre and Performance* (Manchester: Manchester University Press, 2004).
Gilder, Rosamond, *Enter the Actress – The First Women in the Theatre* (George A. Harrap, 1931).
Gillis, John, *A World of Their Own Making* (Oxford: Oxford University Press, 1997).
Goreau, Angeline, *Reconstructing Aphra* (Oxford: Oxford University Press, 1980).
Gosse, Edmund, *Restoration Plays* (J. M. Dent, 1932).
Greer, Germaine, *Slip-Shod Sibyls* (1995), reprinted Penguin Books, 1996.
Harbage, A., *Annals of English Drama 975–1700*, revised S. Schoenbaum (Methuen, 1964).
Highfill, Philip H. (ed.), *A Biographical Dictionary of Actors, Actresses, Musicians, Dancers, Managers and Other Stage Personnel in London 1660–1800* (Carbondale: Southern Illinois University Press, 1973), 16 vols.
Hill, Christopher, *The Century of Revolution* (1961), reprinted Routledge, 1993.
Hobby, Elaine, *Virtue of Necessity* (Virago, 1988).
Hodges, John, C. (ed.), *William Congreve: Letters and Documents* (Macmillan, 1964).
Holland, Peter, *The Ornament of Action* (Cambridge: Cambridge University Press, 1979).
Hook, Lucyle, 'Mrs. Elizabeth Barry and Mrs. Anne Bracegirdle, Actresses: Their Careers from 1672 to 1695; A Study in Influence', unpublished PhD dissertation, New York University, 1945.
——— 'James Brydges Drops in at the Theater' *Huntington Library Quarterly*, 8 (1946), pp. 306–311.
——— 'Anne Bracegirdle's First Appearance', *Theatre Notebook*, 13 (1958), pp. 133–137.
——— 'Portraits of Elizabeth Barry and Anne Bracegirdle', *Theatre Notebook*, 15 (1960), pp. 129–37.
——— (ed.), and Introduction to *The Female Wits* (1704), The Augustan Reprint Society (Los Angeles: University of California, 1967).

Hotson, Leslie, *The Commonwealth and Restoration Stage* (Cambridge, MA: Harvard University Press, 1928).
Howe, Elizabeth, *The First English Actresses – Women and Drama 1660–1700* (Cambridge: Cambridge University Press, 1992).
Hughes, Derek, *English Drama 1660–1700* (Oxford: Clarendon Press, 1996).
—— (ed.), *Eighteenth-century Women Playwrights* (Pickering and Chatto, 2001), 6 vols.
Hume, Robert D., 'A Revival of *The Way of the World* in December 1701 or January 1702', *Theatre Notebook*, 26 (1971), pp. 30–36.
—— *The Development of English Drama in the Late Seventeenth Century* (Oxford: Oxford University Press, 1976).
—— (ed.), *The London Theatre World 1660–1800* (Carbondale: Southern Illinois University Press, 1980).
—— 'The Origins of the Actor Benefit in London', *Theatre Research International*, 9: 2 (1981), pp. 99–111.
—— *Reconstructing Contexts: The Aims and Principles of Archeo-historicism* (New York: Oxford University Press, 1999).
Hunt, Hugh, 'Restoration Acting' in *Restoration Theatre*, Stratford-upon-Avon Studies, 6, ed. John Russell Brown and Bernard Harris (Edward Arnold, 1965), pp. 179–192.
Hutner, Heidi (ed.), *Rereading Aphra Behn* (Charlottesville: University Press of Virginia, 1993).
Jackson, Alfred, 'The Stage and the Authorities, 1600–1714 (as revealed in the Newspapers)', *Review of English Studies*, 14 (1938), pp. 53–62.
Jensby, Wesley Joe, 'A Historical Study of the Characteristics of Acting During the Restoration Period in England (1660–1710)', unpublished PhD dissertation, University of Southern California, 1963.
Kavenik, Frances M., 'Aphra Behn: The Playwright as "Breeches Part"', in *Curtain Calls: British and American Women and the Theater, 1660–1820*, ed. Mary Anne Schofield and Cecilia Macheski (Athens: Ohio University Press, 1991), pp. 177–191.
Keeble, N. H. (ed.), *The Cultural Identity of Seventeenth Century Woman: A Reader* (Routledge, 1994).
Kendall, Kathryn McQueen, 'Theatre, Society, and Women Playwrights in London from 1695 Through the Queen Anne Era', unpublished PhD dissertation, University of Texas at Austin, 1986.
—— *Love and Thunder – Plays by Women in the Age of Queen Anne* (Methuen Drama, 1988).

—— 'Finding the Good Parts: Sexuality in Women's Tragedies in the Time of Queen Anne' in *Curtain Calls: British and American Women and the Theater, 1660–1820*, ed. Mary Anne Schofield and Cecilia Macheski (Athens: Ohio University Press, 1991), pp. 165–176.

Kennedy, Dennis (ed.), *The Oxford Encyclopaedia of Theatre and Performance* (Oxford: Oxford University Press, 2003), 2 vols.

Kenny, S. S., "Theatrical Warfare, 1695–1710", *Theatre Notebook*, 27 (1973), pp. 130–145.

King, Thomas A., "'As if (she) were made on purpose to put the whole world into good humour": Reconstructing the First English Actresses', *The Drama Review*, 36 (fall 1992), pp. 78–101.

Kline, Richard, B., 'Anne Oldfield and Mary de la Riviere Manley: The Unnoticed Reconciliation', *Restoration and 18th Century Theatre Research*, 14 (November 1975), pp. 53–58.

Krutch, Joseph Wood, *Comedy and Conscience After the Restoration* (New York: Columbia University Press, 1924), revised 1949.

Langhans, Edward, A., 'Notes on the Reconstruction of the Lincoln's Inn Fields Theatre' *Theatre Notebook*, 10 (1956), pp. 112–114.

—— 'The Vere Street and Lincoln's Inn Fields Theatres in Pictures', *Educational Theatre Journal*, 20 (1968), pp. 171–185.

Leacroft, Richard, *The Development of The English Playhouse* (Methuen, 1973).

Lewcock, Dawn, 'More for Seeing than Hearing: Behn and the Use of Theatre' in *Aphra Behn Studies*, ed. Janet Todd (Cambridge: Cambridge University Press, 1996), pp. 66–83.

Love, Harold, 'The Myth of the Restoration Audience', *Komos*, 1 (1967), pp. 49–56.

Lowe, R. W. (ed.), *Doran's Annals of the English Stage* (John C. Nimmo, 1888), 3 vols.

—— (ed.), *An Apology for the Life of Mr. Colley Cibber* (John C. Nimmo, 1889), 2 vols.

Lyons, Paddy, and Fidelis Morgan (ed.), *Female Playwrights of the Restoration* (J. M. Dent, 1994).

McAfee, Helen, *Pepys on the Restoration Stage* (New Haven: Yale University Press, 1916).

McDowell, Paula, *The Women of Grub Street* (Oxford: Clarendon Press, 1998).

Mann, David (ed.), *Women Playwrights in England, Ireland and Scotland 1660–Bloomington*: (Indiana University Press, 1996).

Marsden, Jean I., 'Female Spectatorship, Jeremy Collier and the Antitheatrical Debate', *Journal of English Literary History*, 65 (1998), pp. 877–899.

Martin, L. J., 'From Forestage to Proscenium: A Study of Restoration Staging Techniques', *Theatre Survey*, 4 (1963), pp. 3–28.

Maus, Katherine Eisaman, '"Playhouse flesh and blood": Sexual Ideology and the Restoration Actress', *Journal of English Literary History*, 46 (1979), pp. 595–617.

Milhous, Judith, *Thomas Betterton and The Management of Lincoln's Inn Fields 1695–1708* (Carbondale: Southern Illinois University Press, 1979).

—— 'The Profession of Acting in Late Seventeenth-century London' in *Kiss and Tell*, ed. Michael Dixon and Michelle Volansky (Newbury VT: Smith and Kraus, 1993), pp. xxv–xxxi.

Milhous, Judith, and Robert D. Hume, *Producible Interpretation: Eight English Plays 1675–1707* (Carbondale and Edwardsville: Southern Illinois University Press, 1985).

—— (ed.), Downes *Roscius Anglicanus* (1708), *A New Edition* (The Society for Theatre Research, 1987).

—— *A Register of English Theatrical Documents 1660–1737* (Carbondale: Southern Illinois University Press, 1991), 2 vols.

Milling, Jane, 'As the Actress Said to the Politician: The Development of Feminine Oratory in Restoration England', *Women and Theatre Occasional Papers* 3, ed. Maggie Gale and Susan Bassnett (Birmingham: Department of Drama and Theatre Arts, University of Birmingham, 1996), pp. 16–29.

Morgan, Fidelis, *The Female Wits–Women Playwrights of the Restoration* (Virago, 1981).

—— *A Woman of No Character: An Autobiography of Mrs Manley* (Faber and Faber, 1986).

Munns, Jessica, '"I by a double right thy bounties claim": Aphra Behn and Sexual Space' in *Curtain Calls: British and American Women and the Theater, 1660–1820*, ed. Mary Anne Schofield and Cecilia Macheski (Athens: Ohio University Press, 1991), pp. 193–201.

Nagler, A. M., *A Source Book in Theatrical History* (New York: Dover Publications Inc., 1952).

Nussbaum, Felicity A., *The Brink of All We Hate* (Lexington, KY: University Press of Kentucky, 1984).

Nicoll, Allardyce, *A History of Restoration Drama, 1660–1700* (Cambridge: Cambridge University Press, 1923).

—— *British Drama: An Historical Survey* (George Harrap, 1926).
—— *A History of English Drama 1660–1900* (Cambridge: Cambridge University Press, 1952), vol. 1, 1660–1700.
Novak, Maximillian E., 'The Closing of Lincoln's Inn Fields Theatre in 1695' *Restoration and 18th Century Theatre Research*, 14: 1, (1975), pp. 51–2.
—— and David Stuart Rodes (ed.), Thomas Southerne, *Oroonoko* (1695) (Edward Arnold, 1977).
O'Connor, Barry, 'Late Seventeenth Century Royal Portraiture and Restoration Staging' in *Theatre Notebook*, 49: 3 (1995), pp. 152–164.
Owen, Susan J., *Restoration Theatre and Crisis* (Oxford: Oxford University Press, 1996).
—— 'Sexual Politics and Party Politics in Behn's Drama, 1678–83' in *Aphra Behn Studies*, ed. Janet Todd (Cambridge, Cambridge University Press, 1996), pp. 15–29.
Parsons, Philip, 'Restoration Melodrama and Its Actors', *Komos*, I (1967), pp. 81–88.
Payne, Deborah, C., 'Reified Object or Emergent Professional? Retheorizing the Restoration Actress' in *Cultural Readings of Restoration and Eighteenth-century English Theater*, ed. J. Douglas Canfield and Deborah C. Payne (Athens, GA: University of Georgia Press, 1995), pp. 13–38.
Pearson, Jacqueline, *The Prostituted Muse: Images of Women and Women Dramatists 1642–1737* (Hemel Hempstead: Harvester Wheatsheaf, 1988).
Peck, James, 'Anne Oldfield's Lady Townly: Consumption, Credit, and the Whig Hegemony of the 1720s', *Theatre Journal*, 49 (1997), pp. 397–416.
Picard, Lisa, *Restoration London* (Wiedenfeld and Nicolson, 1997).
Postlewait, Thomas, 'History, Hermeneutics, and Narrativity,' in *Critical Theory and Performance*, ed. Janelle G. Reinelt and Joseph R. Roach (Ann Arbor: University of Michigan Press, 1998), pp. 356–368.
Postlewait, Thomas, and Bruce A. McConachie (ed.), *Interpreting the Theatrical Past* (Iowa: University of Iowa Press, 1989).
Powell, Jocelyn, *Restoration Theatre Production* (Routledge and Kegan Paul, 1984).
Pullen, Kirsten, *Actresses and Whores: On Stage and in Society* (Cambridge: Cambridge University Press, 2005).
Ray, Karen J., '"The Yielding Moment": A Woman's View of Amorous Females and Fallen Women', *Restoration and 18th Century Theatre Research*, 11: 2 (winter 1996), pp. 39–48.

—— 'Friendly Fire: The Oxymoron of Authority in Catherine Trotter's *Love at a Loss*', *Restoration and 18th Century Theatre Research*, 14: 1 (summer 1999), pp. 74–82.

Reinelt, Janelle G., and Joseph R. Roach (ed.), *Critical Theory and Performance* (1992), and reprinted Ann Arbor: University of Michigan Press, 1998.

Richards, Sandra, *The Rise of the English Actress* (Macmillan Press, 1993).

Roberts, David, *The Ladies: Female Patronage of Restoration Drama 1660–1700* (Oxford: Clarendon Press, 1989).

Rubik, Margarete, *Early Women Dramatists 1500–1800* (Macmillan Press, 1998).

Rubin, Miri, 'What Is Cultural History Now?', in *What Is History Now?* ed. David Cannadine (Palgrave Macmillan, 2002), pp. 80–94.

Sackville-West, V., *Aphra Behn* (Gerald Howe Ltd, 1927).

Sarlos, Robert, K., 'Performance Reconstruction: The Vital Link Between Past and Future' in *Interpreting the Theatrical Past*, ed. Thomas Postlewait and Bruce A. McConachie (Iowa: University of Iowa Press, 1989), pp. 198–229.

Scanlan, E. G., 'Reconstruction of the Duke's Playhouse in Lincoln's Inn Fields, 1661–1671', *Theatre Notebook*, 10 (1956), pp. 48–50.

Schafer, Elizabeth, 'Appropriating Aphra', *Australasian Drama Studies*, 19 (October 1991), pp. 39–49.

Schofield, Mary Anne, and Cecilia Macheski (ed.), *Curtain Calls: British and American Women and the Theater, 1660–1820* (Athens: Ohio University Press, 1991).

Scouten, A. H., 'Notes toward a History of Restoration comedy', *Philological Quarterly*, 45 (1966), pp. 62–70.

Shaaber, M. A., 'A Letter from Mrs. Barry', *University of Pennsylvania Library Chronicle*, 16 (1950), pp. 46–49.

Shepherd, Simon, and Peter Womack, *English Drama: A Cultural History* (Oxford: Blackwell, 1996).

Sinfield, Alan, *Faultlines: Cultural Materialism and the Politics of Dissident Reading* (Oxford: Clarendon Press, 1992).

Smalley, Beryl, 'An Anonymous Poem of the Eighteenth Century', *Review of English Studies*, 19 (1943), p. 70.

Smith, Dane F., *Plays About the Theatre in England 1671–1737* (Oxford: Oxford University Press, 1936).

Southern, Richard, *Changeable Scenery* (Faber and Faber, 1952).

Steeves, Edna L. (ed.), *The Plays of Mary Pix and Catherine Trotter* (New York and London: Garland Publishing Inc., 1982), 2 vols.

BIBLIOGRAPHY

—— 'Dressing to Deceive'. in *Curtain Calls: British and American Women and the Theater, 1660–1820*, ed. Mary Anne Schofield and Cecilia Macheski (Athens: Ohio University Press, 1991), pp. 220–228.
Stern, Tiffany, *Rehearsal from Shakespeare to Sheridan* (Oxford: Clarendon Press, 2000).
Stone, Lawrence, *The Family, Sex and Marriage in England 1500–1800* (1977), abridged and revised (Harmondsworth: Penguin Books, 1979).
Straub, Kristina, *Sexual Suspects: Eighteenth-century Players and Sexual Ideology* (Princeton: Princeton University Press, 1992).
—— 'Actors and Homophobia', in *Cultural Readings of Restoration and Eighteenth-century English Theater*, ed. Douglas Canfield and Deborah Payne (Athens: University of Georgia Press, 1995), pp. 258–280.
Styan, J. L., *Restoration Comedy in Performance* (Cambridge: Cambridge University Press, 1986).
Summers, Montague (ed), *The Works of Aphra Behn* (London: William Heinemann, 1915), reprinted New York: Phaeton, 1967, 6 vols.
—— (ed.), Downes, *Roscius Anglicanus* (Fortune Press, [1928]).
Taney, Retta M., *Restoration Revivals on the British Stage (1944–1979): A Critical Survey*, (Lanham: University Press of America, 1985).
Thomas, David (ed.), *Restoration and Georgian England 1660–1788* (Cambridge: Cambridge University Press, 1989).
—— *William Congreve*, English Dramatists series (Macmillan, 1992).
—— *From Tennis Court to Playhouse* (Warwick: University of Warwick, 1996).
—— 'The Design of the Theatre Du Marais and Wren's Theatre Royal, Drury Lane: A Computer-based Investigation', *Theatre Notebook*, 52: 3 (1999), pp. 127–145.
Thomas, Keith, 'Women and the Civil War Sects', *Past and Present*, 13 (1958), pp. 42–62.
Todd, Janet, *The Secret Life of Aphra Behn* (André Deutsch, 1996).
—— (ed.), *Aphra Behn Studies* (Cambridge, Cambridge University Press, 1996).
—— (ed.), *The Works of Aphra Behn* (William Pickering, 1996), 7 vols.
Tomlinson, Sophie, 'She that Plays the King: Henrietta Maria and the Threat of the Actress in Caroline Culture', in *The Politics of Tragicomedy: Shakespeare and After*, ed. Gordon McMullen and Jonathan Hope (Routledge, 1992) pp. 189–207.

Turner, Dorothy, 'Restoration Drama in the Public Sphere: Propaganda, the Playhouse, and Published Drama', *Restoration and Eighteenth Century Theatre Research*, 12: 1 (summer 1997), pp. 18–39.

Van Lennep, William (ed.), *The London Stage 1660–1800: A Calendar of Plays, Entertainments and Afterpieces Together with Casts, Box-receipts and Contemporary Comment Compiled from the Playbills, Newspapers and Theatrical Diaries of the Period.* Part 1, *1660–1700* (Carbondale: Southern Illinois University Press, 1965).

Weber, Harold M., *The Restoration Rake-hero* (Madison: University of Wisconsin Press, 1986).

Wildeblood, Joan and Peter Brinson, *The Polite World* (Oxford University Press, 1965).

Wiley, Autrey Nell, *Rare Prologues and Epilogues 1642–1700* (Allen and Unwin, 1940).

Wilson, John Harold, 'Rant, Cant, and Tone on the Restoration Stage', *Studies in Philology*, 52 (1955), pp. 592–598.

—— 'Theatre Notes from the Newdigate Newsletters', *Theatre Notebook*, 10 (1956), pp. 79–84.

—— *All the King's Ladies - Actresses of the Restoration* (Chicago: University of Chicago Press, 1958).

Wiseman, S. J., *Aphra Behn: Writers and Their Work* (Plymouth: Northcote House Publishers Ltd, 1996).

Woolf, Virginia, *A Room of One's Own* (1928), reprinted Penguin, 1945.

INDEX

Plays can be found under the names of playwrights.

Actress/whore trope 4, 34, 62, 86–7
Anti-theatricalism 77, 157, 179
  see also Collier, Jeremy
'Ariadne' 114, 120–2
  She Ventures and He Wins 19, 114–20
Aston, Anthony 81

Backscheider, Paula 33
Barry, Elizabeth 10, 17–8, 43, 53–4, 66, 67, 68, 162, 168–70, 188
  as playwright 120–2
  as target of satire 56–62, 179, 189
  benefit with United Company 62–4
  collaboration with Bracegirdle 78–82, 85–92, 100, 115, 127–9, 140–1, 144, 146–53, 172–4, 193–9, 203
  joins the Duke's Company 45–7
  whorish reputation 81–2, 121
Bartholomew fair 64
Bassnett, Susan 12, 13
Behn, Aphra 16, 64, 76, 115, 123–4, 146–7, 171, 188
  Abdelazar 39, 44, 45, 46
  Agnes de Castro 123
  Counterfeit Bridegroom, The 39
  False Count, The 45
  Feign'd Curtezans 43, 115, 122
  first plays produced 29–47
  Forc'd Marriage, The 33, 44
  History of the Nun, The 123
  life and works appropriated by Gildon 123–4
  Lucky Chance, The 68–70
  Oroonoko 123
  Rover, The 46, 68
  Rover II, The 122
  Sir Patient Fancy 43
  Town Fopp, The 39
  Widow Ranter, The 43
  Younger Brother, The 123–4
Bennett, Susan 7, 15, 185, 203–4
Betterton, Mary 33–6, 44, 79–80, 84–5, 93, 98
  training actresses 34
Betterton, Thomas 110–1, 57, 136
  as actor-manager of Duke's Company 10, 28, 44
  as actor-manager of the United Company 51, 56, 78–9, 84, 92, 95–100
  in the Players' Company 107–9, 143, 173, 179, 185, 194, 198–9
Boutell, Elizabeth (Betty) 116
Bowman, Elizabeth 98, 115, 143, 180
Bracegirdle, Anne 10, 17–8, 63, 111, 162, 167, 168–70
  collaboration with Barry 78–82, 85–92, 100, 127–9, 85–92, 140–1, 144, 146–53, 172–4, 193–9, 203
  first appearance 79
  reputation for virtue 80–2, 90–1, 112–4, 179, 188–90
Bratton, Jacky 8–9, 12, 64, 128, 147–8, 159–60
Breeches roles 37, 39, 90, 112, 114, 121, 122, 148, 196–7

Brown, Thomas 188
Burton, Sarah 61
Butler, Charlotte 84

Cavendish, Margaret (Duchess of Newcastle) 32
Centlivre, Susanna 10, 120, 147, 179, 190–1
Gamester, The 195–7
Cibber, Colley 10, 45, 63, 79–81, 87, 96–7, 108, 111, 135–6, 141–2, 144, 194–5
Clark, Constance 119–20, 184
Collier, Jeremy 82, 157–62, 170, 184, 192–3
Comedy 148, 149, 160, 184
   Subordinated to tragedy 87–9
Congreve, William 10, 93–5, 99, 111, 119, 160–1, 165–6, 194
   Mourning Bride, The 144
   Love for Love 109, 111–4
   Old Batchelor, The 94, 135–6
   Way of the World, The 88, 180–1, 184–5
Cooke, Sarah 59, 68
Covent Garden (Royal Opera House) 7–8
Cross-dressing 37
   see also breeches roles
Currer, Elizabeth (Betty) 39–43

Davenant, Alexander 77, 78, 95
Davenant, Charles 51–2, 77
Davenant, Mary (Lady) 28–9, 38, 44, 45, 46, 51, 107
Davenant, Thomas 78, 95
Davenant, William (Sir) 12, 27, 45, 51, 107
Davis, Tracy C. 6
Doggett, Thomas 95, 142
Dorset Gardens (theatre) 29, 51, 79, 107
Downes, John 44, 52, 57, 180, 194

Drury Lane (Theatre Royal) 7, 8, 18, 53, 123
   Backstage tour 1–3, 5, 10, 19
Dryden, John 76
Duke's Company 27–9, 38, 46, 47, 51–4, 77, 85, 107
   Table of actresses in Behn's plays 40–42
D'Urfey, Thomas
   Marriage-Hater Match'd, The 90

Epilogues *see* prologues and epilogues

Female audience 36–8, 82–4, 129
Female managers 28, 64–7
Female Wits, The 137–41
Fitzgerald, Percy 77

Gilder, Rosamond 11, 34–5
Gildon, Charles 123–4
Gould, Robert 55–6, 62
   The Play-House, A Satyr 55–6, 162
Gwynn, Nell 1, 2, 4, 14, 19, 39, 43

Hart, Charles 52, 56,
Holland, Peter 87
Hook, Lucyle 11, 53–4, 79, 82, 86, 100, 138–9, 168–9
Hotson, Leslie 64–6
Howe, Elizabeth 12, 67, 86, 128
Hume, Robert 52–3, 62–3

Killigrew, Charles 51–2
Killigrew, Thomas 1, 2, 12, 27, 51, 53
   see also King's Company
King's Company 27–8, 47, 51–4, 65, 68, 84
Kneller, Sir Godfrey 168–9
Knight, Frances Maria 84–5

INDEX

Langhans, Edward 107
Lee, Mary (Slingsby) 39, 44, 59, 85
Leigh, Anthony 43, 44, 88, 91
Leigh, Elinor 40, 46, 88, 92, 98, 143
Leigh, Elizabeth 64–7, 116
Lincoln's Inn Fields (theatre) 18, 27, 45, 84–5, 99, 107, 109, 143, 160

Manley, Delarivier 118–9, 122–30, 137–41, 165, 198
   Lost Lover, The 125, 137
   Royal Mischief, The 126, 127–30, 137, 164
Marsden, Jean 82–4, 158
Milhous, Judith 19, 51, 52–3, 96–7, 99, 107–8, 126, 141–2, 145, 158, 188, 194–5
Motteux, Pierre 116, 120–1, 146, 151, 167
   Love's a Jest 143
   Loves of Mars and Venus, The 143
Mountfort, Susannah, *see* Percival, Susannah
Mountfort, William 85, 89–92
   Injur'd Lovers, The 85
   murder of 91–3
Mynn (Minn, Minns) Mrs 65

Otway, Thomas 44, 67, 76

Patent Company 108, 111, 123–6, 135, 146, 157, 191–2
Payne, Deborah 14
Pepys, Samuel 32, 36
Percival, Susannah 60, 68, 80, 84, 92–3, 98, 111, 141
Philips, Katherine 31–2, 115, 124–5
Pix, Mary 10, 118–20, 122–30, 137–41, 191
   Beau Defeated, The 181–5
   Deceiver Deceived, The 165–8

Different Widows, The 192
Double Distress, The 187
False Friend, The 180
Innocent Mistress, The 146–53, 182
Queen Catherine 173–4
Spanish Wives, The 145, 147
Players' Company 18–9, Part 2 *passim*
   burlesque of 135–7, 140–2
   disbanding of 197
   formation of 97–100
Postlewait, Thomas 11
Powell, George 136–8, 140, 165–8
Prologues and epilogues 39, 76, 90–1, 110, 111–14, 115–16, 120–1, 135, 141, 151–2, 162–4, 192–3, 198–9
Pullen, Kirsten 4–5

Rehearsal 137–41
Rich, Christopher 78, 95–7, 110, 126
Rochester, John Wilmot Earl of 45, 46
Rogers, Jane 85

Satires and lampoons 13
   Comparison Between Two Stages, A 186–7, 189
   Satyr on the Players, A 56, 57–62
Settle, Elkanah 64–6, 85
Sentimental comedy 87
Shadwell, Thomas
   Scowrers, The 88
She-tragedy, 85
Skipwith, Thomas 78, 95, 142
Southerne, Thomas 123
   Maid's Last Prayer, The 92–3
   Oroonoko 123, 135
   Wives Excuse, The 87
Straub, Kristina 61
Summers, Montague 57, 60

Todd, Janet 29–31, 38, 44, 45
Trotter, Catherine 118–9, 122–30, 137–41
  Fatal Friendship, The 170–2

United Company 56, 68, 76, 77, 80, 84
  dissolution of 95–9
  formation of 51–5
Unnatural Mother, The 164, 180

Vanburgh, John 10, 144, 193–5, 197–8
  Relapse, The 144
  Provok'd Wife, The 144, 162
Verbruggen, John 186, 191–2
Verbruggen, Susannah, see Percival

Wiseman, Jane 188
Wycherley, William 76

EU authorised representative for GPSR:
Easy Access System Europe, Mustamäe tee 50,
10621 Tallinn, Estonia
gpsr.requests@easproject.com

www.ingramcontent.com/pod-product-compliance
Ingram Content Group UK Ltd.
Pitfield, Milton Keynes, MK11 3LW, UK
UKHW020857160426
5217IPUK00035B/1394